Eucharistic Body

Eucharistic Body

Frank C. Senn

Fortress Press
Minneapolis

EUCHARISTIC BODY

Cover image: Christ Blessing, detail from the Altarpiece of the Last Supper, 1464-68 (oil on panel), Bouts, Dirck (c.1415-75) / St. Peter's, Louvain, Belgium / Bridgeman Images
Cover design: Laurie Ingram

Print ISBN: 978-1-5064-1676-2
eBook ISBN: 978-1-5064-2516-0

The paper used in this publication meets the minimum requirements of American National Standard for Information Sciences — Permanence of Paper for Printed Library Materials, ANSI Z329.48-1984.
Manufactured in the U.S.A.

This book was produced using Pressbooks.com, and PDF rendering was done by PrinceXML.

Contents

Acknowledgments

Thanks to New City Press and the Augustinian Heritage Institute for permission to quote from *The Works of St. Augustine: A Translation for the 21st Century.* Ed. John E. Rotelle, OSA. Part 2: *Sermons,* trans. Edmund Hill, OP, 6:254–55. New York: New City Press, 1993. Used with permission.

Thanks to Liturgical Press for permission to cite several texts of eucharistic prayers from *Prayers of the Eucharist: Early and Reformed,* trans. and ed. R. C. D. Jasper and G. J. Cuming. 3rd ed. Collegeville, MN: Liturgical Press, © 1987 by Order of Saint Benedict, Collegeville, Minnesota. Used with permission.

Scripture quotations are from the New Revised Standard Version, © 1989 by the Division of Christian Education of the National Council of Churches of Christ in the U.S.A., and are used with permission.

Thanks to Brian Buesing, photographer, and the Rev. Kristin White, rector of St. Augustine Episcopal Church, Wilmette, IL for permission to use the photograph of the Christmas Eve Eucharist.

Thanks to Joe Simchak, photographer, for permission the use the photograph of the author celebrating the Eucharist at Immanuel Lutheran Church, Evanston, IL.

Thanks to Pastor Sigurður Árni Þórðarson for permission to use the photograph of him and a confirmand celebrating a Confirmation Communion Service in Flatey, Iceland.

Image on next page: Christ the Man of Sorrows from the Utraquist Church of Our Lady before Teyn in Prague, ca. 1470.

Introduction

Three things came together to make possible this little book about the Eucharist. First, I received an invitation to lecture to pastors of the Church of Iceland through my Icelandic friend Pastor Gunnlaugur Garðarsson of Akureyri. I agreed to give lectures on May 29–31, 2016 to pastors meeting for their theological days in Hólár on the north coast of Iceland. This would be my third and possibly last lecture series to Icelandic pastors. Gunnlaugur suggested that I should address some aspects of liturgical renewal that might draw on my life's work. When I asked if that meant injecting some elements of intellectual autobiography into these lectures, he said yes. I thought to myself, "That's the sort of thing you do when you reach the 'golden years' of your career!" But I guess I've arrived at that point.

Second, I would have just finished teaching a doctoral seminar on the Eucharist in the spring term at Garrett-Evangelical Theological Seminary in Evanston, Illinois before departing for Iceland at the end of May. Before that, in January, I taught an intensive course in Reformation Liturgy at Trinity School for Ministry/North American Lutheran Seminary in Ambridge, Pennsylvania, which dealt in part with eucharistic issues of the Reformation era. So I suggested that I would focus on the Eucharist in my lectures at Hólár. I was teaching the Eucharist seminar concurrently with preparing lectures for Iceland, so what I had to present would be very fresh. With the Eucharist as the central focus I promised to address also other related issues of current interest.

Third, I was finishing the editing on my book *Embodied Liturgy*[1] when I responded to the Iceland invitation. In fact, I would be in Iceland

---

1. Frank C. Senn, *Embodied Liturgy: Lessons in Christian Ritual* (Minneapolis: Fortress, 2016).

just at the time Fortress Press was making my book available. So the bodily performance of the liturgy and receiving the sacraments bodily were very much on my mind. I thought I might bring the body into my reflections on the meanings of the Eucharist more thoroughly than has often been the case. This would relate very well to some new studies on the body and presence and memory that have appeared in the last several years. In fact, my own body as a communicant would be the existential and vulnerable starting point for reflection on the eucharistic body. I wove narratives from my personal life into my lectures in Iceland and I took the risk of including them in this book.

I bring three bodies together in this little book: the sacramental body of Christ; the social body of Christ, which is the church that assembles to celebrate the Eucharist; and the body of the communicant who receives the sacramental body into his or her own body as a participant in the social body of the eucharistic assembly.

The first six chapters are based on the Iceland lectures. They explore the relationship of the Eucharist to our lives as pilgrims in this world (chapter 1), to anaphora and the eucharistic life (chapter 2), to cosmology and praise (chapter 3), to the body and its memory (chapter 4), to the interpersonal body of the Spirit-formed community (chapter 5), and to the relationship between Trinitarian doxology and worldview (chapter 6).

A eucharistic life cannot be formed in us unless we participate in the Eucharist regularly, and that cannot happen unless the church celebrates it frequently—every Lord's Day at least. We still have Lutheran congregations in which Holy Communion is not offered every week to those who desire it—contrary to the Augsburg Confession and its Apology, article 24. There are more Protestant congregations that do not have Communion every Sunday than those that do—against the desire of all the Protestant Reformers except Zwingli. Surely the forthcoming five-hundredth anniversary of the Reformation is a time to rectify this sorry situation.[2]

Promoting the Great Thanksgiving is another agenda of this book. An expansive understanding of how the Eucharist relates to the totality of life cannot be expressed without words at the Table that express nothing less than a worldview. Celebrating a non-eucharistic Communion, using only the words of institution, as in many Protestant tradi-

---

2. Simon Chan, *Liturgical Theology: The Church as Worshiping Community* (Downers Grove, IL: IVP Academic, 2006), has caused a stir in the global evangelical/Pentecostal world with his strong endorsement of restoring the Eucharist to the center of the church's life.

tions, deprives the people of a fuller and richer understanding of the Eucharist. Using only some parts of the eucharistic prayer traditions, and perhaps not even in a coherent order, is also not very helpful in forming the faithful into a more expansive but theologically cohesive understanding of the Eucharist.

More ecumenical scholarly work has been done on eucharistic prayers than on any other genre of liturgical texts. I daresay that work on the *Lutheran Book of Worship* eucharistic prayers was state of the art for its time, modified only by what was considered absolutely unacceptable in the Lutheran church bodies that supported the Inter-Lutheran Commission on Worship at that time. Provision still had to be made in LBW for use of the words of institution apart from the context of a eucharistic prayer. A compromise between the words of institution alone and a full eucharistic prayer was the 1942 Swedish prayer that followed the Sanctus and ended with "Amen. Come, Lord Jesus" before the words of institution—thus clearly separating prayer and proclamation to satisfy those Lutherans who insist on that distinction. It is disappointing, in my view, to see little further advance in the eucharistic prayers in *Evangelical Lutheran Worship* (2006) of the Evangelical Lutheran Church in America as well as the idiosyncratic efforts in *Lutheran Service Book* (2006) of the Lutheran Church–Missouri Synod to provide some elements of a eucharistic prayer, but without including the words of institution in any of them. To some extent this is the result of Lutheran church bodies going their separate ways in liturgical work after a century of cooperative inter-Lutheran liturgical work, and intent on pressing their own theological (ideological) agendas.

There are two more lectures in this book. After exploring anaphora traditions we will devote attention to understandings of eucharistic presence in the Western tradition and how those understandings relate to bodily reception of the sacramental. Worship is more than words; we respond with bodily postures and gestures when encountering the divine presence. We receive the body of Christ into our own bodies. We will look at the relationship of body and presence in chapter 7.

Finally, a major issue today is who can come to the Lord's Table. What approach do we take in response to the presence of other Christians and even the unbaptized in our eucharistic assemblies? What should be our practices of hospitality in relation to our stewardship of the mysteries or sacraments instituted by Christ for his church? A Lutheran graduate student in the Eucharist seminar at Garrett-

Evangelical, Shane Brinegar, organized a colloquy on "the open table" at the Lutheran School of Theology at Chicago. Chapter 8 is based on remarks I gave at that colloquy during the spring of 2016. But I also spoke of wider issues of "fencing the table" at the colloquy, such as ecumenical expressions of eucharistic hospitality and eucharistic discipline.

Taken together, these eight chapters go through the complete celebration of the Eucharist from the entrance to the dismissal. I discussed aspects of the Eucharist in greater depth in my large book on *Christian Liturgy—Catholic and Evangelical*,[3] so readers may appreciate this synthesis of my views about the Eucharist.

I think I must also say that while I address issues that are important to Lutherans (the state Church of Iceland is Lutheran), my examples are taken from the whole (i.e., catholic) eucharistic tradition. I hope that ecumenical readers will find ideas and issues in this book that are relevant to them.

My approach to the Eucharist is different today from what it was some thirty years ago. In those days we were focused on texts. What makes the difference now is my "return to the body" that I discussed in the introduction to *Embodied Liturgy*. This book builds on that project.

I did not lead any yoga sequences in Iceland like I did with the students in Indonesia, although I did lead the pastors through a body scan and I made reference to some meditations that focus on the body. But yoga and meditation are ways of getting in touch with our bodies, so I included a few simple sequences and meditation suggestions in this book. People who practice yoga (there are millions of us!) may find these sequences and meditations instructive. They are indicated in italics in the text. But all Christians must realize that the Eucharist is something we do with our bodies, receive into our bodies, and together as those who eat and drink constitute a corporate or social body. The Eucharist is all about bodies.

It remains to thank Pastor Gunnlaugur Garðarsson for inviting me to the Holár conference and driving me all around Iceland; and to Pastors Geir Waage in Reykholt, Þorgrímur Daníelsson of Húsavík, and Floki Kristinsson of Hvanneyri, Borgarfjardarsysla, for inviting me into their homes and introducing me to their unique contributions to Icelandic life: the Snorri Sturluson museum and archives in Reykholt, a body of knowledge for which Geir serves as curator; mountain climbing med-

---

3. Frank C. Senn, *Christian Liturgy—Catholic and Evangelical* (Minneapolis: Fortress, 1997).

itations led by Þorgrímur on Sunday afternoons; and the annual pilgrimage to Skalholt organized by Floki. These Icelanders are all about the body too. As millions of tourists are now discovering, Iceland isn't as cold as its name suggests. I'm grateful that I have also come to know warm Icelandic hearts. And, once again, my thanks to Michael Gibson of Fortress Press for taking on this project.

Frank C. Senn
Evanston, IL
September 28, 2016
Eve of St. Michael and All Angels

1

Ad Altare Dei: Journey into Presence

Introibo ad altare Dei: R/ *Ad Deum qui laetificat juventutem meam* (I will go to the altar of God: to God who gives joy to my youth).

These were the first words of the old Roman Latin Mass after the trinitarian invocation. They were part of the preparatory office usually said by the priest and the server on the steps of the altar before the beginning of the Mass proper with the introit for the Mass. I probably heard these words when I attended Mass for the first time with my Roman Catholic aunt while I was a confirmand in my Lutheran church. I don't claim to remember them—or other Latin words I heard at that Mass. But I begin this book on the Eucharist with them because the God I encountered at the altar indeed gave joy to my youth.

My life with the Eucharist began when I received Holy Communion for the first time on Easter Sunday in 1957. I was thirteen years old, going on fourteen. I had been confirmed on Palm Sunday in 1957 in Tabor Lutheran Church in Buffalo, New York. On Easter Sunday, with my confirmation class, I came forward to the Communion rail, knelt down, and received the white Host and drank a small glass of wine. I remember the strange consistency of the Host; it was pasty and clung to the roof of my mouth. The wine helped it go down my throat, but it also left an astringent burning sensation as it traveled down my esophagus into my stomach. These substances didn't taste like the bread and wine we had at home. I remember the physical sensations of consuming them and later thought about how eating this bread and drinking this wine signified my union with Christ in his body and blood, joined me fully to his body on earth, completing a process of initiation that had begun with my baptism as an infant, and granted forgiveness of my sins. I was well catechized by my parish pastor, Richard Ebel.

My first Communion was the most impressionable religious experience of my early years. It made an impression on me for existential reasons that I shall discuss in later lectures.

My home congregation celebrated Holy Communion once a month, as did many Lutheran congregations in the United States at the time. As I got around to other congregations during my high school and college years, I discovered that Holy Communion could be celebrated more frequently. Because my sense of vocation to ordained ministry was received early in life (perhaps earlier than my confirmation, but definitely during my high school years), I was interested in the wider life of the church, and especially the liturgical practices of other churches and also of the Jewish synagogue, during my high school years.

I attended Hartwick College in Oneonta, New York (1961–1965). I became active in the Lutheran Student Association, and during my third year in college I read Alexander Schmemann's *For the Life of the World*,[1] which was first published in 1963 as a study book for the National Student Christian Federation. It opened up a sacramental worldview that went beyond anything I had heard or read before that point. It has become a classic that I return to again and again. This sacramental worldview opened more fully when, in my senior year, I read Mircea Eliade's *The Sacred and the Profane*.[2] Eliade taught that an earthly object does not cease being an earthly object when it becomes a manifestation of the sacred; rather, a hierophany occurs in which the divine is communicated through this particular stone or tree (or, as I reasoned, through this particular bread and wine) as opposed to all other trees or stones (or bread or wine). As I read Schmemann and Eliade, I thought their understandings of sacrament and the sacred were not very different from my Lutheran understandings of the Eucharist.

In my senior year in college I also read, on the recommendation of a campus pastor, volume 37 of *Luther's Works*, particularly the treatise

1. Alexander Schmemann, *For the Life of the World: Sacraments and Orthodoxy* (Crestwood, NY: St. Vladimir's Seminary Press, 1973).
2. Mircea Eliade, *The Sacred and the Profane: The Nature of Religion*, trans. Willard R. Trask (New York: Harper & Row, 1959).

That These Words of Christ, "This Is My Body," etc., Still Stand Firm against the Fanatics (1537). I understood Luther to be saying that Christ comes to us in the bread and wine that is designated as his body and blood by his words, "This is my body" and "This is my blood," without a change in the elements. If Christ is present everywhere by virtue of the omnipresence of his divine nature, he can also be present in bread and wine. But, wrote Luther, "it is one thing if God is present, and another if he is present for you. He is there for you when he adds his Word and binds himself, saying, 'Here you are to find me.'"[3]

I didn't receive much liturgical education at the Lutheran School of Theology at Chicago (my first two years on the Maywood campus). We had a basic course on worship well taught by our homiletics professor, H. Grady Davis. For that course I had acquired Luther D. Reed's *The Lutheran Liturgy*[4] and I continued to explore my interest by acquiring Gregory Dix's *The Shape of the Liturgy*,[5] which I also enjoyed for its literary quality. But in those days without a liturgics professor on the faculty students who were interested in liturgy had to pick and choose among other course offerings to increase their liturgical knowledge. My Old Testament professor Horace Hummel, who had an interest in liturgy himself, introduced me to the writings of the French oratorian (and ex-Lutheran pastor) Louis Bouyer.[6] In my senior year I took a course from Professor Hummel in the cultic interpretation of the Psalms and from Professor Arthur Vööbus on liturgical material in the synoptic Gospels and in the *Didache*. Most fortuitously, I also took a course in Christian ecumenical dialogue East and West from Professor Robert Tobias, who arranged for Fr. Alexander Schmemann to fly to Chicago every Monday during the term as a co-teacher to give lectures on dialogue topics from the Orthodox perspective. Naturally, in a course in ecumenical dialogue issues surrounding the interpretation of the sacraments were discussed. I spoke with Fr. Schmemann about my interest in liturgical studies, and he encouraged me to apply to Notre Dame and study with Fr. Aidan Kavanagh, OSB. So I applied to Notre Dame and received a full-tuition scholarship. I was also awarded a graduate fellowship from the Board of Theological Education of the Lutheran Church in America, which the board gave to a graduating

---

3. Martin Luther, *That These Words of Christ, "This Is My Body," etc., Still Stand Firm against the Fanatics*, in *Luther's Works*, ed. and trans. Robert H. Fischer (Philadelphia: Muhlenberg, 1961), 37:68.
4. Luther D. Reed, *The Lutheran Liturgy*, 2nd ed. (Philadelphia: Fortress, 1959).
5. Gregory Dix, *The Shape of the Liturgy* (London: Dacre, 1945; repr., Minneapolis: Seabury, 1983).
6. I began with Louis Bouyer, *Liturgical Piety* (Notre Dame: University of Notre Dame Press, 1954). This became my introduction to Odo Casel's mystery theology.

senior from each LCA seminary. An arrangement was worked out by the Rev. Dr. Walter Wick, president of the Indiana-Kentucky Synod of the Lutheran Church in America, whereby I would be called as assistant pastor (part time) of Gloria Dei Lutheran Church in South Bend, Indiana, so that I could also be ordained to the ministry of Word and Sacraments. I was ordained in my home congregation in Buffalo, NY on the Day of Saints Peter and Paul, June 29, 1969.

Weekly Celebration of Holy Communion

My experience and my reading convinced me that the Eucharist should be celebrated every Sunday and festival, and maybe offered on weekdays (although I was also acquiring an appreciation of the value of daily morning and evening prayer, Matins and Vespers, from my experience of these offices in the college and seminary chapels). The Apology of the Augsburg Confession is very clear that "we do not abolish the Mass but religiously retain and defend it. Among us the Mass is celebrated on every Lord's day and on other festivals, when the sacrament is made available to those who wish to partake of it, after they have been examined and absolved."[7]

As I said, most Lutheran congregations celebrated Holy Communion once a month, with Antecommunion (the liturgy of the Word) as the chief service on other Sundays. The confessions of the Lutheran Church teach that Word and Sacrament belong together. Acts 2:42 testifies that those who were baptized on the Day of Pentecost "devoted themselves to the apostles teaching and fellowship, to the breaking of bread and the prayers." A unified liturgy of Word and Meal is the testimony of the ancient church in Justin Martyr's *First Apology*, written around 150 CE.

There may have been practical reasons why weekly Communion was not observed in our churches, such as lack of availability of pastors in early American history to tend to the spiritual needs of congregations in scattered frontier settlements. But the argument that celebrating the sacrament too frequently makes it too ordinary is simply justifying and sanctifying an emergency practice. Communion was intended to be an ordinary part of Christian life.

Later, after seminary and while still in graduate school in the 1970s, I served on the Joint Committee of the American Lutheran Church and

7. *The Book of Concord: The Confessions of the Evangelical Lutheran Church*, ed. Robert Kolb and Timothy J. Wengert (Minneapolis: Fortress, 2000), 258.

the Lutheran Church in America to Study Communion Practices. We pushed for a strong affirmation of weekly Communion on the basis of the Lutheran confessions (Augsburg Confession and Apology Article 24) and the benefits of Holy Communion in Luther's catechisms.

The congregations I served as a pastor (five of them over a forty-year period) all had Holy Communion every Sunday and festival, and I think we experienced the sacrament as extraordinarily ordinary in our common life. I have to admit that I did not institute the practice of weekly Communion in any congregation I served; it was already in place when I was called to these congregations. The one partial exception was that in my last call, to Immanuel in Evanston, I inherited an "interrupted Eucharist" in which on two or three Sundays of every month the congregation was dismissed with a benediction after the liturgy of the Word. The Eucharist was then celebrated and Communion offered to those who remained. I wanted to end this practice, but not right away. I provided the option that people could leave during a hymn before the preface, but taught that the service would continue without interruption into the Eucharist. When I found out that the people who left were enjoying the coffee and refreshments while the rest of us were in worship (this was a Swedish congregation with a sit-down coffee hour with refreshments served on china), I said that they would have to wait until the communing members arrived for the coffee hour. Within a year very few were leaving the service and the full service without interruption was well established. At that point I deleted the interpolated hymn.

I actually had the experience of introducing a weekly Communion Service already in my undergraduate college years. As a leader in the Lutheran Student Association on campus I persuaded the pastor of Atonement Lutheran Church in Oneonta, New York, to provide a Sunday-evening Communion service for students from Hartwick College and the State University of New York every Sunday evening. The Atonement congregation had acquired property at the foot of Oyaron Hill on which Hartwick College was located and built a new facility just off campus. It was notable for having a free-standing altar with a Communion rail encircling it. I had been exposed to aspects of liturgical renewal at regional and national gatherings of the Lutheran student movement, and I wanted to see those practices introduced locally. My idea was to invite some occasional guest celebrants and preachers, particularly campus pastors from Lutheran university ministry centers in upstate New York, who could model for us some of these renewing practices. I give the pastor *loci*, Dr. Harold C. Fry, credit for going along with this scheme and convincing his church council that the students weren't trying to avoid interaction with the resident congregation. In fact, students just didn't get up early on Sunday mornings after being out late on Saturday nights. So providing an evening service could be seen as mission outreach. And, of course, members of the congregation were welcome. The added feature was that the guest presider and preacher would remain after the liturgy for discussion with the students over pizza and soda. We didn't know it at that time in the early 1960s, but we were returning to a more ancient model of Christian gatherings for meal and word—in that order—that has only been explored by liturgical scholars in the last several decades.

The Early Christian Symposium Meal

We know from the book of Acts that the first Christians continued praying in the Jerusalem temple as long as it was available. But they also gathered in one another's homes in which they engaged in meal fellowship and teaching. This became the pattern as Christianity spread beyond Jerusalem and Palestine into the surrounding countries. Converts could pray in the Jewish synagogues as long as they were welcome, but they met in homes of Christians for meal fellowship and mutual edification. What the Acts of the Apostles called "the breaking of bread" St. Paul called the Lord's Supper. The point of the gathering was to share in the meal instituted by our Lord Jesus Christ "on the night when he was betrayed" (1 Cor 11:23).

In the last several decades New Testament and liturgical scholars (both Jewish and Christian) have seen the Greco-Roman banquet, the symposium discussion with meal (*deipnon*), providing the form both of the emerging the Jewish Passover Seder in the diaspora and the Christian gathering for word and meal. The social context of the celebration of the Lord's Supper was a gathering of the church in the house of a member, or in an inn rented for the occasion, as other supper clubs did in the Greco-Roman world, to have a banquet. The form of the banquet was most likely a symposium. A symposium was a meal (*deipnon*), accompanied by entertainment, which was followed by a drinking party in which the guests engaged in discussion, often on a philosophic topic. There were a number of literary symposia from ancient Greece and Rome, of which the most famous is probably Plato's.[8]

---

8. *The Portable Plato*, ed. Scott Buchanan (New York: Viking, 1948), 186–87.

Scholars like Blake Leyerle[9] and Dennis E. Smith,[10] who have studied the meal customs of the ancient Greco-Roman world, see the symposium as the form of the banquet that lies behind the Jewish Passover Seder of the diaspora as well as the Christian Eucharist. Typically a Greek symposium began with the sharing of food and wine, a thanksgiving to the god of the feast, entertainment of some sort in the form of a dance, a poem, a drama, or a philosophic proposition, followed by discussion of what has been presented, accompanied by additional cups of wine (with copious drinking!).

Liturgical scholarship has now accepted as a given that Christianity entered the Greco-Roman world as a table fellowship with the common meal providing the principal reason for gathering.[11] In fact, the Christian gatherings looked to the Roman authorities like a typical supper club. The Lord's Supper was celebrated in the context of a community meal at least until the early second century. As we see from the issues raised by St. Paul in his First Letter to the Corinthians, this arrangement was not without its social problems since the unity of the church as the body of Christ, manifested in the sharing of the one loaf and the one cup (1 Cor 10:16–17), required waiting for all to be present in the assembly and an equal menu for all the social classes. St. Paul implied that the host couldn't serve one menu for his peers (perhaps fellow patrons) and another menu for clients and plebs, with the slaves getting the leftover because they arrived late.[12] The radical inclusiveness of "one baptism" was slow to register with Christians used to a system of social stratification.

Meal and Word

How did it happen that the Eucharist was joined to a liturgy of the Word with Scripture readings, preaching, and common prayers? Liturgical scholars have pointed to two Jewish liturgies as models for Chris-

9. Blake Leyerle, "Meal Customs in the Greco-Roman World," in *Passover and Easter: Origin and History to Modern Times*, vol. 5 of *Two Liturgical Traditions* (Notre Dame: University of Notre Dame Press, 1999), 29–61.
10. Dennis E. Smith, *From Symposium to Eucharist: The Banquet in the Early Christian World* (Minneapolis: Fortress, 2003).
11. See Paul F. Bradshaw and Maxwell E. Johnson, *The Eucharistic Liturgies: Their Evolution and Interpretation* (Collegeville, MN: Liturgical, 2012), 1–11.
12. See Gerd Theissen, *The Social Setting of Pauline Christianity: Essays on Corinth*, ed. and trans. John H. Schütz (Philadelphia: Fortress, 1982), 145–74.

tian liturgy: the synagogue service and domestic meal rituals.[13] But this still leaves unanswered the question of how they were joined together.

A clue emerges once we consider the meal-symposium structure of the early Christian gatherings. In 1 Corinthians 14:26 St. Paul mentions that people brought gifts to share at the supper gathering, for example, "a hymn, a lesson, a revelation, a tongue, or an interpretation." From the diversity of gifts in the church, the members each contributed something to the meeting. The context of the gathering was a meal. To this meal was added singing, Scripture reading, prophesying, speaking in tongues as some were inspired to utter ecstatic speech, but always with interpretation so that people would understand what was being said. Thus the Word was added to the meal—the reverse of Protestant practice of appending the meal to the Word.

Justin Martyr, in his *First Apology* 67, reports that at Sunday gatherings "the memoirs of the apostles" and "the writings of the prophets" were read "as long as time permits," and that the president commented on these readings. Then bread and wine were taken and the president gave thanks to the best of his ability and the elements were shared by the community. The deacons took consecrated elements to the sick and imprisoned after the dismissal.[14]

There is no reference in Justin Martyr's account to singing the "psalms, hymns, and spiritual songs" mentioned in the Pauline Letters (Eph 5:19; Col 3:16) that must have been included in the symposium banquet, as well as sung at home. In his letter to Emperor Trajan (112 CE), Pliny the Younger, governor of Bithynia, reports from his interrogation of Christians that they had given up having a supper club in dutiful response to the imperial ban on such gatherings, but also mentions that they gathered early in the morning to take an oath and sing a hymn to Christ "as to a god."[15] There is evidence of hymns and songs being composed in the second century, such as the Odes of Solomon. Clement of Alexandria, who commented on music in the education of youth, is credited with having written the first Christian strophic hymn ("Shepherd of Tender Youth").[16] We can only conclude that either the Sunday-morning liturgy described by Justin was par-

13. See Louis Bouyer, *Eucharist: Theology and Spirituality of the Eucharistic Prayer*, trans. Charles Underhill Quinn (Notre Dame: University of Notre Dame Press, 1968).
14. Justin Martyr, *First Apology* 67 (*Early Christian Fathers*, trans. Edward Rochie Hardy, Library of Christian Classics 1 (Philadelphia: Westminster, 1953), 287.
15. Pliny, "Letter X (*ad Traj.*)," cxvi. *Documents of the Christian Church*, ed. Henry Bettenson, 2nd ed. (Oxford: Oxford University Press, 1967), 3–4.
16. See the evidence for early Christian songs in John Arthur Smith, *Music in Ancient Judaism and Early Christianity* (Farnham, UK: Ashgate, 2011).

ticularly plain, or else (what I think is more likely the case) it doesn't cover everything that was actually done in the liturgy (which is often the case when simply listing an order of service).

So how did all the singing to which we are accustomed become a regular feature of the eucharistic liturgy? I think the clue is to look at the places in the liturgy that have always included a lot of music: at the entrance, during the offering, and during the administration of Holy Communion. These are all moments in the liturgy during which people are moving. The suggestion would be that when Christian congregations moved out of house churches and into basilicas in the fourth century, the logistics of the larger spaces and bigger assemblies required a devotional way to cover the movement of people: of the ministers at the entrance, of those bringing gifts at the offertory, and of those processing to a Communion station during the distribution. Other music came to cover the movement required for the readings, either to the ambo or with the gospel book to the place where the Gospel would be read. I do not think that all this movement and use of cover music occurred everywhere immediately.[17] But the development of choirs, first in the East and then in Rome and other places in the West, suggests that the use of music was expanding during the fourth century to the point where music leadership was needed. As we might assume from later experience, not everyone was happy with these developments. Some church fathers issued warnings about the songs becoming too decorative and to avoid use of musical instruments associated with pagan cults.[18]

Journey into the Kingdom

It seems to me that the emerging entrance rites in the basilicas during the fourth and fifth centuries paralleled the structure of the pilgrimage rites that emerged in the Holy Land in the fourth century, as reported in Egeria's travel diary (ca. 381–384).[19] Egeria describes how pilgrims gathered at a designated place and processed to the shrine chanting refrains to psalms and hymns. Upon arrival at the shrine, Scripture passages related to the event being commemorated at the site were

---

17. Augustine describes no ceremonial entrance in his comments on worship in Hippo. On the other hand, he loved to hear the people sing both hymns and liturgical responses. See Frederic van der Meer, *Augustine the Bishop*, trans. B. Battershaw and G. R. Lamb (London: Sheed & Ward, 1961), 389–90, 325–37.
18. See Andrew B. McGowan, *Ancient Christian Worship: Early Church Practices in Social, Historical, and Theological Perspective* (Grand Rapids: Baker Academic, 2014), 122–28.
19. *Egeria's Travels*, ed. and trans. John Wilkerson, 3rd ed. (Warminster, UK: Aris & Phillips, 1999).

read, followed by prayers (probably litanies led by deacons with the people responding *Kyrie eleison* to the petitions). Then the Eucharist was celebrated, either in the basilica at the shrine, or at the basilica of the Anastasis (place of the resurrection) back in Jerusalem. In other words, pilgrimage rites, like the full eucharistic liturgies themselves (especially as they emerged in urban centers like Rome and Constantinople, which celebrated liturgies in different station churches[20]), comprised the shape of gathering and processing while singing psalms and hymns, readings with commentary, and prayers, followed by the Eucharist with its Great Thanksgiving, the distribution of the sacramental elements, and dismissal (sending).

Alexander Schmemann has called the entire liturgy a journey into the dimension of the kingdom, which is blessed at the beginning of the Divine Liturgy of St. John Chrysostom. "The Liturgy of the Eucharist is best understood as a journey or procession. It is the journey of the Church into the dimension of the Kingdom. We use this word 'dimension' because it seems the best way to indicate the manner of our sacramental entrance into the risen life of Christ."[21]

Of course, the sacramental entrance into the risen life of Christ begins at baptism, which should be understood as comprehending the entire process of Christian initiation, not only the water rite. As Luther taught in his catechisms, Christians are always returning to their baptism. This is expressed in repentance, a daily dying to sin and rising again in righteousness to live forever in God's kingdom. So while there is a specific process of Christian initiation that we will explore in chapter 8, Christian life itself has an initiatory character. Victor and Edith Turner have noted the initiatory quality of pilgrimages.

> A pilgrim is an initiand, entering into a new, deeper level of existence than he has known in his accustomed milieu. Homologous with the ordeals of tribal initiation are the trials, tribulations, and even temptations of the pilgrim's way. And at the end the pilgrim, like the novice, is exposed to powerful religious sacra (shrines, images, liturgies, curative waters, ritual circumambulations of holy objects, and so on), the beneficial effect of which depends upon the zeal and pertinacity of his quest.[22]

20. See John F. Baldovin, SJ, *Worship: City, Church and Renewal* (Washington, DC: The Pastoral Press, 1991), 3–35; Aidan Kavanagh, *On Liturgical Theology* (New York: Pueblo, 1984), 52–69.
21. Schmemann, *For the Life of the World*, 26.
22. Victor and Edith Turner, *Image and Pilgrimage in Christian Culture: Anthropological Perspectives* (New York: Columbia University Press, 1978), 8.

While there may be other distractions along the pilgrim's way, and awesome sacred objects to behold at the pilgrimage shrine, the Eucharist is the end of the journey.

Pilgrimage is a bodily meditation because pilgrims have to walk to get to their destination. They may walk alone or with a group. Chances are that those who set out walking alone will end up in a group, and bonding with fellow pilgrims will occur. On the way pilgrims may chant psalms and sing hymns and stop for prayers as well as meals, rest, or sleep. As they reach their destination pilgrims will often walk barefoot to the final site. Walking barefoot is an expression of humility but also a sign of penitence. Many people have undertaken pilgrimage as a penance. It has been the custom of the Croagh Patrick pilgrimage in Ireland to climb Ireland's holiest mountain barefoot. This is very arduous and even painful to tender feet because the trail has been degraded by many people walking over it for centuries. About a million people a year visit the Reek, as the statue of St. Patrick is colloquially known. July 25 is designated as "Reek Sunday," and it is visited by thousands of people on that day. For those who make it to the top, there is a modern chapel where confessions are heard and the Mass is celebrated.

One of the most popular pilgrimages today, drawing pilgrims from around the world, is the Camino to Santiago de Compostella in Spain. The destination is believed to be the final burial site of the apostle St. James the Elder, whose day of commemoration is July 25. People begin from various starting points. Some Europeans begin from their homes and walk for months. Many walkers just do the Camino for the hike and the adventure, but that has also been a part of pilgrimages. They end up at the pilgrim basilica in Santiago de Compostella with its gigantic swinging thurible (incense pot) and the celebration of Mass.

A local pilgrimage has developed in Iceland by Pastor Floki Kristinsson that involves a six-day walk to the shrine of St. Thorlak in Skálholt, where there is a modern little cathedral. The aim is to arrive at Skálholt on July 22, which is the feast day of St. Thorlak, whose remains have been uncovered on the cathedral grounds. (Thorlak is Iceland's only canonized saint.) Floki tells me that the pilgrimage helps people to discover themselves when they are removed from the ordinary routines and pressures of their lives, as well as bond with others on the pilgrim way and deepen their spirituality. The pilgrims travel the last mile barefoot and end the pilgrimage with the celebration of the Eucharist in the Skálholt cathedral.

Figure 1a. Pilgrimage to Skálholt.

The pilgrimages actually continue into the shrine churches that are their destinations for the celebration of the Divine Liturgy, the Mass, the Eucharist, the service of Holy Communion (as the liturgy of Word and Eucharistic Meal has been variously called in different traditions). Historically the liturgy continued with the same elements that constituted the songs of the pilgrimage: psalmody (Introit) and litanies (Kyrie Eleison). In the Western liturgy these elements climaxed in the canticle of praise, the Gloria in Excelsis (at least on Sundays and festivals, but in the Roman Mass not necessarily on weekdays).

In the liturgical revisions of the 1970s the introit psalm was usually replaced with a strophic hymn, and the other material (Kyrie, Glory to God, Worthy is Christ, Trisagion) was used as seemed appropriate for the day or season. This shortened the entrance rite and made it more flexible. But what was lost was a sense that crossing the threshold from this world into the dimension of the kingdom might require a little more time to make the adjustment, especially if people have been hurriedly getting into the nave by the starting time of the service while others are drifting in "late."

We settle into our places for the opening prayer and hear the Word of God. By the end of antiquity the Old Testament reading was lost and the liturgy only had the Epistle and Gospel. One of the great achievements of the liturgical revisions that occurred after the Second Vatican Council was to restore the Old Testament reading and a responsorial psalm after it. We have journeyed into the dimension of the kingdom, but in the readings Christ comes to meet us—typologically in the Old Testament readings and psalmody, in apostolic proclamation (*kerygma*) in the New Testament reading, and in Christ's own voice in the Gospel. In the Gospel procession—usually accompanied by lights proclaiming Christ as the light of the world—the living voice of Christ is brought into the midst of the assembly. This has been the structure of the three-year Roman and Revised Common Lectionaries (RCL).

In recent years some Protestants have found fault with the RCL because it doesn't cover enough Scripture. The Reformed tradition historically has preferred a continuous reading of and preaching on whole biblical books while Lutherans and Anglicans were comfortable continuing with the historic one-year lectionary pericope system. Those who opt for other lectionaries (such as the Narrative Lectionary) are usually trying to cover more of the Bible than the standard lectionaries do. But worship is not the same as Bible study. Historically, readings were chosen to fit the event being celebrated. In the pilgrimage rites a reading suitable to what the shrine commemorated was chosen. As the church year developed, in part as a result of pilgrimage rites in the Holy Land, readings were chosen because the church was commemorating Christ's birth or baptism or death or resurrection or ascension or some other biblical event or day of devotion or life of a saint. The liturgical commemoration determined the readings. Thus, the church year is not a reflection of the lectionary but the lectionary is based on the church year and its calendar of commemorations. And the purpose of the gathering is the meal, the Eucharist or Lord's Supper. The readings are brought to the Table. And the priority of the Gospel within the set of readings is to hear the living voice of Christ at the Lord's Table.[23] This purpose of the Gospel reading eludes those who don't proclaim it in the context of the Eucharist.

On the wall of the Skálholt cathedral above the high altar is a mosaic of Christ who seems to be crashing through the wall to enter the church at that altar. Thus one could imagine the pilgrims entering the

23. See Fritz West, *Scripture and Memory: The Ecumenical Hermeneutic of the Three-Year Lectionaries* (Collegeville, MN: Liturgical, 1997).

church at the west end and Christ entering at the east end, all meeting at the altar—the Table of the Word and the Meal.

Figure 1b. The Cathedral Church at Skálholt, Iceland.

Offertory and Great Entrance

We arrive at the place of the eucharistic celebration, but we do not arrive empty-handed. Bread and wine are needed for this celebration. The Christians of antiquity brought bread and wine for the Eucharist and other gifts for the church and their contributions for the poor and the sick. These were offerings for the needs of the body. Against gnostic devaluation of the material creation, including the human body, Irenaeus of Lyons pointed out the offering of material gifts and then the reception of the eucharistic body and blood of Christ as nourishment for human flesh, giving hope for the resurrection of the human body. He asked of the gnostics,

> How can they say that the flesh goes to corruption and does not partake of life, when it is nourished by the Lord's body and blood? Therefore, let them either change their opinion or refrain from offering the things just mentioned. But our opinion agrees with the Eucharist, and the Eucharist in turn confirms our opinion. For we offer to God those things which belong to God, proclaiming fittingly the communion and unity of the flesh and the spirit. For as the bread, which is produced from the earth, when it receives the invocation of God is no longer common bread, but the Eucharist, consisting of two realities, the earthly and the heavenly; so also our bodies, when they receive the Eucharist, are no longer corruptible, but have hope of the resurrection.[24]

To the extent possible, the gifts for the Eucharist were brought to the altar in the basilicas from the fourth century on both in the East and in the West. As we see in the papal Mass in *Ordo Romanus Primus* (ca. 700), the pope, other bishops, the archdeacon, and other deacons received gifts from the nobility and breads from the people that were collected into a sack held by acolytes and flasks of wine that were poured into a large vat.[25] Far more gifts were received than were needed for the celebration. These would be set aside for other celebrations, for the use of the clergy, and for the poor.[26]

While an offertory procession of the faithful continued in the West into the Middle Ages, in the East it proved more practical for the faith-

---

24. Irenaeus, *Adversus haereses* 4.18, trans. from David N. Power, *Irenaeus of Lyons on Baptism and Eucharist*, Alcuin/GROW Joint Liturgical Study 18 (Nottingham, UK: Grove, 1991), 21.
25. G. G. Willis, *Further Essays in Early Roman Liturgy*, Alcuin Club Collections 550 (London: SPCK, 1968), 18–19.
26. See Joseph A. Jungmann, SJ, *The Mass of the Roman Rite: Its Origins and Development*, trans. Francis A. Brunner, CSSR (Westminster, MD: Christian Classics, 1986), 2:7–8.

ful to deposit their gifts in a side room when they arrived in the basilica. The gifts of bread and wine needed for the Eucharist were taken to a sacristy and prepared for use on the paten and in the chalice that would be transferred to the altar in the Great Entrance. This became one of the most dramatic moments in the Divine Liturgy in the Byzantine tradition as the procession of bishop, presbyters, deacons, and acolytes, accompanied by banners, incense, and torches, made its way from the sacristy through the assembly and up through the royal doors while the cherubic hymn was sung.[27]

Joseph A. Jungmann notes that the offering of the faithful in the Western liturgies became bound up with the eucharistic sacrifice. By the eleventh century the bread and wine had ceased to be offered by the laity and they were prepared ahead of the Mass by the priests. At this point the offering of money came to the fore. This took the form especially of offerings for votive Masses for the dead, for the sick, for a good harvest, in honor of a saint, and so on. These intentions were mentioned in the *secreta* (silent) prayers at the offertory and in the *Hanc igitur* portion of the canon (eucharistic prayer). Those who were making a votive offering could bring it up to the altar and "thus join more closely in the sacrifice."[28]

This was precisely why Luther abolished the offertory prayers (calling them "*tota illa abominatio*") as well as the prayers of the canon, except for the words of institution.[29] They were connected with the offering of votive masses, and votive masses suggested the offering of the Eucharist for special intentions not covered in the once-for-all sufficient atoning sacrifice of Christ on the cross, the benefits of which are received in the gift of Communion. The vessels and elements on the altar still needed to be prepared for Holy Communion, but Luther suggested that that preparation could take place while the creed was being sung in both his Latin and German Masses. The effect of eliminating the offertory and making the creed the hinge between the office of the Word and the office of the Sacrament also brought Word and Sacrament into closer temporal juxtaposition. Luther would be surprised by how complicated offertories have become in current Lutheran services of Holy Communion with the collection of money, choir anthems,

---

27. See Robert F. Taft, SJ, *The Great Entrance. A History of the Transfer of the Gifts and Other Preanaphoral Rites of the Liturgy of St. John Chrysostom*, 2nd ed., Orientalia Christiana Analecta 200 (Rome: Pontificium institutum studiorum orientalium, 1978).
28. Jungmann, *Mass of the Roman Rite*, 2:23.
29. See Martin Luther, "An Order of Mass and Communion for the Church at Wittenberg," in *Luther's Works*, ed. Ulrich S. Leupold (Philadelphia: Fortress, 1965), 53:25–26.

special recognitions, offertory processions with plates of money, and sometimes the transfer of bread and wine from the credence table to the altar while an offertory psalm or song is sung.

In the liturgical renewal of the 1960s there was an attempt to revive the offertory procession of the people. This caused some amount of theological controversy in the Church of England and in American Lutheranism in the 1970s.[30] In many congregations the bread and wine is included with the money gifts in the offertory procession to the altar. Of greater consequence is encouraging people to directly provide the bread and wine for the Eucharist.

The offertory prayers in the 1969 Roman Mass remind us of the grain and grapes "that earth has given and human hands have made" into bread and wine. Yes, "earth has given" what we receive; we humans made products from what earth has given and offer them back to God. The gifts of creation are gifts of God's grace. Joseph Sittler suggested that before we consider the quite proper understanding of grace as the overcoming of alienation from God by God's action of forgiveness, we need to discern "grace as the sheer *givenness character* of life, of the world, and the self—the plain *presentedness* of all that is."[31]

In our Eucharists we need to appreciate the earthly gifts which serve as means of grace. It would be well if our churches could get rid of the unleavened wafers and return to the practice of the church members baking the bread for the Eucharist, as is done in the Orthodox churches. We need fresh bread with an aroma that suggests our relationship to the earth and to human touch. We need wine that has been aged with care. We need to treat reverently the bread and wine as gifts we offer to God and gifts that are given back to us as Holy Communion. I once wrote an essay suggesting that our reverential treatment and disposal of the consecrated elements can model our treatment of the earth itself.[32]

Indeed, what liturgy can do is model behavior and form attitude. The behavior liturgy should teach is to handle earthly things with care and reverence; the attitude it should cultivate is appreciation, even gratitude, for the givenness of the things we simply receive by grace. Liturgy can teach us what we should do at every one of our tables at home: receive the things of creation with appreciation and thanksgiv-

---

30. See Frank C. Senn, "The Presentation of the Gifts: The Offertory Reconsidered," in *A Stewardship of the Mysteries* (Mahwah, NJ: Paulist, 1999), 73–80.
31. Joseph Sittler, *Essays on Nature and Grace* (Philadelphia: Fortress, 1972), 88.
32. Frank C. Senn, "'The Care of the Earth' as a Paradigm for the Treatment of the Eucharistic Elements," in *A Stewardship of the Mysteries* (Mahwah, NJ: Paulist, 1999), 175–90.

ing. One of my favorite English authors, G. K. Chesterton, wrote in his *Autobiography* (completed only a few weeks before his death in 1936), "The aim of life is appreciation; there is no sense in not appreciating things; and there is no sense in having more of them if you have less appreciation of them."[33] This eucharistic offering is an expression of the liturgical work of the priesthood of believers, just as it is the work of the lay priesthood to offer intercession for the world (laypeople in liturgical renewal parishes often lead the intercessions). The gifts of bread and wine as part of their offering to God is a tangible expression of the sacrifice of thanksgiving (*sacrificium laudis*) offered by the whole people of God, laity as well as the ordained priesthood. In this act, the people of God are living out their fundamental calling as priests of creation.[34] It is from this act that the term *Eucharistia* is extended to cover the whole order of worship from gathering to sending. In bringing their gifts to the altar, the people are offering themselves in a manner that recalls Christ's own self-sacrifice of his life for the life of the world—the epitome of the gospel that we proclaim and celebrate in the Eucharist.

Altars and Tables

We come now to *ad altare Dei.* Altars in the ancient world were associated with sacrifices. Undoubtedly Christians had no altars as such in their symposium banquets. A table was needed on which to place the food, including the bread and wine for the Eucharist, which would be passed to the reclining communicants by the servants of the church (deacons). A table would always be needed for the eucharistic meal.

Generally Christians prayed facing east toward the rising sun and hailed Christ as the Sun of Righteousness. In the earliest basilicas the altar table was farther out into the nave than was later the case. The standing congregation could be gathered on three sides with *cancelli* (low railings) fencing the altar. The bishop assumed the seat (*cathedra*) of the magistrate or governor in the apse, surrounded on benches by his presbyters. If the apse was on the east end of the building the celebrant faced the apse for prayer, along with the people (*ad orientem*). If east was on the entrance end of the building the celebrant faced the

---

33. G. K. Chesterton, *The Autobiography of G. K. Chesterton* (San Francisco: Ignatius, 2006), 327.
34. Georgia Masters Keightley, "The Church's Laity: Called to Be Creation's Priests," *Worship* 84, no. 4 (July 2010): 309–27.

entrance for prayer, and therefore also faced the people (*versus populum*).

When Christians gathered in cemeteries or underground catacombs they celebrated the Eucharist on the graves of the faithful departed, placing the bread and wine on the flat mensa of the grave marker, just as the Romans did in their *refrigeria*. This had a profound influence on the development of altars in the basilicas. The earliest altars in basilicas were still wooden tables. But eventually they were stone tables that looked like tombs. Indeed, they were tombs because relics of the saints were embedded in the altars. Thus they became a part of the cult of the saints. At the same time, they were the place on which the sacrifice of the Mass was offered, especially votive Masses offered with special intentions for the living and the dead. As the demand for votive Masses increased during the times of plague in the late Middle Ages, the church buildings became ringed with side altars. In addition, medieval altars were adorned with pictures in altar panels rising in the reredos behind the mensa. In John Calvin's interpretation of the Ten Commandments, the prohibition on "graven images" was its own commandment, not just a continuation of the first commandment about "other gods." For all these reasons, as far as the Reformed were concerned, altars had to go; they were too much associated with papal error and superstition. They would be replaced by simple wooden tables from which the Lord's Supper would be administered. In 1550 all altars were dismantled in England and were replaced by communion tables arranged lengthwise in the chancel between choir stalls. The celebrant stood on the north side of the Table facing communicants who had moved into the stalls on the south side. Martin Luther had suggested in his treatise on *The German Mass and Order of Service* (1526) that "the altar should not remain where it is, and the priest should always face the people as Christ doubtlessly did in the Last Supper. But let that await its own time."[35]

The Reformed were especially irked that Lutherans continued to use the pre-Reformation altars, sometimes leaving the relics intact rather than destroying the altar to remove them. Lutherans even built new and bigger altars by the end of the sixteenth century, adorned with new works of art, such as the altar pieces of Lucas Cranach the Younger, which painted scenes of Word and Sacrament rather than of the lives of the saints.[36] This continuing use of pictures also became a

---

35. *Luther's Works*. Vol. 53, *Liturgy and Hymns*, ed. and trans. Ulrich S. Leupold (Philadelphia: Fortress, 1965), 69.

source of contention between Lutherans and Reformed. Martin Luther had counseled freedom in "indifferent matters" (*adiaphora*), things that were neither commanded nor forbidden in Scripture and had nothing to do with salvation. But the resolution of the adiaphoristic controversy in Lutheranism after Luther's death resulted in a confessional position, stated in the Formula of Concord, that "nothing is an indifferent matter in a situation of confession" (*Nihil est adiaphoron in statu confessionis*).[37] So against Reformed demands that altars must be abolished in favor of simple wooden Communion tables, Lutherans argued that their Christian freedom allowed them to continue to use altars since they were no longer the place of the veneration of saints and the sacrifice of the Mass but of prayer and thanksgiving and the Lord's Supper. Moreover, appropriate pictures on the altar reredoses helped to instruct and edify the faithful. There is also something to be said for the beauty of holiness, and Lutherans castigated Reformed churches that looked like horse barns. While Reformed communicants stood before the Communion Table (the practice at Strassburg) or sat around the Communion Table (the practice of the Scots Presbyterians), Lutherans continued to kneel before their ornate altars to receive the true body and blood of Christ.

Catholic altars were also changed by the Reformation, and by changes in architectural styles. Beginning with the Jesuit Church in Rome (Il Gesú, built 1568–1575), the Gothic rood screens and divided choirs that separated people in the nave from the high altar were abandoned. Jesuits had no practice of a choral prayer office, so a divided chancel was not needed. Organ and musical forces were moved into the rear or a side balcony. This enabled the whole sanctuary in the neoclassical church buildings to be opened up and the altar clearly exposed to the congregation.[38] This became the new model of Catholic church architecture after the Council of Trent. By the end of the sixteenth century tabernacles were placed on the altar mensas, which contained the reserved Hosts. This placed the reserved hosts front and center rather than off to the side like in hanging pyxes, sacrament houses, or side-wall ambries. Catholics were encouraged to commune more frequently, but ocular Communion received a boost with the popular devotion of

36. See Bodo Nischan, "Becoming Protestants: Lutheran Altars or Reformed Communion Tables?," in *Worship in Medieval and Early Modern Europe: Change and Continuity in Religious Practice*, ed. Karin Maag and John D. Witvliet (Notre Dame: University of Notre Dame Press, 2004), 84–111.
37. Robert Kolb and Timothy J. Wengert, eds., *The Book of Concord: The Confessions of the Evangelical Lutheran Church* (Minneapolis: Fortress, 2000), 637.
38. James F. White, *Roman Catholic Worship: Trent to Today* (Mahwah, NJ: Paulist, 1995), 6–9.

Benediction of the Blessed Sacrament after Sunday Vespers. Catholics clearly believed that Christ was present and resided in the tabernacle. This prompted genuflection when Catholics passed in front of the altar.

In the liturgical movement of the twentieth century, there was concern to bring the altar toward or even into the assembled congregation with the presiding minister facing the people (*versus populum*) across the altar. This was based on the basilican style in ancient Rome in which some churches had a westward rather than an eastward orientation (*ad orientem*). Pope Benedict XVI (as Joseph Cardinal Ratzinger) made a strong case for celebrant and people turning together toward the coming Lord in prayer. This orientation can be a powerful eschatological symbol.[39] Ratzinger made the point that, in fact, the cross marks the spot: celebrant and people should pray facing the cross, which would direct orientation. However, the point was to face *east*. Over time the altar receded farther and farther into the apse, pushing the bishop or celebrant to the side. If the apse was truly on the east end of the building, the celebrant would face east for prayer (including during the eucharistic prayer) and his back would be toward the people. Eventually the apse was considered the "liturgical east" whether it was the geographic east or not. If the celebrant is facing another actual direction, this undermines the value of orientation.

Orientation is a powerful religious symbol. Jews orient toward Jerusalem in prayer and Muslims orient toward Mecca. If Christians are going to orient toward the east, they should actually be facing east no matter how the worship space is oriented. If the altar is farther out into the midst of the people, the celebrant will also be more in the midst of people, as we see in many church buildings that have been designed since the 1960s. Then it is possible to orient properly and still be in the midst of the people. Praying facing east together emphasizes the eschatological character of Christian liturgy. But gathering around the Table for the eucharistic meal emphasizes the sense of the presence of the Lord among us.

---

39. Joseph Cardinal Ratzinger, *The Feast of Faith: Approaches to a Theology of the Liturgy*, trans. Graham Harrison (San Francisco: Ignatius, 1986), 139–45.

Figure 1c. The Jesuit Church Il Gesú in Rome (built 1568–1575) is noted for its open approach to the altar. It became a model for Catholic church architecture after the Council of Trent.

Behind the new design of liturgical spaces is a change of what Lawrence Hoffman called the master cultural image from transcendence to immanence.[40] In these new or renewed spaces the emphasis is not on worshiping a transcendent God "out there" but on experiencing God present "among us." This is a change in the location of what Rudolf Otto called "the numinous." Beginning in the 1950s with the growth of the suburbs, the new master image for our experience of the numinous has become what we call "community." "Community" here is not understood as the town or city neighborhood in which one lives but as a group that is like an extended family bound together not by blood but by mutual concerns and commitments.

So by community I mean what the anthropologist Victor Turner called *communitas*—a social setting in which class structures are removed and social distance is diminished.[41] The master image of community emphasizes a group experience that is characterized by words like *openness, relationships, sharing.* Immanence is becoming a more universal master image for churches and religions. It has implications for how people participate in worship and how we experience presence. "Real presence" is not "up there" but "down here," among us and within us—which is what we have always believed about Holy Communion. Our liturgical journey, enacting our earthly pilgrimage, is a journey into the divine presence. But the Lord whom we seek also comes to tabernacle among us. We meet him and one another *ad altare Dei.*

40. Lawrence A. Hoffman, *Beyond the Text: A Holistic Approach to Liturgy* (Bloomington and Indianapolis: Indiana University Press, 1987), 149–71.
41. Victor Turner, *The Ritual Process: Structure and Anti-structure* (Chicago: Aldine, 1969), 126–30.

2

Anaphora: A Eucharistic Life

We have seen how the word was joined to the eucharistic meal and eventually formed a unified liturgy of Word and Meal by the second century of the church's life. The only liturgical texts we have from these meal gatherings in the early Christian centuries are the eucharistic prayers, which gave their name to the whole liturgical order: *Eucharistia*. We have eucharistic prayers in the late first-century church manual known as the *Didache*, chapters 9 and 10,[1] which are very much patterned after the kind of Jewish table blessings (*berakhot*) over the first cup and shared loaf at the beginning of the meal and the concluding thanksgiving after the supper (*birkat ha-mazon*) that are later mentioned in the Mishnah (ca. 200 CE).

There has been debate over whether the table prayers in the *Didache* are for an Agape meal or the Eucharist. The rubric at the beginning of chapter 9 clearly says, "Concerning the Eucharist." Earlier scholars had difficulty imagining the Eucharist or Lord's Supper in the context of an actual meal.[2] They were attracted to the fact that chapter 14:1 states, "Assembling on every Sunday of the Lord, break bread and give thanks, confessing your faults beforehand, so that your sacrifice may be pure."[3]

---

1. Kurt Niederwimmer, *The Didache: A Commentary*, trans. Linda M. Maloney, Hermeneia (Minneapolis: Fortress, 1998), 144, 155.
2. See, for example, J.-P. Audet, *La Didachè: Instructions des Apôtres* (Paris: Cerf, 1958).
3. Niederwimmer, *The Didache*, 194.

Since the next verse states, "Let no one engaged in a dispute with his comrade join you until they have been reconciled," I think it is more likely that chapter 14 is concerned about eucharistic discipline than about the Eucharist itself. I accept the conclusion of my seminary professor, Arthur Vööbus, that the table prayers in chapters 9-10 belong to the Eucharist.[4] The next oldest extant eucharistic prayer is the third-century East Syrian Anaphora of Addai and Mari.[5] It shows some characteristics of Semitic prayers and is still used, in a more developed version, in the Syro-Malabar Church in India. In its original form it is a series of separate prayers, as in *The Didache*. This explains why the first prayer can be addressed to the Father "who created the world in his lovingkindness" while the second prayer is addressed to the Son in thanksgiving for his great grace "in that you have clothed yourself in our humanity so as to enliven us with your divinity." It is possible, as Emmanuel Cutrone suggested, that the Lord's Supper was shared after the epiclesis of the Holy Spirit and that the final thanksgiving was offered after the meal.[6]

Another eucharistic prayer that was thought to date from the early third century, but that probably received its final form in the fourth century (although some parts might be as old as the second), is the anaphora in the church order known as the *Apostolic Tradition*, which was once attributed to Hippolytus of Rome.[7] This anaphora caught the imagination of modern liturgical committees and found entré, in whole or in part, into several late twentieth century eucharistic liturgies, including Roman Catholic, Lutheran, and Episcopal. In actuality, whether it was composed by Hippolytus or not, it was most likely a model prayer rather than an actual one.

Because the eucharistic prayer was the central text of the eucharistic liturgies, it received a lot of attention as a liturgical genre from liturgical scholars. When I began graduate work in liturgical studies at the University of Notre Dame in 1969 a lot of attention was given to eucharistic prayers in the course on ancient Christian liturgy. The

---

4. Arthur Vööbus, *Liturgical Traditions in the Didache* (Stockholm: Estonian Theological Society in Exile, 1968).

5. W. F. Macomber, "The Oldest Known Text of the Anaphora of the Holy Apostles Addai and Mari," *Orientalia Christiana Periodica* 32 (1966): 335-37; Bryan D. Spinks, ed., *Addai and Mari—The Anaphora of the Apostles: A Text for Students* (Bramcote, UK: Grove, 1980); Sarhad Jammo, "The Anaphora of the Apostles Addai and Mari: A Study of Structure and Background," *Orientalia Christiana Periodica* 68 (2002): 5-35.

6. E. J. Cutrone, "The Anaphora of the Apostles: Implications of the Mar Esa'ya Text, *Theological Studies* 34 (1973): 624-42.

7. Paul F. Bradshaw, Maxwell E. Johnson, and L. Edward Phillips, *The Apostolic Tradition: A Commentary*, Hermeneia (Minneapolis: Fortress, 2002), 38-41.

anthology of eucharistic texts edited by Anton Hänggi and Irmgard Pahl had just been published.[8] At the same time, Louis Bouyer's *Eucharist* had just been published in English translation by the University of Notre Dame Press, and we gave some attention in the doctoral liturgy seminar to checking out his sources (or lack thereof).[9]

In the early 1970s I became involved in the liturgical work of the Lutheran Church while still a graduate student. I was appointed to the Consulting Committee on Worship of the Lutheran Church in America. Our major task in those days was to review the proposals of the Inter-Lutheran Commission on Worship (ILCW) that would lead to a new inter-Lutheran worship book, the *Lutheran Book of Worship* (1978), as well as other documents, such as a proposed Statement on Communion Practices that I already mentioned. Eugene Brand, the project director of the Inter-Lutheran Committee on Worship, secured my appointment on several working subcommittees of the ILCW, including the one on eucharistic prayers as it neared the completion of its tasks.

The use of a full eucharistic prayer emerged as one of the most controversial issues in the ILCW's work in the 1970s, in spite of the fact that the Common Liturgy in the *Service Book and Hymnal* (1958), used by the eight Lutheran churches that merged into the ALC (1960) and LCA (1962), included the option of a full eucharistic prayer. The *Worship Supplement* published by the Commission on Worship of the Lutheran Church–Missouri Synod in 1969 included four full eucharistic prayers, one of which was the so-called Anaphora of Hippolytus (*Apostolic Tradition*). Nevertheless, the use of a full eucharistic prayer became the subject of debate. In particular there was a series of theological exchanges between LCA theologian Robert W. Jenson and ALC theologian Gerhard Forde in papers prepared for the ILCW and included in the minutes of the Commission.[10] It would take us too far afield to rehearse here the detailed arguments and specific proposals of Jenson and Forde, but in general Jenson appealed to the Eastern traditions as models for new Lutheran Eucharistic prayers, especially the use of the Epiclesis of the Spirit to enliven the Words of Christ, and Forde insisted that a distinction must be made between prayer and proclamation, with the Words of Institution in the category of proclamation. There must be an

---

8. Anton Hänggi and Irmgard Pahl, eds., *Prex Eucharistica: Textus e Variis Liturgiis Antiquioribus Selecti* (Fribourg: Éditions Universitaires Fribourg Suisse, 1968).
9. Louis Bouyer, *Eucharist: Theology and Spirituality of the Eucharistic Prayer*, trans. Charles Underhill Quinn (Notre Dame: University of Notre Dame Press, 1968).
10. See "Forde-Jenson Papers," Record Group #31: roll #10

"Amen" to a previous prayer before continuing with the Words of Institution.

The ILCW had published in *Contemporary Worship-10: The Great Thanksgiving* a set of ten eucharistic prayers for trial use. I was added to the subcommittee on eucharistic prayers after the publication of *CW-10*. From this base our subcommittee prepared four full eucharistic prayers that the ILCW approved for inclusion in the *Lutheran Book of Worship*, leaders' edition: an emendation of the Great Thanksgiving in *CW-2: The Service of Holy Communion* (1970); a revision of "the prayer of many parts" in *CW-10: The Great Thanksgiving* (1976), which was my task; a slight emending of the Prayer of Thanksgiving from the *Service Book and Hymnal* (1958), attributed to Luther D. Reed; and the so-called Anaphora of Hippolytus, translated by Gordon Lathrop.[11]

Doctoral Dissertation on the Swedish Reformation Eucharist

Because this work on the eucharistic prayers was going on with its attendant controversies, I decided to focus on some area of the Eucharist for my doctoral dissertation. Lutheran liturgy had not had a full eucharistic prayer until the twentieth century; it had focused instead on the *Verba Testamenti* (words of institution). Consecration was understood to be the proclamation of these words of Christ (also called the institution narrative). In Luther's Latin Mass (*Formula Missae et Communionis* [1523]) the institution narrative was attached to the common eucharistic preface with a *qui*-clause (who on the night in which he was betrayed . . .) and was therefore within the context of prayer. In his German Mass (*Deutsche Messe und Gottesdienst* [1526]) the institution narrative stood alone and was chanted to the same tone as the gospel chant. Typical Lutheran Communion services based on the German church orders included the preface dialogue (Sursum Corda), the common or a proper preface leading to the Sanctus, and then either the Lord's Prayer and institution narrative or the institution narrative and the Lord's Prayer (different church orders followed different sequences). As I noted, the *Service Book and Hymnal of the Lutheran Church in America* included the option of a full eucharistic prayer of classical design that included the institution narrative. This prayer was attributed to Luther D. Reed (although it may originally have been

11. This process is described by Gail Ramshaw-Schmidt, "Toward Lutheran Eucharistic Prayers," in Frank C. Senn, ed., *New Eucharistic Prayers: An Ecumenical Study of Their Development and Structure* (Mahwah, NJ: Paulist, 1987), 74–79.

the work of Paul Strodach). Lutheran liturgical work in Europe had also been reconsidering the use of eucharistic prayer. An example of a Lutheran eucharistic prayer from the Reformation period would carry great weight for contemporary Lutheran consideration.

The Swedish Mass always had a fuller eucharistic expression than German Mass orders. The Swedish Mass of Olavus Petri (1531) and subsequent editions up through the Church Order of Archbishop Laurentius Petri (1571) followed the pattern of Luther's *Formula Missae*. It had an expanded eucharistic preface based on the paschal preface leading into the institution narrative, which was followed by the Sanctus and Benedictus.

But in 1576 there appeared a Swedish-Latin Liturgy with a full eucharistic prayer in the so-called Red Book (*Den röde boken*) of King Johan III. The ordo of this Liturgy followed that of Luther's *Formula Missae* and Olavus Petri's *Swedish Mass* with preface dialogue, preface, Words of Institution, and Sanctus and Benedictus. In addition to Petri's paschal preface and a second common preface for weekdays the Liturgy of King Johan III provided eight proper prefaces for Christmas, Epiphany, the Annunciation, Passiontide, Easter, the Ascension, Pentecost, and Trinity. During the singing of the Sanctus the celebrant offered four prayers in a quiet voice: *Memores igitur, Et supplices te, Nobis quoque peccatoribus,* and *Per quem Domine.*

When I saw this liturgy and its eucharistic prayer in an anthology of texts on the Mass in Sweden by Eric Yelverton, I knew this had to be my dissertation topic.[12] It required learning some Swedish and improving my Latin (although the primary sources were in sixteenth century versions of these languages). I received a small travel grant from the LCA Board of Theological Education and spent six weeks in Uppsala using Carolina Rediviva (the famed university library) and taking a side trip to Turku, Finland to visit the Åbo Akademie and pay a call on Professor Sigtrygg Serenius, who had written a dissertation on *Liturgia svecanae ecclesiae catholicae et orthodoxae conformis.*[13]

---

12. Eric E. Yelverton, *The Mass in Sweden: Its Development from the Latin Rite from 1531 to 1917*, Henry Bradshaw Society 57 (London: Harrison & Sons, 1920), 78–120. I published a synopsis of my dissertation in an article in *Studia Liturgica*. Large segments of it were included in my book *Christian Liturgy: Catholic and Evangelical*. For both, see Frank C. Senn, "Liturgia Svecanae Ecclesiae: An Attempt at Eucharistic Restoration during the Swedish Reformation," *Studia Liturgica* 14 (1980–1981): 20–36; Senn, *Christian Liturgy: Catholic and Evangelical* (Minneapolis: Fortress, 1997), 399–476.

13. Sigtrygg Serenius, *Liturgia svecanae ecclesiae catholicae et orthodoxae conformis: En liturgihistorisk undersökning med särskild hänsyn till struktur och förloagor* (Åbo, Finland: Åbo Akademi, 1966). Johan III had been Duke of Finland before succeeding his deposed brother Erik XIV as king and was held in higher esteem by the Finns than by the Swedes.

In order to demonstrate that this Liturgy could be regarded as evangelical as well as Catholic, I needed to immerse myself in a study of the Reformation in Sweden. The Reformation pursued a more irenic course in Sweden than in Germany because Gustav I Vasa used the Reformation to achieve the political ends of national independence and financial self-sufficiency. Because no confession of faith was adopted until the end of the sixteenth century (at the Uppsala synod in 1593), a number of theological options existed side by side within one national church: primarily the Lutheranism of Olavus and Laurentius Petri, but also Reform-Catholicism (manifested in the *Missa Lincopensis*), Calvinism (under Erik XIV and Karl IX), and the George Cassander–inspired mediating theology of Johan III with its desire for reconciliation between Rome and Wittenberg on the basis of the *consensus quinquasaecularis* (consensus of the first five centuries). Swedish liturgical development in the sixteenth century must be seen in this context.

While the Swedish Mass of Olavus Petri (1531) followed the structure of Luther's *Formula Missae*, it was more directly influenced by Döber's Nuremberg Mass. Over a period of forty years Archbishop Laurentius Petri amalgamated the Swedish Mass with the Latin Mass until the Swedish *högmässa* was definitively ordered in the 1571 *Church Order*. Johan III intended to continue the Melanchthonian orientation of Laurentius Petri, but in such a way as to move toward evangelical-Catholic reunion by returning to the fathers. *Nova ordinantia ecclesiastica* (1575) reflected this tendency, but on the whole it must be regarded as a compromise between Johan III and the bishops (thus Roland Persson[14]). *Liturgia svecanae ecclesiae catholicae et orthodoxae conformis* (1576) can be taken much more as an expression of Johan's mediating theology.

The liturgy (the Red Book) immediately aroused the antagonism of an "antiliturgist" party because of its ceremonial richness and expression of eucharistic offering of the Son of God (*eudem filium . . . offerimus tibi*). Because of the presence of Jesuits at Johan's court and because of Johan's clandestine negotiations with the papacy over the assets of his wife, Queen Katarina Jagellonica of Poland, the liturgy was viewed by the antiliturgists as a Jesuit product. Recent research has shown that the liturgy is not just a conflation of "two heterogeneous elements" (*Missale Romanum* 1570 and *Svenska Mässan* 1557)—the opinion of older Swedish scholars; it also shows the influence of medieval Swedish missal traditions, conservative German church orders, the Anglican

---

14. Roland Persson, *Johan III och Noca Ordinantia* (Lund: CWK Gleerup, 1973).

Book of Common Prayer, and a conscious use of Eastern and early church sources (thus Sigtrygg Serenius[15]). The offertory and eucharistic prayers in the Red Book were carefully crafted to express an evangelical theology.

Even so, is it possible to have a full eucharistic prayer in the Lutheran liturgy because of the problem of eucharistic sacrifice? Some have said no. Sixteenth-century polemics make it difficult to delineate the issues involved. There was, of course, the issue of the transactional character of the votive Mass, which was the most frequently celebrated type of Mass in the Middle Ages. But there was also what Ferdinand Pratzner called the "crisis of the sacramental idea,"[16] which resulted in the historicization of the sacrifice of the cross in medieval and Reformation theology. This was caused by concern to protect the doctrine of the real presence in medieval theology. It led to rendering asunder *sacramentum et res, figura et veritas.*

The major problem is an offering of the bread and wine after the words of institution. The classical eucharistic prayers have, after the institution narrative, a remembrance of Christ's saving work and offering an offering of bread and wine: *memores . . . offerimus.* If the *Verba Christi* are seen as consecratory, the oblation after the *Verba* would be understood to be the body and blood of Christ. Objecting that the body and blood of Christ cannot be offered to God, Luther rejected any liturgical offering of the elements after the consecratory words of institution. In his 1520 *Prelude to the Babylonian Captivity of the Church,* Luther wrote:

> Therefore, let the priests who offer the sacrifice of the mass in these corrupt and most perilous times take heed, first, that they do not refer to the sacrament the words of the greater or lesser canon [offertory and eucharistic prayers], together with the collects, because they smack too strongly of sacrifice. They should refer them instead to the bread and wine to be consecrated, or to their own prayers. For the bread and wine are offered beforehand for blessing in order that they may be sanctified by the word and by prayer [1 Tim 4:5], but after they have been blessed and consecrated they are no longer offered, but received as a gift from God.[17]

15. Sigtrygg Serenius, *Liturgia svecanae ecclesiae catholicae et orthodoxae conformis: En liturgihistorisk undersökning med särskild hänsyn till struktur och förloagor* (Åbo, Finland: Åbo Akademi, 1966).
16. Ferdinand Pratzner, *Messe und Kreuzopfer. Die Krise der Sakramentalen Idee bei Luther und in der Mittelalterlichen Scholastik* (Wien: Herder, 1970).
17. Martin Luther, *The Babylonian Captivity of the Church,* in *Luther's Works,* ed. Abdel Ross Wentz (Philadelphia: Muhlenberg, 1961), 36:84.

What Luther is saying regarding liturgical order is that after the con-secration of the bread and wine (which, following the Western under-standing from Ambrose via Thomas Aquinas, was identified with the words of Christ), the elements are the body and blood of Christ, they can no longer be offered to God; that would be a blasphemous reversal of the "direction" of the sacrament. The elements are to be received by the communicants as the gift of Communion.[18]

However, in his writings concerning the *use* of the sacrament as the gift of Communion, Luther was able to see how the dimension of sac-rifice pervaded the whole Mass. In his *Admonition concerning the Sacra-ment* of 1530 Luther held that the act of "remembrance" (*anamnesis*) and the "sacrament" are two different things. "The memorial [*Gedächt-nis*] is indeed supposed to be a sacrifice of thanksgiving; but the sacra-ment itself [*das Sacrament selbst*] should not be a sacrifice, but a gift of God which he has given to us and which we should take and receive with thanks." Luther continues:

> For this reason I think that the ancients called this office *eucharistia* or *sacramentum eucharistie*, that is, a thanksgiving. For in this sacrament we should thank God according to the command of Christ, and we should use and receive the sacrament with thanks. . . .
>
> As a result of such an understanding I believe that many hymns were included and retained in the mass which deal with thanking and praising [God] in a wonderful and excellent way, as for example, the Gloria in excelsis, the Alleluia, the Lord's Prayer [Luther said *Patrem*, which should refer to the creed, not the Lord's Prayer; the translation is not correct], the Preface, the Sanctus, the Benedictus, and the Agnus Dei. In these var-ious parts you find nothing about a sacrifice but only praise and thanks. Therefore we have also kept them in our mass.[19]

Philipp Melanchthon also turned to ancient and Eastern liturgies to find models of a proper Eucharistic sacrifice. In the Apology of the Augsburg Confession, article 24, he notes that

> The Greek canon also says a lot about an offering; but it clearly shows that it is not talking about the body and blood of the Lord in particular, but about the entire service, about the prayers and thanksgivings. This is what it says: "And make us worthy to come to offer you entreaties and supplications and bloodless sacrifices for all the people" [from the Divine

---

18. See Carl F. Wisløff, *The Gift of Communion: Luther's Controversy with Rome on the Eucharistic Sacrifice*, trans. Joseph M. Shaw (Minneapolis: Augsburg, 1958).
19. Martin Luther, *Admonition concerning the Sacrament*, in *Luther's Works*, ed. Martin E. Lehmann (Philadelphia: Fortress, 1971), 38:122–23.

Liturgy of St. John Chrysostom, cited in Greek]. Properly understood, this is not offensive. It prays that we might be made worthy to offer prayers and supplications and bloodless sacrifices for the people. [Melanchthon is here translating his quote into Latin.] It calls even prayers "bloodless sacrifices." It also says this a little later: "We offer you this reasonable and bloodless service" [liturgy]. It is a misinterpretation to translate this as a "reasonable victim" and to apply it to the body of Christ itself [as in the Roman canon]. For the [Greek] canon is talking about the entire service; and by "reasonable service" [Rom 12:1] Paul meant the service of the mind, fear, faith, prayer, thanksgiving, and the like, in opposition to a theory of *ex opera operato*.[20]

Since the Apology of the Augsburg Confession is a confessional writing included in the Book of Concord, we may say that Lutheranism has a positive confessional evaluation of the Greek anaphoras in the West Syrian family of prayers in its symbolical books, and particularly their understanding of the eucharistic sacrifice, and therefore those eucharistic prayer traditions should be available as models for Lutheran eucharistic prayers. The liturgical movement had taken a special interest in the West Syrian anaphoras because of their trinitarian structure and narrative elements. This structure includes:

Introductory praise of the Father for the work of creation
    Leading to the Sanctus
Remembrance of the saving work of the Son
    Leading to the words of institution (institution narrative)
Anamnesis statement
    Leading to the offering of the gifts of bread and wine
Epiclesis of the Holy Spirit
    Leading to the intercessions and commemorations
Concluding trinitarian doxology

The positive interpretations of eucharistic memorial and sacrifice that the Apology notes in the "Greek canons" were present in the writings of the Swedish Reformers, especially Archbishop Laurentius Petri, and they are given liturgical expression in the Liturgy of Johan III. Laurentius Petri had taught that the Eucharist can be called a sacrifice "because the priest and the congregation interpose it between the wrath of God and their sins."[21] The same idea is expressed in the

---

20. Robert Kolb and Timothy J. Wengert, eds., *The Book of Concord* (Minneapolis: Fortress, 2000), 274.
21. Cited in Gustaf Aulén, *Eucharist and Sacrifice*, trans. Eric H. Wahlstrom (Philadelphia: Muhlenberg, 1958), 98.

Liturgy of King Johan III. After the preface and institution narrative, while the choir sings the Sanctus and Benedictus (it follows the order of the Swedish Mass of Olavus Petri), the celebrant continues with a revised *Memores igitur*:

> Therefore we also remember, O Lord God, this blessed command and the same thy son our Lord Jesus Christ's holy passion and death, his resurrection and ascension. And this thy son thou hast in thy boundless mercy sent and given unto us, that he might be an offering for our sins, and by his one offering on the cross pay the price of our redemption, fulfill thy justice and make perfect such an offering as might serve for the welfare of all the elect unto the end of the world. The same thy Son, the same offering, which is a pure, holy and undefiled offering, set before us for our reconciliation, our shield, defense, and covering against thy wrath, against the terror of sins and of death, we take and receive with faith and offer before thy glorious majesty with our humble supplications. For these thy great benefits we give thee fervent thanks with heart and mouth, yet not as our bounden duty is but according to our power.[22]

The oblation here is not the bread and wine, much less the body and blood of Christ, but rather the offering of the Son to the Father, which "we take and receive with faith." Remembering the sacrifice of the Son to the Father is for the purpose of appealing to his atoning sacrifice as the basis of our trust in the benefits we receive in the gift of Communion. Gustaf Aulén would argue, on the basis of this Swedish eucharistic tradition, that the real presence of Christ also implies the presence of his atoning sacrifice.[23] I argued in my dissertation that the Red Book expressed an understanding of the presence of Christ's sacrifice in the Mass that is compatible with the evangelical theology as taught by the Swedish Reformers. It is a different approach to eucharistic sacrifice than the German tradition, but it is an approach available to us as we work on eucharistic prayers.[24]

Anaphoral Theology

Lutherans may have had difficulties with eucharistic sacrifice, but not with all aspects of it. Most Lutheran Mass orders have included the preface dialogue, often referred to simply as the Sursum Corda, the

22. Yelverton, *The Mass in Sweden*, 106–7.
23. Aulén, *Eucharist and Sacrifice*, 100.
24. See Frank C. Senn, "Toward a Different Anaphoral Structure," *Worship* 58 (1984), 346–58; included in Frank C. Senn, *A Stewardship of the Mysteries* (New York and Mahwah, NJ: Paulist, 1999), 81–94.

preface (with variable propers), and the Sanctus. The Eastern eucharistic prayers are called "anaphora" after the Sursum Corda. Hence, we speak of the Anaphoras of St. Mark, St. James, St. Basil, St. John Chrysostom, and so on.

The lines of dialogue between the presider and the assembly before the Great Thanksgiving are common to all the classical eucharistic prayers from the third or fourth century on. From the Anaphora of St. John Chrysostom and St. Basil:

Ἱερεύς· Ἄνω σχῶμεν τὰς καρδίας.
Λαός· Ἔχομεν πρὸς τὸν Κύριον.

The Latin version in the Roman canon is:

Priest: Sursum corda.
People: Habemus ad Dominum.

The English is:

P: Lift up your hearts.
C: We lift them to the Lord.

Ἄνω suggests an offering since it is a lifting up, drawing on the Old Testament image of the heave offering. But instead of lifting up bread and wine (or money) we are to lift up our hearts. Lifting our hearts is a metaphorical expression. The term "heart" (Hebrew *leb*, Greek *kardia*) is used more than a thousand times in the Bible. Its metaphorical uses are diverse but not unrelated to the bodily organ, and by easy transition to those experiences that affect or are affected by the body. Emotions such as fear, love, courage, anger, joy, sorrow, hatred are always ascribed to the heart—especially in the Old Testament Psalms. As representing the human person, the heart was considered to be the seat of emotions (Lev 19:17—hatred in the heart), but also the center of moral, spiritual, and intellectual life. Sometimes *leb* is rendered as "mind." The Anaphora in Book 8 of the fourth-century Syriac *Apostolic Constitutions* has "lift up your minds." The Anaphora of St. James used in Jerusalem compromises with the double "Let us lift up our mind and our hearts." But all other anaphoras have "lift up your hearts."

The heart is our human core. Deuteronomy commands, "You shall love YHWH your God with all your heart, and with all your soul, and with all your might" (Deut 6:5). Heart takes the first place in the series and is the term that remains unchanged in the New Testament renditions (cf. Matt 22:37; Mark 12:30, 33; Luke 10:27). To put it colloquially, heart is what makes us tick; it's what we are all about. What we are invited to offer to the Lord is ourselves. St. Augustine commented on the Sursum Corda in *Sermon* 227 and elsewhere, finding in it the Pauline injunction to "seek the things that are above" (Col 3:1–2).[25] In the catechetical *Sermon* 227 to the newly baptized Augustine explains that

> you are urged to lift up your hearts; that's only for the members of Christ. After all if you have become members of Christ, where is your head? Members have a head. If the head hadn't gone before you, the members would never follow. Where has our head gone? What did you give back in the creed? "On the third day he rose again from the dead, he ascended into heaven, he is seated at the right hand of the Father." So our head is in heaven. That's why, after the words "Lift up your hearts," you reply, "We have lifted them up to the Lord."
>
> And you mustn't attribute to your own powers, your own merits, your own efforts, this lifting up of your hearts to the Lord, because it is God's gift that you should have your heart up above.[26]

Augustine's interpretation may have inspired the Protestant Reformers' views of the Sursum Corda. It became an important part of their understanding of the Eucharist and retained a place in the texts of their liturgies, even if not always in the traditional way. Only Ulrich Zwingli, who first retained the Sursum Corda in an *Attack on the Canon of the Mass* (1523), totally deleted it in his *Action or Use of the Lord's Supper Easter* (1525).[27] On the other hand, Martin Luther, Martin Bucer, and John Calvin preserved the Sursum Corda. Luther in his *Formula Missae* (1523) retained the Sursum Corda in the preface dialogue, as in the traditional eucharistic prayers: "Lift up your hearts. R/ We lift them to the Lord." Later, in his *Deutsche Messe* (1526), Luther's Sursum Corda moves from the role of an opening dialogue to the eucharistic prayer to the Admonition to the communicants: "I admonish you first of all to lift up your hearts to God to pray with me the Lord's Prayer."[28] Although it is

25. Philip H. Pfatteicher, *Commentary on the Lutheran Book of Worship* (Minneapolis: Augsburg Fortress, 1990), 159.
26. Augustine, *Sermon* 227 (*Sermons 184–229Z*, ed. John E. Rotelle, OSA, trans. Edmund Hill, OP, Works of St. Augustine III/6 (New York: New City Press, 1993), 255; cited in J.-M.-R. Tillard, *Flesh of the Church, Flesh of Christ: At the Source of the Ecclesiology of Communion*, trans. Madeleine Beaumont (Collegeville, MN: Liturgical, 2001), 40.
27. R. C. D. Jasper and G. J. Cuming, eds., *Prayers of the Eucharist: Early and Reformed*, 3rd ed. (Collegeville, MN: Liturgical, 1992), 181–82.
28. Ibid., 196.

no longer part of the dialogue, Luther still uses it as an expression of prayerful trust to God. Martin Bucer's solution was to make the Sursum Corda part of the prayers of intercession and consecration: "To the end that, by all means, we as thine obedient children may ever lift our hearts and souls unto thee in true childlike trust."[29] Luther and Bucer place the Sursum Corda in different positions, but both still use it as an expression of the prayer of faith in the eucharistic rite.

Unlike Luther and Bucer, for Calvin the Sursum Corda is not an invitation to prayer but an "orientation" for the celebration of the sacrament. In his *Form of Church Prayers* (Geneva, 1542), Calvin puts the Reformed Sursum Corda after the words of institution in the Exhortation: "Let us lift our spirits and hearts on high where Jesus Christ is in the glory of his Father, whence we expect him at our redemption."[30] Thus all communicants listen to the Sursum Corda before receiving the bread and wine and are invited to lift their thoughts to where Christ is "on high."[31] Martha Moore-Keish contends that Calvin's Sursum Corda is intended to inspire "a particular attitude in the worshiper."[32] The Sursum Corda's words ("therefore, lift up your hearts on high, seeking the heavenly things in heaven . . . do not fix your eyes on the visible signs") helps participants avoid a "false understanding" of the Lord's Supper and leads their eyes toward Christ in heaven, not toward the eucharistic elements on the earth.[33] "Let us not be fascinated by these earthly and corruptible elements which we see with our eyes and touch with our hands, seeking Him there as though He were enclosed in the bread or wine. . . . Let us be content to have the bread and wine as signs and witnesses, seeking the truth spiritually where the Word of God promises that we shall find it."[34] So central to Calvin's theology of the Eucharist do worship scholars consider the Sursum Corda to be that a recent book on worship in Calvin's Geneva is titled *Lifting Hearts to the Lord*.[35]

Contrary to Augustine's and Calvin's interpretation, there is nothing in the invitation that implies lifting up our heart *to heaven*, especially if

29. Bard Thompson, *Liturgies of the Western Church* (Cleveland: World, 1961; repr., Philadelphia: Fortress, 1989), 173.
30. Ibid., 207.
31. Ibid., 223.
32. Martha L. Moore-Keish, *Do This in Remembrance of Me: A Ritual Approach to Reformed Eucharistic Theology* (Grand Rapids: Eerdmans, 2008), 26.
33. Ibid., 223.
34. Ibid., 207.
35. Karin Maag, *Lifting Hearts to the Lord: Worship with John Calvin in Sixteenth-Century Geneva* (Grand Rapids: Eerdmans, 2016).

we expect to receive Christ in the earthly signs of this sacrament. The Sursum Corda can be understood both as the offering of ourselves as a living sacrifice (Rom 12:1) and also as the opening of our hearts to God in anticipation of what we shall receive in the gift of Communion. The current English translation of the preface dialogue avoids the repetition of the word "up" in the response: "Lift up your hearts. R/ We lift them to the Lord." The invitation to "lift up your hearts" is an invitation to offer our whole lives to the Lord, of which the bread and wine and other gifts offered just prior to the Great Thanksgiving are a token of gratitude for the life we have been given.

Opening the Heart Center

In recent years I have taken up the practice of yoga. At first it was a way of rehabbing my physical body after a year of chemotherapy. But I found that it also sharpened my mind and consciousness, which had been dulled by the chemo experience (the so-called "chemo brain"). Yoga is not just an exercise program. The historical practices of yoga were spiritual practices to train the body and mind to self-observe and become aware of one's relationships with divinity and the surrounding world.

Yoga places a great deal of emphasis on "the heart center." We have three different hearts. Of course, there is the physical heart that pumps blood to our whole body, to all our organs and to the brain. We also refer to the heart as the seat of our emotions, both negative and positive. When we love, hate, are fearful or excited, feel shame or pride, we feel this in our emotional heart. Our innermost heart (Sanskrit *hrdaya*) is our spiritual heart. The English term *heart* is derived from the Sanskrit root *hrt*, which means "the innermost."

In the yoga Tantra tradition this is referred to as the heart chakra (*anahata*) within the subtle body. It is located between the lower three earthly chakras (pelvic floor, sacral area, solar plexus, which deal with the worldly concerns of security, procreation, and personal power) and the upper three spiritual chakras (throat, third eye, crown of the head, which deal with the higher concerns of creative expression, insight, and enlightenment). Without opening and balancing the heart chakra it is difficult to balance the other chakras, and the flow from the lower to the upper chakras and from the upper to the lower chakras is diminished or blocked.[36]

Anahata, as the spiritual heart, relates to *bhakti*—devotion, love, service to others, worship of God. Opening the heart is an important aspect of yoga. Many yoga poses (*asanas*) that open the heart are backbends that thrust forward the chest.

Among them are cobra, standing backbend, warrior 1, camel, bridge, and wheel. An anahata yoga sequence could be this vinyasa: move from table pose to child pose. Slide forward to cobra, first a low cobra then a high cobra. Reach back to grab your ankles for bow pose or come up on your knees for camel pose. Then move into extended puppy pose with knees on the ground and butt in the air, forehead on the ground, arms extended forward, and elbows off the floor (anahatasana). Roll over on back for bridge pose. Then savasana.

In *bhakti* yoga these poses, fueled by the breath (*prana*), are not ends in themselves, but ways of offering to God who and what we are. I think a yoga practice that opens the heart could be a way of embodying an anaphoral theology: lifting up the heart in a sacrifice of love and praise to God the Father, through Jesus Christ, in the Holy Spirit.

I once participated in a workshop taught by the renowned yoga teacher Rod Stryker on "Tantra: Awakening the Sacred Channel." He said that one should bring whatever *bhakti* one knows to one's yoga practice and see if one's yoga practice enriches one's *bhakti*. My *bhakti* is orthodox Christianity. It took me a while to understand why he said this. It is because yoga is not a religion in itself, but its techniques have been employed in the service of several religions. This also means that "Christian yoga" is not needed, only yoga practiced by Christians. Among other benefits yoga trains one to connect breath and posture, which can be helpful in performing liturgy.

The Sursum Corda dialogue invites bodily gestures. If the presiding minister extends his or her hands and arms toward the congregation when saying "The Lord be with you," the congregation should return the gesture when saying "And also with you/And with your spirit." With the invitation to "lift up your hearts," the presiding minister should lift up his arms and hands, thus thrusting his chest slightly forward. In the response, "we have, to the Lord," the congregation should do likewise. At the invitation, "Let us give thanks to the Lord our God," the presiding minister could bring his hands to the heart in prayer position. Mirroring this gesture, the congregation responds: "It is right and just so to do." Doing the gestures makes us aware of the meanings of the phrases. Since this dialogue is usually chanted, breath needs to be added to movements. Chanting the dialogue also allows time

---

36. On the chakras and the subtle body see Georg Feuerstein, *Tantra: The Path of Ecstasy* (Boston: Shambhala, 1998), 139–64.

to incorporate these gestures. Anything sung over and over helps to cement the words in the conscious mind. Like all lines of dialogue, it is done more dynamically if the presiding minister and congregation can face each other without scripts in hand.

Eucharistic Life

The Sursum Corda exchange is the center of this dialogue. The other lines of dialogue also occur before other prayers, but the Sursum Corda only occurs before the eucharistic prayer. It invites us to open our hearts to receive our Lord who comes to us in this holy sacrament. But it also suggests an opening to the eucharistic life—the life we live when we are dismissed and sent back into the world. I will focus on that in the last chapter. This book is an invitation to see the connections between the Eucharist and the whole of life.

I am interested in a particular way of living the eucharistic life that I will explore in further chapters. Andrea Bieler and Luise Schottroff have suggested that "the Eucharistic life is embedded in micro- and macro-structures that shape individual bodies as much as they shape the global economy."[37]

The issue of embodiment in liturgy has interested me in recent years as I returned to the body—especially my body—after experiencing nearly a year of chemotherapy following a diagnosis of stage 2 colon cancer, and recalling bodily events in my life—among them the occurrences that made my first Communion so memorable. After years of paying little attention to my body, I became interested in everything about my body—what it was going through physically at the time I was receiving chemotherapy but also the history of my life in the body. My meditations on my body brought to mind experiences both good and bad that were rooted in the body's memory, and experiences both good and bad that concerned my body. I came to see both the bad and the good experiences filtered through my eucharistic Communions in my early adolescence, and I will relate those experiences in this book. My meditations brought to mind also how, in my teen years, I experienced the presence of God in worship more profoundly as I put myself bodily into the liturgy. While exploring the impact of bodily postures such as standing, kneeling, bowing I became aware of how they made me more mindful of what I was doing in worship (although I wouldn't have

---

37. Andrea Bieler and Luise Schottroff, *The Eucharist: Bodies, Bread, and Resurrection* (Minneapolis: Fortress, 2007), 4.

used the word "mindful" in those years). In the process of reflecting on these impressions from my youth I returned to liturgical interests from my earlier years—liturgy as a ritual act involving the body.[38]

I was able to unpack this renewed interest in the body in my book on *Embodied Liturgy*.[39] I won't repeat here what you can read there. I will simply note in a summary way that we are created as bodily creatures who have only our bodies with which to serve God in worship and take care of the neighbor; and that God connects with us as bodily creatures through earthly sacramental signs that affect our bodies both externally (water and oil) and internally (bread and wine). By means of our bodies we connect with the earth from which we were created, hold memories of our life before God as we remember the sacrifice of Christ's life in his body, and interact with others in the community of faith. All of these aspects of life are brought together in the Eucharist and are articulated in the Anaphora or Great Thanksgiving.

Figure 2. Praying the Anaphora or Great Thanksgiving at St. Augustine's Episcopal Church in Wilmette, IL. The rector, the Rev. Kristin White, invites all of the children and anyone else to gather at the altar during the eucharistic prayer and to pray with hands uplifted in the orans or "prayer" position. The deacon holding the child is the Rev. Bryan Cones.

38. See especially Frank C. Senn, *The Pastor as Worship Leader: A Manual for Corporate Worship* (Minneapolis: Augsburg, 1977), 143–44.
39. See Frank C. Senn, *Embodied Liturgy: Lessons in Christian Ritual* (Minneapolis: Fortress, 2016).

41

3

Preface and Sanctus: Cosmology and Praise

In the summer of my fifteenth year I spent a week in a wilderness area known as Zoar Valley south of Buffalo, New York, with three other Boy Scout buddies. Our parents were willing to let us stay in the cabin our Scout troop had constructed on wilderness land that we had been given permission to use. Our fathers drove us down from Buffalo (about an hour's drive), dropped in during the week to make sure we were okay, and picked us up at the end of the week. Otherwise we were on our own.

We spent the days hiking up and down the deep gorge carved by the rapidly flowing stream of the south branch of the Cattaraugus Creek on its way to the main stream and ultimately to Lake Erie. One day we hiked farther upstream than we had before and came to an area where the whole torrent of the creek rushed through a water-smoothed rock chasm about four to five feet in width and emptied into a deep pool. Such a pool invited a swim on a warm summer day, so we shed our clothes and jumped in. We didn't think twice about "skinny-dipping" since we had been swimming naked together all year in high-school freshman swimming class as well as in the YMCA pool at Scout swim nights. (It was actually required that boys swim naked at the YMCA and in high school swimming classes up until the early 1970s.) This was the summer of 1958, and we were four teenage boys skinny-dipping in the cold waters of a wilderness creek on warm summer days and then lying alongside the creek on sun-warmed rock worn smooth by count-less spring torrents just as nature's God had created us. There was a water snake in our little Eden. The pool was the snake's and we were probably laying on its sun-warmed rock, but we didn't converse with the serpent and it went its way.

We returned to our swimming hole every day after that. I think nakedness afforded a way to be immersed sensuously in the natural world. In my skin I could feel the coolness of the water, the warmth of the sun, the smoothness of the rock, and perhaps even sense a relation-ship with that snake who also encountered the world in its bare skin. We also experienced bonding among ourselves as we cooked together, hiked along the creek bed, swam naked in our own water hole (well, the snake's actually), and lay sunning ourselves on the rocks fully exposed to God.

I remember this event vividly for the memory of the physical con-nection with an awesome natural place and a creature for which it was home. Perhaps this fits the category of Robert Bellah's "unitive" expe-rience in which we are entirely at one with our experience.[1] I experi-enced a connection between my body and the space it was inhabiting. Sacredness accrued to this place in my memory not only because of its striking natural features but also because of our group experience of it. Ritual, including Christian worship, requires a sense of connected-ness of persons to places, of bodies to spaces. It is easy to see this in the example of the relationship of the body to a natural environment. But we also develop a bodily relationship with the human places we inhabit and the religious spaces we experience in worship.

Recovering a Doctrine of Creation

A popular writer on college campuses in the early 1960s was Loren Eiseley (1907–1977). He was an American anthropologist, educator, philosopher, and natural science writer, whose book on evolution *The Immense Journey* (1957), was being read by everyone on campuses at that time. I particularly enjoyed *The Firmament of Time* (1960), which I read at the same time. It consists of a series of lectures on the history of science Eiseley gave in 1959 to honor the one hundredth anniversary of Darwin's *The Origin of Species*. The lectures explore our human relation-ship to historical time and the natural world, or rather our growing dis-

1. Robert N. Bellah, *Religion in Human Evolution: From the Paleolithic to the Axial Age* (Cambridge, MA: Belknap Press of Harvard University Press, 2011), 13.

connectedness from both as we live in an increasingly artificial world alienated from both history and nature. Eiseley wrote that "man has a belief in seen and unseen nature. He is both pragmatist and mystic."[2] Eiseley himself, a fossil hunter, was a mystic. He could float down the Platte River in Nebraska or ride a horse up a Colorado mountain immersed both in the time that had passed historically and the nature that was present.

This way of connecting with historical time and the natural world is not accessible to everyone. But I was learning in those days another approach to connecting with history and nature that is accessible to everyone in the liturgy of the church. In the fall of 1963 or 1964 I had a chance to hear the then-young Yale professor Jaroslav Pelikan (1923–2006) speak at a pastors' conference in Albany, New York, on Catholic substance and Protestant principle in Luther's Reformation (some of which was included in his book *Obedient Rebel*).[3]

One of Pelikan's lectures had to do with Catholic substance and Protestant principle in Luther's approach to liturgy. One of the points that interested me was Pelikan's discussion of the cosmological setting of worship in Luther's commentaries on Genesis and the Psalms. Even though as an Old Testament scholar Luther knew the dangers of too close a link between nature and biblical religion, he had an appreciation of God's creation. In his commentary on Genesis Luther imagined Adam preaching on Psalm 148, praising God "for entrusting him with the rule of all the creatures on earth." Thus, said Luther, "Psalms 148 and 149 set forth a sort of liturgy of this thanksgiving, where the sun, the moon, the stars, the fish, and the dragons are all commanded to praise the Lord."[4] Pelikan also suggested that liturgy relates to the world of nature through its use of earthly elements in the sacraments, in following the natural cycles of the year in the liturgical calendar, in sanctifying night and day in the daily prayer offices, and in the use of architectural design.

Pelikan's attention to the cosmological element in Luther's thought may have been inspired by his former colleague at the University of Chicago Divinity School, Joseph Sittler (1904–1987), who had given attention to connections between nature and grace in his collection of university sermons titled after one of the sermons, *The Care of the*

---

2. Loren Eiseley, *The Firmament of Time* (New York: Atheneum, 1960), 4.
3. Jaroslav Pelikan, *Obedient Rebel: Catholic Substance and Protestant Principle in Luther's Reformation* (New York: Harper & Row, 1964).
4. Cited in ibid., 89.

Earth.[5] I learned of Sittler's collection of sermons from a Lutheran campus pastor, Clyde McCormick at Northwestern University (who also introduced me to the writings of Mircea Eliade), and the next school year (1964–1965) he sent to me a copy of Sittler's "Called to Unity," an address to the 1961 New Delhi Assembly of the World Council of Churches. I was bowled over by the christology of nature Sittler proposed in his address. He noted that the scope of grace had retreated in the face of the scientific advances in the modern world. As a result, Sittler said,

> Our vocabulary of praise has become personal, pastoral, too purely spiritual, static. We have not affirmed as inherent in Christ—God's proper man for man's proper selfhood and society—the world political, the world economical, the world aesthetic, and all other commanded orderings of actuality that flow from the ancient summons to tend this garden of the Lord. When atoms are disposable to the ultimate hurt the very atoms must be reclaimed for God and his will.[6]

To me, this was a mind-blowing statement. Sittler's point was that the order of redemption must be big enough to redeem the order of creation from the bondage to human sin to which it has been subjected. Since we praise God as our Redeemer as well as our Creator, Sittler went on to suggest that a depleted cosmology also depletes our vocabulary of praise. Christian orthodoxy depends on this vocabulary of praise, because *orthodoxia* is "right praise" as well as "right teaching." The two are inseparable.[7]

Since the age of Enlightenment the churches had given in bit by bit to the scientific worldview. While claiming to glorify God as the Creator, a little bit of faith has retreated with each scientific discovery, like the tide Matthew Arnold saw receding from Dover Beach, so that by the twentieth century the church was left only with the personal dimension of faith and a diminished vocabulary of praise. The only way to expand our vocabulary of praise, said Sittler, is to expand our cosmology.

In fact, our commonly accepted cosmology has expanded vastly in the twentieth century from what it was before the seventeenth century.[8] Scientific consensus has developed about the beginning of our

---

5. Joseph Sittler, *The Care of the Earth and Other University Sermons* (Philadelphia: Fortress, 1964) appeared at the same time as Pelikan's *Obedient Rebel.*
6. Joseph Sittler, "Called to Unity," *Ecumenical Review* 14 (1962): 175–87.
7. See Jaroslav Pelikan, *The Melody of Theology: A Philosophical Dictionary* (Cambridge, MA: Harvard University Press, 1988), 187.

universe from particles of matter and light expanding away from an original hot point some 13.7 billion years ago, followed by the formation of galaxies and stars, one of which was our star, the sun, which in turn spun out planets, one of which is our earth. The first cell life appeared on the earth about 4 billion years ago and the first humans (*homo habilis*) about 2.6 million years ago. Consequential human activity on the earth, what Brian Schwimme and Mary Tucker call "becoming a planetary presence," began around 12,000 BCE.[9]

For an expanded vocabulary of praise adequate to our expanded cosmology Sittler turned to the poets, artists, composers, and architects because insights into human participation in the world of nature were coming from them, not from theologians. Only through poets, artists, composers, and architects could Western theology and liturgy catch up with Eastern Christianity's celebration of the material creation as the sacramental means of the divine presence. Poets of faith like Gerard Manley Hopkins could exult in "God's Grandeur."

> The world is charged with the grandeur of God.
>   It will flame out, like shining from shook foil;
>   It gathers to a greatness, like the ooze of oil
> Crushed. Why do men then now not reck his rod?
> Generations have trod, have trod, have trod;
>   And all is seared with trade; bleared, smeared with toil;
>   And wears man's smudge and shares man's smell: the soil
> Is bare now, nor can foot feel, being shod.
>
> And for all this, nature is never spent;
>   There lives the dearest freshness deep down things;
> And though the last lights off the black West went
>   Oh, morning, at the brown brink eastward, springs—
> Because the Holy Ghost over the bent
>   World broods with warm breast and with ah! bright wings.[10]

Hopkins saw God's grandeur in the world; we must see it in the universe. Our shod feet have left "a planetary presence." As Brian Swimme and Mary Tucker observed, "Every place we went, we became that

---

8. For an accessible presentation on the emergence of scientific theories that contributed to our current cosmology see Stephen W. Hawking, *A Brief History of Time: From the Big Bang to Black Holes, with an Introduction by Carl Sagan* (New York: Bantam, 1988).

9. Brian Thomas Swimme and Mary Evelyn Tucker, *Journey of the Universe* (New Haven and London: Yale University Press, 2011).

10. Gerard Manley Hopkins, *A Selection of His Poems and Prose*, ed. with Introduction by W. H. Gardner (Baltimore: Penguin, 1953), 27.

place."[11] We humans have dominated every place we have settled, but without a clear sense of destiny for ourselves, the other species with which we come into contact, and our planet. The planet will be safe from our adventures only if we can retain a sense of wonder at what is around us and utter the praise that opens our heart to the universe and its Creator.

The Eucharistic Vocabulary of Praise

The eucharistic prayer traditions, particularly the Eastern anaphoras, provide us with a vocabulary of praise that is lacking in the Western liturgical traditions. We call the opening part of the prayer "preface," from the Latin *praefari*. This does not mean "introduction" but "to pray aloud"—that is, to chant. No matter how quietly the rest of the eucharistic prayer is prayed, the preface is sung aloud as an ecstatic act of praise.

In the eucharistic preface the cosmos is the subject of our praise. The Greek word *kosmos* means order; cosmology is the study of the order of things. It is the area of scientific study particularly today associated with astrophysics. But the ancient myth-makers were also scientists of a sort, trying to discern the order of things and expressing in their myths and rituals a comprehensive worldview that made sense of reality as it was encountered and experienced.

The eucharistic prayers in the *Didache* make reference to "the broken bread that was scattered over the mountains, and when brought together became one" as an analogy to the church being "brought together from the ends of the earth into your kingdom" (chapter 9). In the thanksgiving after supper (chapter 10) God is acknowledged as the One who "created all things for the sake of your Name, and gave food and drink to mankind for their enjoyment, that they might give you thanks; but to us you have granted spiritual food and drink and eternal life through your child Jesus." This acknowledgment of the food and drink does not come first, as it might in the comparable Jewish table prayer, but second in order after thanksgiving for the "holy Name which you have enshrined in our hearts, and the knowledge and faith and immortality which you have made known to us through your child Jesus."[12] It is a christology of creation.

---

11. Swimme and Tucker, *Journey of the Universe*, 93.
12. R. C. D. Jasper and G. J. Cuming, eds., *Prayers of the Eucharist: Early and Reformed*, 3rd ed. (Collegeville, MN: Liturgical, 1992), 23–24.

Interestingly, the third-century Syriac Anaphora of Addai and Mari also begins by extolling "the adorable and glorious Name," to which may have later been specified "of the Father and of the Son and of the Holy Spirit." It goes on to say that "He created the world through his grace and its inhabitants in his compassion."[13] This might have served as a cue to add in the fourth century the Sanctus with its surrounding cosmology of the heavenly hosts.

I think a case can be made that the addition of the Sanctus increased the cosmological element in the eucharistic tradition. In other words, the grand vision of the heavenly worship would not be in the eucharistic prayers apart from the inclusion of the Sanctus of Isaiah's vision. The anaphora in the *Apostolic Tradition* lacks a Sanctus and also a cosmological element. It begins with christology, giving thanks to God "through your beloved child Jesus Christ, whom in the last times you sent to us as a savior and redeemer and angel [messenger] of your will." The only cosmological hint is "through whom you made all things."[14] The much later Roman canon also begins on a christological note in its various proper prefaces. The prefaces all give praise and thanks to the Father "through your Son Jesus Christ our Lord, *who . . .*" (fill in the proper reason for praising God for what he has done in Christ). The only cosmological element is the invitation at the end of the preface to join our praise "with the angels and archangels and all the company of heaven." But this was surely added to provide a fitting lead into the Sanctus hymn when it was inserted into the old Roman anaphora. One could omit the Sanctus and move from the content of the proper preface to the *Te igitur clementissime Pater* and the prayer would be much more flowing. E. C. Ratcliff has suggested that in some eucharistic prayer traditions the Sanctus would fit better at the end as part of the concluding doxology.[15]

Gregory Dix suggested that the Sanctus first entered the eucharistic tradition in Egypt, where it was borrowed from the synagogue liturgy.[16] This place of origin was affirmed by Robert Taft,[17] who argued that the Sanctus fit into the fourth-century Egyptian prayers, such as the Anaphoras of St. Mark, of Sarapion of Thmuis, and of St. Basil of Cae-

13. Ibid., 34.
14. Ibid., 35.
15. E. C. Ratcliff, "The Sanctus and the Pattern of the Early Anaphora," *Journal of Ecclesiastical History* 1 (1950): 29–36, 125–34.
16. Gregory Dix, "Primitive Consecration Prayers," *Theology* 37 (1938): 261–83.
17. Robert Taft, "The Interpolation of the Sanctus into the Anaphora: When and Where; An Interpretation of the Dossier," Part 1, *Orientalia Christiana Periodica*, part 1: 57 (1991): 281–308; part 2: 58 (1992): 531–52.

sarea, without seeming to be an interpolation, as it is in the Roman canon. In Sarapion and St. Mark the Sanctus is lacking the Benedictus ("Blessed is he who comes in the Name of the Lord"), although it is included in St. Basil. Bryan Spinks disagreed with all of this in his study *The Sanctus in the Eucharistic Prayer*,[18] although later he softened some of his positions.[19] Gabrielle Winkler has joined Spinks in seeing Syria as the place of origin of the Sanctus in the eucharistic tradition, including in Addai and Mari. Her sources are wide-ranging, including mystagogical catecheses from the church fathers. Paul Bradshaw and Maxwell Johnson find Winkler's arguments compelling because she provides a theological rationale for the inclusion of the Sanctus in the Christian eucharistic tradition, which became "*the* primary location and manifestation of the presence of Christ, the very dwelling of the *Shekinah* here and now."[20] In other words, the Sanctus would be an appropriate christological hymn, with or without the Benedictus.

Whether the Sanctus emerged in Christian prayer in Egypt or Syria, it obviously found a secure place in Egyptian and Syrian anaphoras in the fourth century. Alexandria and Antioch were both centers of Jewish thought and practice, but it seems to me that relations between Christians and Jews were better in Alexandria, where Origen was studying Hebrew with a rabbi. He left a comment on Isaiah's vision of the heavenly worship in *De Principiis* 4.3, 14. Commenting on Isaiah 6:2–3 Origen writes,

> For because the two seraphim alone have their wings over the face of God and over his feet, we may venture to declare that neither the armies of the holy angels nor the holy thrones, nor the dominions, nor principalities, nor powers can wholly know the beginnings of all things and the ends of the universe.[21]

The introduction to the Sanctus and the post-Sanctus in the Anaphora of Sarapion is as follows:

> For you are above all rule and authority and power and dominion and every name which is named, not only in this age but also in the coming

18. Bryan D. Spinks, *The Sanctus in the Eucharistic Prayer* (Cambridge: Cambridge University Press, 1991).
19. Bryan D. Spinks, "The Integrity of the Anaphora of Sarapion of Thmuis and Liturgical Methodology," *Journal of Theological Studies* 49 (1998): 136–45, here at 141.
20. Paul F. Bradshaw and Maxwell E. Johnson, *The Eucharistic Liturgies: Their Evolution and Interpretation* (Collegeville, MN: Liturgical, 2012), 118.
21. Cited in ibid., 113.

one. Beside you stand a thousand thousands and a myriad myriads of angels, archangels, thrones, dominions, principalities and powers.

Beside you stand the two most-honored six-winged seraphim. With two wings they cover the face, and with two the feet, and with two they fly, sanctifying. With them receive also our sanctification as we say:

Holy, holy, holy Lord of Sabbaoth; heaven and earth are full of your glory.

Full is heaven and full also is the earth of your majestic glory, Lord of powers.[22]

It is not necessary to say that the Sanctus first appeared in an Egyptian prayer like Sarapion's, who served as bishop of Thmuis in the Nile delta and was a friend and follower of Athanasius of Alexandria, to see here the influence of the great Origen.

The emergence of the Sanctus also in the synagogue liturgy is an interesting question, as fraught with scholarly debate among Jewish liturgists as among Christian. To cut to the chase, contemporary Jewish scholars like Lawrence A. Hoffman see the origin of the synagogue Sanctus (*Kedushah*) in a group of Jewish mystics known as *yordei merkavah*, or "those who go down into the chariot." *Kedush* could serve as a chanted mantra whose cognitive meaning was less important than the rhythmic affective function. Hoffman writes,

> More striking was the fact that these prayers were apparently recited—at least by some—after several days of fasting, and in a bodily position marked by placing the head between the knees, thus allowing the blood to rush quickly to the brain. Behind the praxis was a cosmology that pictured our world in the center, with seven heavens surrounding it. In the furthermost heaven sat God enthroned in a chariot of glory, surrounded by angels giving praise, in the very words of the *Kedushah*. Worship's task was to transport the mystics to the seventh heaven, where they would join the heavenly band of laudators.[23]

The title of Hoffman's book is *Beyond the Text: A Holistic Approach to Liturgy*. His interest in how the text is embodied should be of interest to us also, because it also became the practice among Christians, or at least the ministers at the altar, to cross their arms and hands over their breasts and bow profoundly during the singing of the Sanctus (and after fasting before receiving Communion!). Inversions with the

22. Cited in ibid.
23. Lawrence A. Hoffman, *Beyond the Text: A Holistic Approach to Liturgy* (Bloomington and Indianapolis: Indiana University Press, 1987), 155.

head upside down and the blood rushing to the brain have long been practiced by mystics in different religions as a way into spiritual vision or enlightenment. Some form of prostration with one's head on the floor is practiced by Hindus, Buddhists, Muslims, Orthodox Christians, as well as in martial arts and yoga. In the Christian eucharistic tradition the ministers bow profoundly with arms crossed over their chest as the "Holy, holy, holy" is sung and stand upright for "Blessed is he who comes . . ." while making the sign of the cross on themselves.

I do not want to leave the Egyptian eucharistic tradition without noting the attention to the earthly cosmology in the Anaphora of St. Mark. A unique feature of the Egyptian tradition is the inclusion of the intercessions within the preface. Supplication is often the other side of praise. In the Anaphora of St. Mark the standard acknowledgment of God as the maker of heaven and earth is amplified with reference to what is on the earth, "the seas, the rivers, the fountains, the lakes and all things that are therein"[24]—all references to water. Then in the supplications that follow the praise there is a series of petitions (perhaps used as needed). In the liturgies of the Coptic Orthodox Church the litany of the water is prayed from June 19 to October 19, the litany of the plants is prayed from October 20 to January 18, and the litany of the crops is prayed from January 19 to June 18. The appropriate litany concludes:

> Bless them to their fullness, and give happiness unto the face of the earth. May its furrows be watered, and its fruits be plentiful, make it ready for sowing and harvesting, and dispose our lives according to your will.[25]

Here are concerns quite relevant to the countries along the Nile, which depend on the regularity of the great river for good harvests, expressed in this living anaphora used in the Coptic Church of Egypt and the Church of Ethiopia.

I also note that the anaphora in Book 8 of the Syrian *Apostolic Constitutions*, which includes just about everything that could possibly be said in a eucharistic prayer, begins its long narrative recital after the Sursum Corda with a complete description of the creation of the world through the only-begotten Son, the Word, and gives detailed descriptions of all the aspects of that creative work mentioned in Genesis 1.

From here I wish to jump to Western Europe, which has expressed a

---

24. *The Liturgies of the Coptic Orthodox Church* (Hinsdale, IL: St. Mark and St. Bishoy Coptic Orthodox Church, 1987), 190.
25. Ibid., 69.

great sense of bonding with the earth in its cosmology. I noted the limited expression of cosmology in the Roman canon. However, there are instances of cosmology in the old Gallican rite. The Gallican and Visigothic eucharistic prayers were prayers of many parts, all of which were changeable, and therefore not many examples survive.[26] One remarkable survival is provided by R. C. D. Jasper and G. J. Cuming in their collection of *Prayers of the Eucharist*, assembled from several manuscripts.

> It is fitting and right, just and right, here and everywhere to give you thanks, Lord, holy Father, eternal God; you snatched us from perpetual death and the last darkness of hell, and gave mortal matter, put together from the liquid mud, to your Son and to eternity. Who is acceptable to tell your praises, who can make a full declaration of your works? Every tongue marvels at you, all priests extol your glory.
>
> When you had overcome chaos and the confused elements and the darkness in which things swam, you gave wonderful forms to the amazed elements: the tender world blushed at the fires of the sun, and the rude earth wondered at the dealings of the moon. And lest no inhabitant should adorn all this, and the sun's orb shine on emptiness, your hands made from clay a more excellent likeness, which a holy fire quickened within, and a lively soul brought to life throughout its idle parts. We may not look, Father, into the inner mysteries. To you alone is known the majesty of your work: what there is in man, that the blood held in the veins washes the fearful limbs and the living earth; that the loose appearances of bodies are held together by tightening nerves, and the individual bones gain strength from the organs within.
>
> But whence comes so great a bounty to miserable men, that we should be formed in the likeness of you and your Son, that an earthly thing should be eternal? We abandoned the commandments of your blessed majesty; we were plunged, mortal once more, into the earth from which we came, and mourned the loss of the eternal comfort of your gift. But your manifold goodness and inestimable majesty sent the saving Word from heaven, that he should be made flesh by taking a human body, and should care for that which the age had lost and the ancient wounds. Therefore all the angels, with the manifold multitude of the saints, praise him with unceasing voice, saying:
>
> Holy, holy, [holy, lord God of Sabbaoth . . .][27]

It would be interesting to know how many more anaphora "parts" like this one there might be or might have been used that express such a

26. See Walter Howard Frere, *The Anaphora or Great Eucharistic Prayer: An Irenical Study in Liturgical History* (London: Society for Promoting Christian Knowledge; New York: Macmillan, 1938), 94–116.
27. Jasper and Cuming, *Prayers of the Eucharist*, 148–49.

sense of relationship with the creation. The problem with the survival of the Gallican prayers is that each part of the anaphora was variable in each local church. Unless a text is copied over and over again (like the Roman Canon that first appears in the Gelasian Sacramentary of *Codex Reginensis* 316), the chances of its survival over the centuries is slim.

But there is evidence of other texts in Western European liturgies that also point to the Western European delight in the natural world. In the Visigothic rite in Spain the canticle *Benedicite opera omnia* ("All you works of the Lord, bless the Lord") was sung between the Epistle and the Gospel. We have the Latin poetry of Venantius Honorius Clementianus Fortunatus (ca. 530–ca. 600/609), who was born in Italy and later served the Merovingian court at Metz, whose *Salve feste dies* became the medieval Easter processional hymn. The stanzas of "Hail thee, festival day" were set to a tune by Ralph Vaughan Williams in the 1906 *English Hymnal* for use as a processional hymn on Easter, Ascension, and Pentecost. The refrain and first stanza is:

Refrain: Hail thee, festival day!
Blest day that art hallowed forever;
day wherein Christ arose,
breaking the kingdom of death.

Lo, the fair beauty of earth,
from the death of the winter arising,
every good gift of the year
now with its Master returns. *Refrain*

Across the water in Ireland we have the Gaelic lyrics of "St. Patrick's Breastplate," translated by Cecil Alexander in 1889 as "I bind unto myself today, the strong name of the Trinity," and set to a tune by Charles Villiers Stanford. It's a sturdy trinitarian hymn, but also includes this stanza:

I bind unto myself today
The virtues of the star lit heaven,
The glorious sun's life giving ray,
The whiteness of the moon at even,
The flashing of the lightning free,
The whirling wind's tempestuous shocks,
The stable earth, the deep salt sea
Around the old eternal rocks.

Against this background maybe St. Francis of Assisi's *Canticle of the Sun* (or *Canticle of the Creatures*) doesn't seem so solitary a witness of Western medieval bonding with the natural world. The title and opening words of Pope Francis's recent encyclical, *Laudato Si'* (Praise be you), which deals with our global environmental crisis, evoke his namesake's canticle. In his canticle St. Francis praises God whose glory is reflected in "Brother Sun" and "Sister Moon," "Brother Fire" and "Sister Water," and "our sister, Mother Earth, who sustains and governs us, and who produces various fruits with colored flowers and herbs," and "Sister Death," who takes home to God the child of God. The canticle is incomplete, though, without St. Francis's praise of human beings "who give pardon," bear infirmity, and live in peace. St. Francis not only lived in harmony with creation but also served the poor. And that is the reason this pope, who considers himself a friend of the poor, has gotten into the climate-change debate, because he asserts that changes in our earthly environment are having an adverse effect especially on the poor.

Because concern over the degradation of our earthly environment has been building for a long time, new eucharistic prayers composed since the 1960s have sought to include a cosmological element. In terms of the typical structure of the eucharistic prayer, and the preference in the Western churches for variable proper christological prefaces, the options are to include a brief cosmological statement in the narrative after the Sanctus or to write an invariable preface. Probably the most famous of these efforts is Prayer C in Rite II of the Book of Common Prayer of The Episcopal Church USA. This eucharistic prayer, penned by Howard Galley, has been called jokingly "the Star Trek anaphora," but it is still a powerful text.

> God of all power, Ruler of the Universe, you are worthy of glory and praise.
> *Glory to you forever and ever.*

> At your command all things came to be: the vast expanse of interstellar space, galaxies, suns, the planets in their courses, and this fragile earth, our island home.
> *By your will they were created and have their being.*

> From the primal elements you brought forth the human race, and blessed us with memory, reason, and skill. You made us the rulers of creation. But we turned against you, and betrayed your trust; and we turned against one another.
> *Have mercy, Lord, for we are sinners in your sight.*[28]

The late H. Boone Porter summed up the virtues of this prayer in these words: "The litany-like exchange between priest and congregation throughout this prayer gives it, in actual use, a remarkable dramatic movement. The extended references to creation in the lengthy and unchanging preface reflect the scientific interest of many people and the desire to see God's purposes carried out in our stewardship of the natural world."[29] But this prayer also appeals to our common cosmology, which has given us a more magnificent and awesome way to speak of God as creator, redeemer, and sanctifier and a graver sense of our stewardship of the creation.[30] A eucharistic prayer that had a fulsome cosmology in its invariable preface is in the Holy Eucharist III in *The Worship Supplement* authorized by the Commission on Worship of the Lutheran Church–Missouri Synod (1969).

> We thank you, almighty Lord, that you are a God of all mankind, that you are not ashamed to be called our God, that you know us by our name, that you keep the world in your hands. For you have made us and called us in this life to be united to you, to be your people on this earth. Blessed are you, Maker of all that exists. Blessed are you, who have given us space and time to live in. Blessed are you for the light of our eyes and the air we breathe. We thank you for the whole creation, for the works of your hands, for all that you have done in our midst, through Jesus Christ our Lord. Therefore we praise your Majesty, almighty God, with all your faithful people; therefore we bow before you and adore you with the words:
> Holy, holy, holy . . .[31]

This text has some of the character of Luther's explanation to the first article of the Creed in the *Small Catechism* in which the created order is personalized. There is a subtle reference to the posture of bowing during the Sanctus in the phrase that leads into the Sanctus. Lacking here is a reference to the heavenly worship.

Another example of a eucharistic prayer that draws cosmological elements into the preface is Eucharistic Prayer 2 from the *Enriching Our Worship* resource of The Episcopal Church. This preface might be used on Sundays in ordinary time after Pentecost.

28. *The Book of Common Prayer* (New York: The Church Hymnal Corporation and Seabury, 1977), 370.
29. H. Boone Porter, "Episcopal Anaphoral Prayers," in *New Eucharistic Prayers: An Ecumenical Study of Their Development and Structure* (Mahwah, NJ: Paulist, 1987), 69.
30. See Sallie McFague, *The Body of God: An Ecological Theology* (Minneapolis: Fortress, 1993).
31. *Worship Supplement* (St. Louis: Concordia, 1969), 65.

We praise you and we bless you, holy and gracious God, source of
  life abundant.
From before time you made ready the creation.
Your Spirit moved over the deep, and brought all things into being:
Sun, moon, and stars; earth, winds, and waters; and every living thing.
You made us in your image, and taught us to walk in your ways.
But we rebelled against you, and wandered far away;
And yet, as a mother cares for her children, you would not forget us.
Time and again you called us to live in the fullness of your love.
And so this day we join with Saints and Angels
in the chorus of praise that rings through eternity,
lifting our voices to magnify you as we sing:
Holy, holy, holy . . .

Embodied Praise

The preface praises God the Father for his work of creation by employ-
ing our whole body: we chant ecstatic speech, standing with arms
uplifted in the orans position, and bowing profoundly at the Sanctus.
This praise is not just a mental exercise; it is embodied in voice and
posture.

Some thoughtful people are suggesting that the environmental crisis
that afflicts the world today is really a crisis of embodiment. In the
modern technological world we have lost our connection to our own
bodies and our relation to the earth from which they are formed. Especially since René Descartes in the seventeenth century we have been
into our minds at the expense of our bodies. When Descartes searched
for the one thing he could be certain about, he landed in his mind. In
his *Meditations on First Philosophy* (1641) he persued a rigorous "method
of doubt" to determine what could not be doubted, and he concluded
that what could not be doubted was that he was thinking. "At last I
have discovered it—thought; this alone is inseparable from me. . . .
I am, then, in the strict sense only a thing that thinks."[32] Cogito *ergo
sum*—"I think, therefore I am." The consequence of Cartesian certainty
is we don't experience things as much as think about them. When we
do that, we disembody. The earth, its resources, and even other people
cease to be subjects to us and become objects. And when we objectify,
we ask how resources and people may serve us. This leads to exploitation. And that brings us to our present environmental crisis.

The Buddhist scholar Reginald A. Ray makes the accusation that "we

32. René Descartes, *Philosophical Writings* II (Cambridge: Cambridge University Press, 1958), 18.

disembody, and this is intimately tied up with the fact that, as modern people, we live in a culture that survives through exploitation. Wittingly or not, we are all exploiters." Whether we lost our connection with others and turned them into objects, or fell into a pattern of exploitation and then lost our connection, Ray says, "we find ourselves in a pattern whereby every person, every thing, every situation, and every occurrence in our life, even the earth itself, is viewed as an object that could serve or thwart our interests, our ambitions, for fulfillment."[33]

If to be disembodied is to be disconnected from the world, to be reconnected means also to return to the body as a living, breathing embodiment of the earth itself from which we were created. Our body is composed of the same elements found in the earth—and in the universe, for that matter.

To return to the body is to turn from the world as the object of our thoughts and uses and to regard it as subject of our worship and stewardship. It is the subject that evokes our praise for its beauty sculpted by wind and water and summons our gratitude for its blessings, for example, for a snake that gave up its swimming hole for our recreation, a smooth rock on which to lay naked in the sun, and to the sun for warming the rock and our bodies. We are moved from a feeling of identification with the creation to a desire to care for it.

We need to reconnect with the earth. The second creation story, in Genesis 2, pictures the Lord creating Adam (the man) from the dust of the earth and the spring of water that welled up. Whatever is in the earth is in our bodies. So whatever else might be said about humankind, we are earthly creatures. Our destiny is not some other world, but this one. "We wait for new heavens and a new earth, where righteousness is at home" (2 Pet 3:13). The book of Revelation pictures the heavenly city, the new Jerusalem, coming down to earth. The earth is our present home and, if Christians took their Bible seriously, it is also our eternal home.[34] We should take delight in the home we have, feel at home in it, explore its wonders great and small, and strive to preserve it for future generations.

There has also been growing research that suggests that touching the earth with our bare body has health benefits. The earth has an

33. Reginald A. Ray, *Touching Enlightenment: Finding Realization in the Body* (Boulder, CO: Sounds True, 2008, 2014), 23.
34. See N. T. Wright, *Surprised by Hope: Rethinking Heaven, the Resurrection, and the Mission of the Church* (San Francisco: HarperOne, 2008), 114–17.

electrical field, and by touching the earth with our bare skin, being "grounded," negative electrical charges are sent into the body. Daniel Chong, a medical doctor, writes, "When you touch the earth with your skin or through material that does not insulate you from its energy field (grounding or 'Earthing'), you literally absorb electrons from its surface into your body. This process has many powerful effects on you, the details of which we have only recently begun to understand."[35] He mentions stress reduction, anti-inflammatory responses, and less-clogged blood flow, all of which increase energy. There is something to be said for the health benefits of walking barefoot outdoors. Removing our shoes on "holy ground" (Exod 3:10) may turn out to be not only an act of respect for God's holy presence but also a way of giving our engagement in worship an electrical charge. Is the energetic Christian worship in Africa related to unshod worshipers standing and dancing on bare ground? Hundreds of millions of Muslims remove their shoes five times a day for prayer. I had my own experience of preaching and worshiping without shoes in a Mar Thoma Syro-Malabar congregation in Singapore. South Asians do not wear shoes into their holy places, including their homes. The very bodily act of removing our shoes for worship makes us mindful that worship occurs in a zone of holiness around God's presence.

The most fundamental thing we can say about ourselves as human beings is that we are creatures of the earth. But of all the creatures of the earth we have the honor of joining "the angels and archangels and all the company of heaven" in praising God. Since the rise of modern science we have defined ourselves as *Homo sapiens*, thinking humans. But from the beginning we were created to be *Homo adorans*, worshiping humans. As Alexander Schmemann reminds us, we were created as the priests who receive the world from God but also offer it back with thanksgiving. And by "filling the world with eucharist," the priest "transforms his life, the one that he receives from the world, into life in God, into communion with God. The world was created as the 'matter,' the material of one all-embracing eucharist, and man was created as the priest of this cosmic sacrament."[36]

There is an advantage to reconnecting with the earth and feeling ourselves to be a part of it since both the cosmology of Genesis 2 and

---

35. Daniel Chong, "Three Reasons Why You Need to Reconnect with the Earth," *MindBodyGreen*, February 17, 2012, http://tinyurl.com/ksvndn5. See also Clinton Ober, Stephen T. Sinatra, and Martin Zucker, *Earthing: The Most Important Health Discovery Ever* (Laguna Beach, CA: Basic Health, 2010).
36. Alexander Schmemann, *For the Life of the World: Sacraments and Orthodoxy* (Crestwood, NY: St. Vladimir's Seminary Press, 1973), 15.

the common cosmology of our modern world hold that we are created from the earth, indeed, from the same materials as the stars. Reginald Ray developed a meditation that helps us connect with the earth—the "Earth Descent," he called it—that consists of making contact with the earth by imagining sinking down into it.[37]

Sitting crossed-legged or lying on the ground settle your body by breathing in and out evenly. Then imagine sinking into the earth 5 feet, 10 feet, 20 feet, 100 feet, 500 feet, 1,000 feet, a mile, five miles, etc. If we inhale and exhale evenly during this meditation we should connect each exhale with the thought of sinking down into the earth and we will actually feel it in our bodies.

If we are sitting during this meditation our perineum makes contact with the earth. This is the anal and genital area of our bodies where we are often uptight and hold things in. In the yoga or Tantric subtle body, the root chakra (*Muladhara*) located in the perineum relates to our concerns for safety and security on our earthly journey. The yogis believed that opening this chakra creates stability in your life. When our basic needs are met, including food and water, shelter and clothing, we feel safe and tend to worry less day to day.

Yoga poses that open the nether regions of the torso can be helpful in our meditation on these issues. A vinyasa could include standing poses like lunge, warrior 1 and warrior 2, and triangle (both sides) and ending in goddess pose. Then squat down on your way to lying down. These are poses in which the legs are spread apart and the perineum is stretched. A final pose is lying on your back with legs spread open and feet touching (butterfly pose). Slowly bring your legs together so that your knees touch. If you do this slowly enough your inner thigh muscles will experience shakiness. Then drop your knees and repeat this several times. You could add to this a pelvic lock (mula bandha) as you bring your knees together and release it when you lower your knees. This exercise should end with a final relaxation (savasana or corpse pose).

As we meditate on our relationship to the earth and to the universe beyond, focus on how we are supported on the earth by a Creator who provides what we need from day to day in the created world. From that realization the attitude of gratitude wells up within us. There is much to be learned from the lower realms of existence and the shadow side of life if we give attention to them.

---

37. Ray, *Touching Enlightenment*, 361–66.

Figure 3. Meditating at Ankgor Wat in Thailand. Hindus, Buddhists, Jains, and New Agers practice meditation that connects them with the earth. Each tradition has its own understanding of meditation and connections with the earth. For Christians the purpose of an earth meditation is to contemplate the creation of our bodies and the earth from the same materials by our Creator God. Photo by Balint Földesi.

4

Anamnesis: Body and Memory

The body can be a real problem for a thirteen-year-old. It's changing faster than one can adjust to it, and that messes with the mind. As puberty was setting in, my voice was starting to change, just when I was going to be singing in a children's operetta at the Buffalo Science Museum and in the spring concert of the Singing Boys of Buffalo at Kleinhans Music Hall. My body was growing, but not enough to my mind in comparison with the bodies of my buddies. Gym class was a mixture of successes and failures. I landed a spot in the boys' gymnastics show in the seventh and eighth grades. But sports that required hand-eye coordination were a disaster for me because I was nearsighted. It was actually the school music teacher who suggested to my mother when I was in the seventh grade that I needed to have my eyes examined because my sight-reading was atrocious. Yes, I really needed glasses. But then I was the little kid with glasses who became a prime target for bullying on the way home from school.

And, of course, my sexuality was emerging. Like every boy going through puberty, I experienced sensations that I didn't understand, nor did I ask. Adolescents don't want to talk about these mysterious body things with their parents, and we had no sex education in school. Most information would come from more "knowledgeable" friends. My mother had a medical dictionary, so I looked up "masturbation." What I read horrified me. It said that masturbation could produce nearsightedness, pimples, and obsessive-compulsive behavior, among other things. An encyclopedia at the public library reported that the Catholic Church considered masturbation a sin because it is "disordered sex" and called it "self-abuse." I wasn't a Catholic and I didn't understand "disordered sex," but I thought this probably applied also to me. So I felt doomed in this world and the next. Like many other kids, I kept all this terror to myself.

Worst of all, my parents' upstairs tenant recognized what was happening in my body and took advantage of it. The couple had me babysit their infant one night when they stepped out. Since they were late returning I fell asleep on their sofa. I woke up groggily with the sensation of warmth around my groin and realized that the man was rubbing my penis while his wife was getting ready for bed. Seeing me awakening he bent over and whispered, "Does this feel good? Don't you like to do this to yourself?" His wife asked what was keeping him so long and told him to come to bed. As soon as he went to bed I ran upstairs to the attic bedroom I shared with my brother and jumped into bed with him. I don't know why I did that. Perhaps for security. Sure enough, the man followed me upstairs; I suppose to make sure I was all right. I'm sure he saw me in bed with my brother. I was terrified by what had happened but didn't tell anyone about it.

The man came home from work just before I came home from school. He began coming up to my bedroom when I came home after school. Since we dressed better for school in those days than kids do now, I usually changed my clothes when I got home. I might have been sitting on my bed only in my briefs, but he came in unannounced and stood there watching me and chatting, as if he belonged there. The guy was creepy, and I was so relieved when that family finally moved out a few months later!

I'm sorry to have to tell these embarrassing adolescent things in an academic and pastoral work, but these were real-life experiences that were occurring in the weeks and months before my Confirmation and first Communion and contributed to making my first Communion at Easter a powerful experience for me. Communicants will bring their real-life experiences, including their bodily experiences, to the eucharistic Meal.

Communion in the Context of the Passion of Our Lord

My issues had to do with my body, so, yes, my focus was very much on my body when I came to the Communion rail that Easter Day, knelt down, and heard the pastor say, "The body of Christ, given for you," as I put the wafer in my mouth, and "The blood of Christ, shed for you," as I drank wine from the little glass.

Before Communion we sang (in old English set to the old Braunschweig tune), "O Christ, Thou Lamb of God, that takest away the sins of the world, have mercy upon us. O Christ, Thou Lamb of God, that takest away the sins of the world, have mercy upon. O Christ, Thou Lamb of God, that takest away the sins of the world, grant us thy peace. Amen." I thought about Christ's suffering on the cross to take away my sins. We didn't have a crucifix in our church, but we had just been through Lent and Holy Week. I had attended Lenten Wednesday Vespers throughout Lent at which the History of the Passion (a seventeenth-century Lutheran harmonization of the four Gospel passion narratives) had been read and preached on; and I had been to church twice on Good Friday: once at the Kensington Methodist Church for the community Good Friday service at noon at which my pastor preached, and then again in the evening at Tabor Lutheran Church for the Good Friday service. But I was hearing about the passion of Christ and what he suffered in the body as I went through my adolescent body issues that spring. It was fresh in my mind on that Easter morning when we sang the Agnus Dei and I went forward to receive my first Communion with my fellow confirmands. I believed that my sins—real or imagined—were forgiven, and that I was saved by the blood of Christ shed on the cross of suffering when his body was tortured and killed. In my adolescent mind I made some connection between the suffering body of Christ and my body that was pummeled by bullies and violated by a child molester.

Eucharistic Sacrifice

The sacrificial death of Christ became a main understanding of the Eucharist, especially in Western Christianity. Both the doctrines of the real presence of Christ and the eucharistic sacrifice became divisive at the time of the Reformation. Protestants could only allow a sacrifice of praise and thanksgiving in the eucharistic celebration. Tridentine Roman Catholicism asserted the relationship between the Mass and the propitiatory sacrifice of Christ on the cross. Yet Protestants did not deny the relationship between the atoning sacrifice of Christ on the cross and Holy Communion. How do we receive the forgiveness of sins and salvation except because of the propitiatory sacrifice of Christ? And if we don't receive those benefits in Holy Communion, how can the sacrament be considered a means of grace?

An ecumenical breakthrough over the impasse of the Reformation on Eucharist and sacrifice has occurred in the dialogues of the twentieth century. Edward Kilmartin, SJ, summed up the emerging ecumenical consensus on the basis of New Testament and patristic studies.

> Sacrifice in the New Testament understanding—and thus in its Christian understanding—is, in the first place, the self-offering of the Father in the gift of his Son, and in the second place the unique response of the Son in his humanity to the Father, and in the third place, the self-offering of believers in union with Christ by which they share in his covenant relationship with the Father.
>
> The Holy Spirit brings about the presence of the historical sacrifice of Christ, and acts through it as source of the transmission of the sacrificial attitudes of Christ that enable the liturgical assembly to participate in Christ's self-offering through the medium of the Eucharistic prayer. . . .
>
> The Eucharistic sacrifice, just as the historical sacrifice of the cross, is grounded in the initiative of the Father. The whole point of the Eucharist is the participation in Christ's Passover from suffering to glory. This is only possible because of the Father's self-gift in the sending of the Son and the response of the Son in his humanity, and the sanctifying work of the Holy Spirit in the Incarnation and in the life of faith of Jesus.[1]

The tendency in modern theology has been to see the whole life of Christ, the whole of the incarnation, as a sacrifice of the Son to the Father, and to emphasize the resurrection as the reason for joy and celebration, thereby diminishing the gloom and sobriety that characterized so many celebrations of the Lord's Supper, especially in Protestant traditions. These ideas were embedded in the prayer I worked on for the *Lutheran Book of Worship*, Great Thanksgiving II.

> Therefore, O God,
>   with this bread and cup
>   we remember the incarnation of your Son:
>   his human birth

---

1. Edward J. Kilmartin, SJ, *The Eucharist in the West: History and Theology*, ed. Robert J. Daly, SJ (Collegeville, MN: Liturgical, 1998), 381–82.

and the covenant he made with us.
We remember the sacrifice of his life:
   his eating with outcasts and sinners,
   and his acceptance of death.
But chiefly [on this day = Easter, Sundays]
   we remember his rising from the tomb,
   his ascension to the seat of power,
   and his sending of the holy and life-giving Spirit.
We cry out for the resurrection of our lives,
   when Christ will come again in beauty and power
   to share with us the great and promised feast.[2]

Feminist theology in particular has been critical of any sacrificial understanding of the saving work of Christ. This critique was applied especially to sacrificial terminology in the eucharistic institution narratives, such as "handed over" and "blood of the covenant . . . poured out for many for the forgiveness of sins" (Matt 26:19) because of its images of brutality and violence.[3]

There is no dogma of the atonement in Christian thought, only theories of the atonement based on various images and metaphors. In the Eucharist we are not obliged to accept any one theory (ransom theory, satisfaction theory, moral influence theory, penal-substitutionary theory, Christus Victor, etc.) as the only correct one (although evangelicals seem to have fastened on the penal-substitution theory); but neither should we deny the reality that these theories are seeking to explicate, namely, how the saving work of Christ reconciles sinful humanity to our holy God and offers forgiveness of sins through the sacraments of the church.

The language of the atoning sacrifice was applied to the crucifixion of Christ in the New Testament on the basis of Christ as the fulfillment of the Scriptures, and therefore also the fulfillment of the sacrificial cult instituted by God through Moses and Aaron for the people of Israel. No reason is given in the Torah as to why God instituted the sacrificial cult. This cultus, which was not unlike other sacrificial systems in the ancient world, was given to Israel as a way for the people to relate to God by expressing thanksgiving, celebrating communion, dealing with personal sin and guilt, and atoning for the sins of the nation.[4]

2. *Lutheran Book of Worship*, leaders ed. (Minneapolis: Augsburg, 1978), 222.
3. See Andrea Bieler and Luise Schottroff, *The Eucharist: Bodies, Bread, and Resurrection* (Minneapolis: Fortress, 2007), 146.

I do not believe that we can understand the crucifixion of Christ (which was, after all, to all appearances an ordinary brutal Roman execution) in sacrificial terms apart from the purposes of the Old Testament sacrifices to effect reconciliation, establish communion between God and his people, and provide for atonement. The sacrifice of Yom Kippur provided a scapegoat to cover the sins of the people. The fact that the sacrifice of Christ is proclaimed as "once for all" means that from the Christian perspective no further scapegoating is needed.[5]

We cannot disconnect the Last Supper, and its command for repetition in our celebration of the Lord's Supper, from the memorial of Christ's death. Receiving Holy Communion on Good Friday in commemoration of the passion of Christ became a major devotion for Christians generally and for Lutherans in particular. In Orthodoxy and Catholicism, which did not celebrate the Eucharist on Good Friday because it was a fast day, Holy Communion was provided in the liturgy of the presanctified at the end of the Good Friday liturgy. The Lutheran tradition provided for a full celebration of the service of Holy Communion with its own set of propers (Introit, Collect, Epistle, Gradual, and Gospel).[6] This had been the biggest Communion day in the church year in German Protestantism.

The Suffering Body

Focus on the bodily sufferings of Christ, in all their brutality, have brought comfort and hope to many people who have suffered bodily for the sake of Christ, but also to those who have experienced affliction on and in their bodies. My adolescent body issues were not so severe in the big scheme of things, but they presented big enough concerns for a thirteen-year-old. As I got older I forgot about these issues entirely as I focused less on my body and more on matters of the mind. In fact, I really didn't think much about my body at all—until a diagnosis of colon cancer hit me squarely in the solar plexus in 2006. Then I thought about my body a lot, especially as it began to deteriorate from the onslaught of a year's worth of chemotherapy. But during that time the

4. See H. H. Rowley, *Worship in Ancient Israel: Its Forms and Meaning* (Philadelphia: Fortress, 1967), 111–43.
5. This was the lifetime work of the French philosopher René Girard. See *The Girard Reader*, ed. James G. Williams (New York: Crossroad, 1996).
6. See *Common Service Book of the Lutheran Church* (Philadelphia: The Board of Publications of the United Lutheran Church in America, 1917), 79–80, and *Service Book and Hymnal of the Lutheran Church in America* (Minneapolis: Augsburg, 1958), 87–88. These were the two worship books used in my congregation in my youth.

sacrament was there for me again with the intensity with which I had experienced it as an adolescent. The body of Christ entered my deteriorating body as a sign of wellness and wholeness. The sacramental body was more real than my ghostly chemo body. At the time the body of Christ was pretty substantial for me; my chemo body was pretty insubstantial, I thought.

Charlene Spretnak wrote about "the resurgence of the real" in postmodernism. She singled out for special attention "the knowing body," "the creative cosmos," and "the complex sense of place." Here I focus on the rediscovery of "the knowing body."[7] Beginning in the 1970s we were learning from alternative medicine that the ills of the body could be treated holistically even though the medical establishment wasn't buying it. By the 1980s the alarming increase in health-care costs was forcing many people to try the less expensive alternative medicines, and they began treating physical ailments with herbs instead of drugs, often to good effect. The mind-body dualism was breaking down, and by the 1990s the psychosomatic approach to wellness was becoming more accepted by medical professionals. Some insurance companies were even recommending that their clients try meditation (although they didn't pay for it!).

There are various ways in which we discover what the body knows, certainly through psychotherapy but also through some massage therapies and somatic bodywork. Sigmund Freud noticed long ago that if we know how to look at the ego in the right way, we can see all the traumatic experiences buried "down below" kind of compressed and welling up into pathological behavior. Body workers have come to see that suppressed traumas, either to the psyche or the body, can result in chronic bodily conditions, for example, back pains. This is because the body retains knowledge of things that the mind has suppressed.

The pioneering body worker Deane Juhan, author of the classic body work manual *Job's Body*, wrote in a blog article titled "Reaching the Mind with Touch" that "the skin is the surface of the brain; to touch the surface is to stir the depths. I cannot touch an organism's skin anywhere without arousing that organism's entirety. That is to say, the skin on one hand is a primary boundary of our physical selves, and on the other hand a primary threshold of interactions that connect our inner world with the world around us in many ways."[8] He stirs the mind as he reaches down into the body to manipulate the connective

---

7. Charlene Spretnak, *The Resurgence of the Real: Body, Nature, and Place in a Hypermodern World* (Reading, MA: Addison-Wesley, 1997), 14–20.

tissues, the neuropeptides, the nerves and muscles. He writes: "'Mind' is vastly more extensive than 'brain.' Mind involves the whole of our landscape, and all of the internal and external ecological processes that are fused into those mysteries and miracles that we call life and consciousness. We are moved by all levels of our feelings, ideas and beliefs, our current assessments, needs and intentions, and by all of the countless processes that underlie them."[9]

Touching the body in both gentle and deep ways can stir the body's memory of past experiences. Perhaps as psychotherapy and somatic body work was becoming more accepted and as people got more into the memories of their bodies, traumas of the past, such as child sexual abuse, began to surface, particularly the widespread instances of sexual abuse of children, especially boys—altar boys!—by priests. The harassment and molesting I experienced from my parents' tenant was fleeting in comparison with some of the stories of child and youth sexual abuse that have emerged in the last twenty years. We know now that children and youth were sexually assaulted by family members, teachers, coaches, friends, neighbors—almost anyone. But being abused by your priest has to be the worst of all because the priest serves the sacrament of the body and blood of Christ *in persona Christi*. Receiving Holy Communion became very comforting to me. But I was not abused by my pastor in the sacristy before I went out to serve Mass with him at the altar. I didn't receive the body of Christ from the hand that had fondled my body in an unwelcome way.

You would think that boys and girls abused by priests would stay away from the Eucharist and from church itself. Professor Robert Orsi, who holds the chair of Catholic Studies at Northwestern University, studied such cases, which he calls "events of abundant evil," and reports in his new book, *History and Presence*, that many of those abused by priests continued to go to Mass. "The Eucharist was not safe for survivors," he wrote; but they went anyway.[10] As I read his case studies I wondered: Do they find solace in identifying with the bodily sufferings of Christ? Do they find healing in receiving the broken body of Christ into their violated bodies?

We need Christ's real presence within us as well as for us if real healing (salvation) is to occur in the Eucharist. I will discuss this more in

---

8. Deane Juhan, "Reaching the Mind with Touch," Job's Body, October 12, 2010, http://tinyurl.com/kga3fye.
9. Ibid.
10. Robert A. Orsi, *History and Presence* (Cambridge, MA: Belknap Press of Harvard University Press, 2016), 221.

the chapter on Communion. But it begins with the sense that Christ must be bodily present—body and blood—in the act of remembrance (anamnesis). We especially remember that he instituted the Lord's Supper "on the night in which he was betrayed" when he himself was agitated by what lay ahead. According to the Synoptic Gospels, at the Passover Seder Jesus focused on the broken loaf and said, "This is my body," and on the cup of blessing at the end of the meal, saying "This is the new covenant in my blood." He was saying that the bread and cup was him. Since he was physically at table with them, it is a mystery how these words should be interpreted in that context. I see no reason why, in faith, the disciples could not have received Christ into their bodies as bread and wine at the last supper even though he was physically present among them. On the other hand, the Last Supper could not have been the fullness of the Eucharist of the church since Christ had not yet offered himself on the altar of the cross or risen from the dead and ascended into heaven. About that post-resurrection Eucharist both Luke and Paul include in their traditions of the institution the command of Jesus, "Do this for the remembrance [anamnēsis] of me"[11] (in connection with the bread in Luke 22:19; in connection with both the bread and cup in 1 Cor 11:24–25).

Remembering the Body

Anamnēsis means "remembrance" in the sense of "reactualization" or "re-presentation" rather than in the sense of dramatic portrayal (mimēsis). But what is reactualized or re-presented in the eucharistic memorial?

To some extent, what is re-presented by anamnēsis is governed by the text. If we have only the institution narrative, as is the case of many Protestant liturgies, we are reactualizing the institution of the Lord's Supper at the "Last Supper" of Jesus and his disciples on the night before his death. A full anaphora will provide a fuller remembrance of the saving work of God in Christ, and not only in the section after the institution narrative that liturgists have called the anamnesis.

In the Eucharist we are remembering Jesus before God (Jeremias, see note 11) by performing the ritual of taking bread and cup, giving thanks over them (although that is not always done), breaking the

---

11. The form of the command in *Lutheran Book of Worship* (1978) and *The Book of Common Prayer* (1979). The wording is based on the proposal of Joachim Jeremias, *The Eucharistic Words of Jesus*, rev. ed., trans. Norman Perrin (New York: Charles Scribner's Sons, 1966) that the command for repetition may be understood as "This do, that God may remember me" (p. 252).

bread, and giving the elements to the communicants (the fourfold shape of the liturgy popularized by Gregory Dix).[12] When St. Paul says in 1 Corinthians 11:26, "For as often as you eat this bread and drink the cup, you proclaim the Lord's death until he comes," he is saying that the action of eating and drinking becomes a remembrance of Christ's death. This is so whether the words of institution are recited or not. We have early eucharistic prayers in the *Didache* and in the East Syrian tradition, such as the Anaphora of Addai and Mari, in which there is no institution narrative—and no evidence that the Words of Institution were used in the rite. But when the institution narrative was added to the anaphora, words of *anamnēsis* followed.

In the *Apostolic Tradition* the command "When you do this, you make my remembrance" is followed by "Remembering therefore his death and resurrection. . . ." The introductory part of the prayer had mentioned the incarnation in the Virgin's womb and the Son's suffering to "destroy death," "break the bonds of the devil," "tread down hell," "shine upon the righteous, and fix a term, and manifest the resurrection."[13]

These things that we remember were performed by Christ in his body. This was the theme of the treatise *On the Incarnation* by St. Athanasius of Alexandria, written around 320. Writing to a cultural skeptic, of which there must have been many in the intellectual center that was Alexandria, he wrote:

> As, then, he who desires to see God Who by nature is invisible and not to be beheld, may yet perceive and know Him through His works, so too let him who does not see Christ with his understanding at least consider Him in His bodily works and test whether they be of man or God. If they be of man, then let him scoff; but if they be of God, let him not mock at things which are no fit subject for scorn, but rather let him recognize the fact and marvel that things divine have been revealed to us by such humble means, that through death deathlessness has been made known to us, and through the Incarnation of the Word the Mind whence all things proceed has been declared, and its Agent and Ordainer, the Word of God Himself. He, indeed, assumed humanity that we might become God. He manifested Himself by means of a body that we might perceive the Mind of the unseen Father. He endured shame from men that we might inherit immortality.[14]

---

12. Gregory Dix, *The Shape of the Liturgy* (London: Dacre, 1945; repr., Minneapolis: Seabury, 1983), 48.

13. R. C. D. Jasper and G. J. Cuming, *Prayers of the Eucharist: Early and Reformed*, 3rd ed. (Collegeville, MN: Liturgical, 1992), 35.

14. St. Athanasius, *On the Incarnation*, with an Introduction by C. S. Lewis (Crestwood, NY: St. Vladimir's Seminary Press, 1953), 92–93.

Athanasius is saying that if you want to know the mind of God, as pertains to our salvation, look to what Christ did in the body; and what Athanasius highlights, among Christ's many bodily works, are his incarnation in the womb of the Virgin, his suffering, death, and resurrection.

These are also the main aspects of the life and work of Christ remembered in the emerging eucharistic prayers of the fourth century. Look at the Egyptian Anaphora of St. Basil as an example. The narrative after the Sanctus emphasizes the incarnation, crucifixion, descent into hell, resurrection on the third day, ascension into heaven and session at the right hand of the Father, and coming day of judgment. These items are remembered again after the institution narrative, which includes the dominical command and St. Paul's gloss from 1 Corinthians 11:26.

> We therefore, remembering his holy sufferings, and his resurrection from the dead, and his ascension into heaven, and his session at the right hand of the Father, and his glorious and fearful coming to us (again), have set before you from your own gifts, this bread and this cup.[15]

This same list of the works of Christ will be repeated in all the West Syrian anaphoras, of which the Byzantine St. Basil and St. John Chrysostom are the two used in the Orthodox Divine Liturgy.

We also note that these same works of Christ are listed in the Nicene Creed as being done "for us and for our salvation": his incarnation in the Virgin Mary, his crucifixion under Pontius Pilate, his death and burial, his resurrection on the third day, his ascension into heaven and session at the right hand of the Father, and his coming again in glory to judge the living and the dead.

These are all works that Christ performed in his body. In fact, these chief works were performed by Christ in his naked body, which was then clothed. Athanasius wrote that "He endured shame from men," but he was not ashamed before God because unlike the first Adam the new Adam was obedient. The body that is naked before the Lord is also clothed by the Lord.[16] Christ came into the world as a naked baby, as we all do, and was then wrapped in swaddling cloths. Christ's "suffering" under Pontius Pilate was his flogging, which was administered to naked victims according to Roman practice, after which he was draped in a purple cloak in mockery of his purported kingship. He was hung

---

15. Jasper and Cuming, *Prayers of the Eucharist*, 71.
16. See Frank C. Senn, *Embodied Liturgy: Lessons in Christian Ritual* (Minneapolis: Fortress, 2016), 53–89.

on the cross stark naked. Roman crucifixions were intended to inflict maximal humiliation, and the crucified victims did not have their genitals discreetly covered by a loincloth; they were exposed for all to see (see figure 4a). But then Christ's naked body was taken down from the cross and wrapped in burial cloths. When Christ rose from the dead he must have emerged naked because when Peter and John went into the empty tomb they found the grave clothes rolled up in a place by themselves. Michelangelo portrayed Christ naked in his sculpture of the risen Christ (although a seventeenth-century pope ordered the figure's genitals covered with a bronze cloth). There was no need for the coverings of this world in the resurrection of the dead—just as Michelangelo painted nude bodies of humanity rising naked in his painting of the last judgment on the walls of the Sistine Chapel above the altar, and being judged by a naked Christ. There is no sin-induced body shame in Christ's works in his naked body. There is no shame for the redeemed in the resurrection, but we shall nevertheless be clothed in white festal garments. Our salvation in Christ is all about his body, but his saving work is applied to our bodies in the sacraments of Holy Baptism and Holy Communion. Not just our souls but also our bodies are sanctified in our reception of the sacraments of Christ.

There is nothing in the creed about Christ's teachings or healing works. For those other works of Christ we have the readings of the Gospels in the liturgy. The works of Christ, also performed on bodies in acts of healing and exorcism, are not to be minimized. They were signs of the intended wholeness of creation in God's Kingdom. Jesus's teachings instruct us in the way of the kingdom of God, and his healing acts encourage us in our sufferings. But Christianity is a religion of salvation, and that was accomplished in the paschal mystery of Christ's Passover from death to life. Contemporary Western liturgies have incorporated as congregational interjections modeled in the ancient Egyptian anaphoras at the place of the anamnesis in our eucharistic prayers memorial acclamations such as "Christ has died. Christ is risen. Christ will come again."

Human suffering and death are not ignored in Christianity; it is present at the center of our most important ritual act—our taking bread and a cup of wine in remembrance of Christ's suffering and death, resurrection and ascension, and promise to come again. In proclaiming the paschal mystery of faith, we connect the threads of our present lives and hopes for the future to what the saving work of Christ was all about in the mind of God.

We have even brought suffering and death to our altars. We recall that altars on which the body and blood of Christ are placed were at first the mensas or tabletops of the graves of the martyrs and other faithful Christians, and the Eucharist was celebrated in the cemeteries at night like other Roman *refrigeria* (meals with the dead). When basilicas were built for Christian worship in the fourth century the altars were often erected over the graves of the martyrs (like St. Peter's on the Vatican Hill—originally a necropolis); or else relics of the martyrs were entombed in the altars. The presence of this cloud of witnesses is also an encouragement to the faithful who suffer in their own bodies.

So the remembrance of Christ's suffering and death is a focus of the Eucharist, for which in the Western church the crucifix on or above the altar served as a visual reminder. The visual representations of the process of the state-sponsored torture and execution of Jesus, expressing realistic agony in medieval woodcarvings, have been toned down in modern representations. The flogging in Mel Gibson's 2004 film, *The Passion of the Christ*, with Jim Caviezel playing Jesus, was prolonged and shockingly graphic (although it was not so graphic as to portray Jesus completely naked, as would have been historically accurate). We confess in the Apostles' Creed that "he suffered under Pontius Pilate," which makes the flogging of Jesus an article of faith for Christians. Flogging preceded all Roman crucifixions. It was designed to weaken the victims. The intensity of the flogging depended on how long they wanted the victims to linger on the cross. Flogging has been an object of meditation, including its reenactment in flagellant processions since the late Middle Ages and today in some Catholic countries like the Philippines. But flogging is also a punishment that continues to be inflicted in many countries in today's world where people are assigned fifty, one hundred, or one thousand lashes.

Contrary to our popular portrayals, victims did not carry or drag the entire cross. The upright post was left in place, and the victim only carried the crossbeam. The fact that Jesus was not able to carry the crossbeam, requiring the soldiers to press the bystander Simon of Cyrene into service, suggests that Jesus was in a very weakened condition from the flogging.

In spite of the prevalence of crucifixions in the Roman world, detailed descriptions of it are few; contemporary writers seem to have avoided the subject. Luke is no exception. In his Gospel he covers the event in one line: "When they came to the place that is called The Skull, they crucified Jesus there with the criminals, one on his right and one on his left" (Luke 23:33). We have some descriptions of crucifixions from the Jewish historian Josephus, including a historical corroboration of the crucifixion of Jesus. And recent archaeological discoveries, including skeletal remains of a crucified man in first-century Jerusalem, have added to our knowledge of the act. The victim was stripped, and whatever clothes he had were divided among the squad of soldiers. Since the victim's arms were usually tied with ropes to the crossbeam he was carrying, nailing the hands (or more likely the wrists) served only to inflict pain by damaging nerves. If Jesus had not been carrying his crossbeam, his arms wouldn't have been tied to it. This would have required nailing. The victim, fastened to the crossbeam, was hoisted into place on the upright post. The crosses were probably only high enough for the victim's feet to be off the ground since the victim had to be pulled up into position. The feet straddled the upright post, and the skeletal remains of the crucified man shows that his feet were nailed through his heels to the post. To prevent the body from slipping forward, the upright post often had a small pole or seat on which the victim uncomfortably sat. It was not a footrest, as artists' portrayals often show. This made the cross Jesus's throne and being hoisted up onto it his enthronement. A sign affixed to the cross or hanging around his neck proclaimed, "This is the King of the Jews." The Gospel of John says in it was written in Hebrew, Greek, and Latin so that Jesus's enthronement was proclaimed to the whole world.

The Italian artist Mario Donizetti painted a crucifixion (not necessarily Jesus) in 1969, drawing on recent archaeological and historical evidence, that visually demonstrates a Roman crucifixion victim.

Reclaiming Bodies

The church throughout its history has turned bodies over to the state for the application of capital punishment, preserving for itself the cure of souls. This was done especially in the torture and burning of heretics in the society of Christendom. But what happens when the bodies of Christians are apprehended and tortured by the state and made to disappear? This was the situation in Chile under the dictatorship of General Augusto Pinochet, which was especially gruesome. Thousands of civilians were rounded up and detained in detention centers where they were systematically given electrical shocks through electrodes attached to sensitive areas of the body like genitals, waterboarded, had their heads forced into buckets of urine and excrement, suffocated with bags, hanged by their feet or hands and beaten, raped (both men and women), or killed (disappeared). The whole point was to rule by fear.

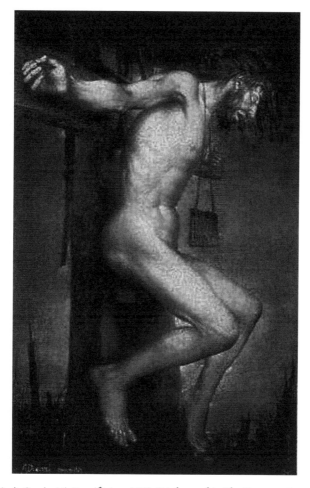

Figure 4a. Mario Donizetti, Crucifixion, 1969. It is housed in The Treasury Museum of the Vatican Basilica.

William T. Cavanaugh studied this situation and in his dissertation, published in book form as *Torture and Eucharist*, proposed that the eucharistic anamnesis is a narrative that does not suppress the reality of state torture. Rather, he claims that the Eucharist was the church's "counter-politics" set against the politics of torture. The eucharistic memorial is a counternarrative of body and pain. The state is conducting a kind of perverse liturgy of its own in the ritual processes of torture. The Eucharist is the church's liturgy set against the state's anti-liturgy. Where the state's anti-liturgy attempts to destroy community by setting people against one another, the eucharistic liturgy draws people into the community of communion. Where the state breaks bodies, the Eucharist holds up the broken body of Christ as the source of healing. Cavanaugh writes:

> Where torture is an anti-liturgy for the realization of the state's power on the bodies of others, Eucharist is the liturgical realization of Christ's suffering and redemptive body in the bodies of his followers. Torture creates fearful and isolated bodies, bodies docile to the purpose of the regime; the Eucharist effects the body of Christ, a body marked by resistance to worldly power. Torture creates victims; Eucharist creates witnesses, *martyrs*. Isolation is overcome in the Eucharist by the building of a communal body which resists the state's attempt to disappear it.[17]

The goal of torture is to destroy social life and through fear create individuals incapable of group associations. It results in the weakening of social institutions (especially the church) and the transferring of individuals' loyalty to the state.[18] The Eucharist as embodied communion makes us mindful of these threats and counters them by creating a community that embraces individuals. Cavanaugh develops his understanding of the eucharistic communion in terms of the true body of Christ, which is "neither purely mystical nor simply analogous to the modern state," because "in the Eucharist the kingdom of God irrupts into time and confuses the spiritual and the temporal."[19]

Cavanaugh seeks to present the idea of the church as the true body of Christ in place of the mystical body ecclesiology. In order to understand these ideas accurately, we must understand correctly the various theological terms for the body of Christ. On the basis of the works of Henri de Lubac, Cavanaugh speaks of a threefold distinction of Christ's body: (1) the historical body, meaning the physical body of Jesus of Nazareth; (2) the sacramental body, or Christ as present in the eucharistic elements; and (3) the ecclesial body, that is, the church.[20]

17. William T. Cavanaugh, *Torture and Eucharist: Theology, Politics, and the Body of Christ* (Malden, MA: Blackwell, 2000), 206.
18. Ibid., 3.
19. Ibid., 206.
20. Ibid., 212. See Henri de Lubac, *Corpus Mysticum: The Eucharist and the Church in the Middle Ages*, trans. Gemma Simmonds, with Richard Price and Christopher Stephens, ed. Laurence Paul Hemming and Susan Frank Parsons (Notre Dame: University of Notre Dame Press, 2006), 28–30, 256.

In the Eucharist, these three aspects of the body of Christ become one, in a real though mysterious manner. Cavanaugh argues that the *corpus mysticum* (the mystical body of Christ as the church) should be identified with the sacramental body, the *corpus verum* (the true body of Christ), not with the institutional body identified with the Roman hierarchy.[21] The points that Cavanaugh emphasizes here are, first, that "the body of Christ is liturgically enacted, not institutionally guaranteed," and second, that "eucharistic resistance to the state must abolish the idea of the temporal and the spiritual as two distinct spaces and recover the eschatological dimension of time."[22] In other words, communion in Christ's body is efficacious not because of the institutional church but because of the sacrament of the Eucharist. The Eucharist is understood as a mystical space where the spiritual and the temporal are merged together in eschatological hope.

On the basis of the church as the true body of Christ, Cavanaugh describes the Eucharist as "a resource for Christian social practice."[23] The church, which shares the nature of Christ, is required to do in reality what Jesus did and does. Specifically, the church should identify itself with suffering people, just as Jesus himself in his passion identified with the afflicted.

A Role for Lament

The Roman Catholic theologian David Power has suggested that anamnesis could relate even more to human suffering if eucharistic praying admitted the element of lament as well as thanksgiving. He notes the juxtaposition of lament and praise in many of the Psalms (such as Psalm 22, the psalm of the passion); and also of complaints against God in Job 29–31 and in Psalm 44. In an essay he wrote for a collection of essays I assembled titled *New Eucharistic Prayers* from the eucharistic prayer study group of the North American Academy of Liturgy, he wondered how, in the face of evil of such magnitude as the Holocaust or mutually assured destruction, we can give thanks without also lamenting the human situation in which we find ourselves. He writes:

> For Christians who gather together in the memory of Jesus Christ, there is a new consciousness today of evil which makes it difficult to name God, and so to make thanksgiving. This consciousness has to do with Chris-

21. Ibid., 218.
22. Ibid., 221.
23. Ibid., 251.

tianity's own pathologies, pathologies which show that those who have engaged in the naming of God in Jesus Christ have been privy to the destructive forces that threaten not only humanity's but the earth's existence. The effect of this is not only to call us to the confession of sin but to make us ask whether the church has even named God aright. It is not easy to render thanks to an absent or to a badly named God.[24]

How do we give thanks in an age in which we remember the Holocaust, apartheid, sexism, the contempt for planet earth, and other evils that Christians have participated in? Power suggests that we need words of lament as well as praise in our eucharistic prayers. He provided one such model in his essay, from which I quote the anamnesis section that follows the institution narrative.

> Remembering, compassionate and loving God, we proclaim the presence of your Word in our human flesh. We proclaim the Spirit who settled upon him, drove him into the wilderness to wrestle with profane hopes, and led him into the company of the blind, the lame, the diseased, the imprisoned, and the very dead. We remember your Word bursting asunder the bonds of death, and rising to your right hand, so that through the Spirit he might continue to live amid the struggles of the torn world.
>
> Taking this bread of tears and happiness, taking this cup of sorrow and inebriation, united with the blessings of Jesus over the bread and cup, we offer you all there ever has been of human sorrow, struggle and hope, longing to be joined together where your folly holds sway in human hearts.[25]

The Body's Memory

Anamnesis is an embodied practice.[26] It is not just a matter of listening to words that evoke the stories of salvation and of the need for healing. Anamnesis relates to the reception of Holy Communion as much as to the recitation of the words of institution and whatever words of the remembrance of Christ that may surround them. In reception of Holy Communion, anamnesis is embedded in the body's memory, not just considered with the mind. The body remembers other times we have gone to the altar and other occasions that brought us there.

Contemporary cognitive science suggests that the mind is not a sep-

---

24. David M. Power, "The Eucharistic Prayer; Another Look," in *New Eucharistic Prayers: An Ecumenical Study of Their Development and Structure*, ed. Frank C. Senn (Mahwah, NJ: Paulist, 1987), 250.
25. Ibid., 253–54. For another sample of this kind of writing see David N. Power, *The Eucharistic Mystery: Revitalizing the Tradition* (New York: Crossroad, 1995), 336–38.
26. See Bieler and Schottroff, *Eucharist*, 170–96.

arate faculty from the rest of the body, as Western philosophy since René Descartes ("I think, therefore I am") has assumed. Evidence suggests that the mind (reason) is not autonomous from bodily capacities such as perception and movement (thus Maurice Merleau-Ponty; see below), emotion and sensory awareness. Rather, as George Lakoff and Mark Johnson report, "From a biological perspective, it is eminently plausible that reason has grown out of the sensory and motor systems and that it still uses those systems or structures developed from them."[27]

David Hogue reports that neuroscientists say that the "visual details, sounds, smells, and touch dimensions of a particular memory . . . are each stored in their own locations in the brain and pulled together to reconstruct a representation of the event."[28] This suggests that when we come to receive the sacrament of the altar the various sensory stimuli and motor motions work together in the brain to well up memories of past communions and maybe even of unrelated events. This is memory as anamnesis because it is reactualization; it becomes real again for us in the present.

Bessel van der Kolk, MD, has specialized in understanding the causes and consequences of traumas suffered in the body and affecting the mind. Since the 1990s brain-imaging tools have disclosed what actually happens in the brains of traumatized people—how brains and the way they store memories are changed by the damage inflicted by traumas. As a result of his studies he reports that "we have . . . begun to understand how overwhelming experiences affect our innermost sensations and our relationship to our physical reality—the core of who we are. We have learned that trauma is not just an event that took place sometime in the past; it is also the imprint left by that experience on mind, brain, and body."[29]

We bring to the eucharistic table our actual bodies with all their sensory perceptions and physical movements. As the senses are stimulated by what we hear, what we see, what we smell, what we touch, what we taste, memories in the body and the mind are stirred up. The Eucharist is a very sensual event. We hear the words of institution and of administration. We see the bread and cup of wine as it is elevated at the con-

27. See George Lakoff and Mark Johnson, *Philosophy in the Flesh: The Embodied Mind and Its Challenges to Western Thought* (New York: Basic Books, 1999), 43.
28. David A. Hogue, *Remembering the Future, Imagining the Past: Story, Ritual and the Human Brain* (Cleveland: Pilgrim, 2003), 60.
29. Bessel van der Kolk, M.D., *The Body Keeps the Score: Brain, Mind, and Body in the Healing of Trauma* (New York: Viking, 2014), 21.

cluding doxology of the eucharistic prayer. We smell the aroma of the freshly baked bread and the poured out wine. We may also smell the burning candles on the altar or the incense from the censing of the Table or the flowers arranged around the altar. We taste the bread and wine on our lips and in our mouths. We touch the bread as it is placed in our hands and the chalice as we take hold of it to drink. What we hear, see, smell, touch, and taste is crucial to our way of remembering Christ at the Eucharist. Anamnesis cannot be considered apart from the whole experience of eating and drinking.

The body is also in motion in the eucharistic celebration. We walk forward to the Communion rail or the Communion station. We may kneel down at the rail or stand at a station. We extend our hands to receive the bread and cup. We bow as we leave the altar. We return to our place and sit or kneel in prayer and then join the congregation in singing hymns during the continuing distribution of the elements to the congregation.

As Maurice Merleau-Ponty postulated in his *Phenomenology of Perception*, our bodily experience of the world is such that we can take up a multiplicity of perspectives on it. By means of "motor intentionality" we cause the world to exist for us by moving toward or away from something or moving the object itself. But there is not first a perception and then a movement. Rather, "the perception and the movement form a system that is modified as a whole."[30] That is, we are perceiving meaning and acting on it simultaneously and a change in circumstances can modify either the action and/or the perceived meaning.

The motor memory of the body recollects other times we have gone forward to receive the sacrament. Some of those walks to the altar were occasions of joy; others were occasions of sorrow. Some were occasions of apprehension and uncertainty about what we would experience, like our first Communion or receiving Communion in another congregation of the body of Christ, or—dare I say it?—receiving the sacrament from the hand of the priest who abused me. All these motor acts remind us of what we are doing and what we are receiving—that in faith we may transcend the worst of our experiences and receive the body of Christ as the bread of companionship rather than the bread of affliction. But motor actions also release the body's stored memories.

We need to know our bodies and come to terms with whatever body issues we may have. This is not easy because we live our lives in the

---

30. Maurice Merleau-Ponty, *Phenomenology of Perception*, trans. Donald A. Landes (London and New York: Routledge, 2012), 113.

modern world divested of our bodies. It's not that we don't *think* about our bodies. We think about them all the time. We think about our aches and pains, or how much weight we are gaining or losing, or what we shall eat or what we shall wear. But when we are *thinking* about our bodies we are still in our heads. We are not necessarily paying attention to what our bodies know and what they remember.

As Carl Gustav Jung has suggested, there are shadows buried in our bodies that need to be encountered.[31] The Buddhist teacher of meditation Reginald Ray, in promoting somatic bodywork, has suggested, first, that there are shadow elements in our bodies that lie in deep darkness and are not ready to be received by our conscious mind; but second, there are those shadowy aspects that are beginning to approach consciousness. "In contrast to the deep darkness, what lies in the shadows always has a quality of directionality toward consciousness—it wants to be known now and integrated with conscious awareness."[32] Ray thinks that these are parts of what he calls our "Buddha nature"—"a profound and irresistible longing" at our very root and core.[33] I suggest that if there are some aspects of us that need to see the light of day in our consciousness, it is so these aspects can be confessed, forgiven, reconciled, justified, or sanctified, as the case may be. But I agree with Ray that they can be brought to light through the bodywork of somatic meditation.

A simple body scan can help us to reconnect with our bodies. This consists of lying on the floor or sitting or standing with eyes closed to shut out outside sensations and mentally reviewing your body slowly from head to toe, missing no part.[34] *Notice whatever sensations arise in each part of the body but move on without judging them. "Whatever needs to come through to our conscious self is able to flow freely in an immediate and abundant way."*[35]

We do the Eucharist to remember Christ; but the stimulation of the senses and the engagement of motor actions also produce our own memories. Some released memories are comforting; others may be scary or even dangerous. In what ways can the sufferings of Christ be related to our own sufferings in body, mind, or spirit in the reception of the sacramental elements?

Some churches have instituted the practice of having lay or ordained

---

31. Jolande Jacobi, *The Psychology of C. G. Jung* (New Haven: Yale University Press, 1973), 109.
32. Reginald A. Ray, *Touching Enlightenment: Finding Realization in the Body* (Boulder, CO: Sounds True, 2008), 266.
33. Ibid., 14.
34. I provided a body scan meditation in *Embodied Liturgy*, 10–12.
35. Ray, *Touching Enlightenment*, 230.

ministers available for prayer, anointing, or the laying on of hands as communicants return to their places after receiving Holy Communion. Providing this ministry of healing in connection with receiving Holy Communion is not just a matter of finding a way to do both in a way that will not prolong the service. Pastoral experience certifies that issues of the past, often buried in the body's memory, come to the surface in the act of receiving Holy Communion. Pastoral wisdom suggests that we should be prepared to help people deal with them then and there. Pastoral testimony reports that people have found great comfort in the laying on of hands in blessing.[36] It is affirming and consoling to experience this loving human touch accompanying a prayer for healing. The relationship between the laying on of hands and anointing and receiving Holy Communion is embedded in the tradition of the postbaptismal laying on of hands and anointing that became the sacrament of confirmation in the Western churches or chrismation in the Eastern Orthodox churches. Since reception of Holy Communion is itself an affirmation of baptism, it is appropriate that the laying on of hands and anointing for the healing—the work of the Holy Spirit—also occur in relation to receiving Holy Communion in the assembly as well as on the sick bed in time of need.

Figure 4b. "This is my Body." The author showing the host during the Words of Institution at a Eucharist in Ordinary Time in his former congregation, Immanuel Lutheran Church in Evanston, IL. The assisting minister is congregation member Margaret Wold. The photo was taken by congregation member Joe Simchak.

36. See Heidi Haverkamp, "Take and Eat? When Church Members Prefer Just a Blessing," *Christian Century* 133, no. 16 (2016): 20–22.

5

Epiclesis: Spirit and Community

As I have related, the experience of my first Holy Communion was the most profound religious experience of my early life. My understanding of the Eucharist grew exponentially during my high school and college years as I ventured beyond my home congregation and experienced the sacrament in other Lutheran congregations and in other faith communities. I encountered different ways of performing the same Common Service in different Lutheran congregations. I experienced the Roman Catholic Mass at a time when some vernacular elements were creeping in (1962) and altars were being pulled away from the so-called east wall (*ad orientem*) and the celebrant faced the people across the table (*versus populum*). The Atonement Lutheran congregation in Oneonta, New York, erected a new building in 1963 and had a freestanding altar with a Communion rail encircling it. On several occasions I visited the Holy Trinity Russian Orthodox Monastery in Jordanville, New York, with my German professor at Hartwick, Dr. Boris Svrakov and his family (he was a Bulgarian), where even young children received Communion. I experienced a campus ministry house church Eucharist. In these various ways I was becoming impressed by the communal character of Holy Communion.

We often go into ourselves in Holy Communion. For Protestants, and certainly also for many Catholics, Holy Communion focuses on the sacrifice of Christ and what that means for us. Martin Luther emphasized in his catechisms that the way to be prepared to worthily receive the body and blood of Christ is to believe the words of Christ, "given and shed for you for the remission of sins."

In Lutheran practice, the decision to receive the sacrament was an individual matter. In traditional Lutheran practice one reported to the pastor in the sacristy on Saturday that one intended to receive the sacrament on Sunday and was often catechized ("Can you recite the Words of Institution?") and examined in terms of one's life and conduct (sometimes a review of one's life in the light of the Ten Commandments). Sometimes an individual confession was then made. Communion seemed like an individual act in which a personal relationship is experienced with Jesus as his body comes into our bodies. We have not usually considered that if I am being united with Jesus Christ by receiving into my body his body and blood, I am also being united with all the other communicants at the table who are also receiving the same sacrament, and that through this means we are forming the church as the body of Christ at the altar and, upon dismissal, in the world.

For many Christians, especially Protestants, the Lord's Supper (*kyriakos deipnon*, 1 Cor 11:20) looks back to the Last Supper of Jesus with his disciples on the night before his death. Because the Lord's Supper focuses on the suffering and death of Jesus as an act of atonement for our sins, the observance often takes on a solemn tone. Faith communities often regard it as a time to focus on confession of sins and personal identification with the sufferings of Jesus in the choice of hymns (e.g., "Just as I am, without one plea"). In my home congregation we used the order for corporate confession on Communion Sundays (in the *Service Book and Hymnal*), which employed the personal pronoun "I" instead of the communal "we" in the prayer of confession. This was followed by a declarative absolution ("I forgive you all your sins") and the "binding word" to the unrepentant ("On the other hand and by the same authority, I declare unto the impenitent and unbelieving . . .").[1]

Liturgical material in the orders of service of many Reformation churches (both Lutheran and Reformed) includes exhortations to the communicants and the Words of Institution alone as a form of consecration (Luther's *Deutsche Messe*) or the institution narrative as a warrant for doing the dominical ordinance followed by exhortation to the communicants (Calvin's *Form and Manner of Prayer*).

Lutheran orders have historically tended to also include a note of

---

1. *Service Book and Hymnal of the Lutheran Church in America* (Minneapolis: Augsburg, 1958), 252.

thanksgiving (*eucharistesas*) by retaining the Preface and Sanctus. This use was assured in American Lutheranism in the Common Service of 1888 and the subsequent inclusion and adaptation of the Common Service in various synodical worship books. This suggests that there is something to celebrate as well as to repent of at the celebration of Holy Communion. Luther's eucharistic hymn *Gott sei gelobet* ("O Lord we praise you, bless you, and adore you"), based on Thomas Aquinas's Corpus Christi sequence *Lauda Sion*, balances the solemn tone with a note of celebration during the administration of the elements. To this consideration should be added the factor that, as neuroscientist and former studio musician Daniel Levitin says, "Singing together releases oxytocin, a neurochemical now known to be involved in establishing bonds of trust between people."[2] If we want to promote the communal character of Holy Communion, it helps to have singing during Communion—by the participants!

Communion implies community. The celebration of the Eucharist has been a corporate act of liturgical worship. It has been an expression of the fellowship (*koinonia*) of the church as the whole congregation participates together in receiving the bread and wine. Private Masses with just a celebrant and a server were regarded as an aberration by the Reformers. I believe I felt that corporate aspect of Holy Communion as I began communing with those in my confirmation class, with my parents, and with the rest of the congregation. Our practice in my home congregation was to come forward to the Communion rail "one table" at a time, which meant as many as could fit at the Communion rail. Each "table" was dismissed with a blessing. Theoretically there should have been an even stronger sense of the corporate character of Holy Communion when the practice changed in most congregations during the 1960s and 1970s and the whole congregation processed forward to the altar, standing at or about it, and then returned to their places to make a place for the next communicant after receiving both elements—all the while supposedly singing the Communion hymns—with the whole congregation receiving the Communion blessing at the end of the administration. But there had also been a sense of small group intimacy when we communed "table by table."

The communion or fellowship dimension of the Eucharist relates to the human condition for which God created us. "It is not good that the

---

2. Daniel J. Levitin, *The World in Six Songs: How the Musical Brain Created Human Nature* (New York: Dutton, 2008), 50–51.

man should be alone; I will make him a helper as his partner," said the Lord God (Gen 2:18). "No man is an island entire to himself," wrote the seventeenth-century English priest and poet John Donne. We are created for and we desire community.

The Interpersonal Body

We may think of our bodies as self-contained units, separated from the rest of the world by our skin. But it's not true, not even biologically. We were all conceived in and born from our mother's womb. The biological elements of our biological parents are a part of our biological makeup. We share that same biological makeup with our siblings—and beyond our immediate nuclear family with grandparents and aunts and uncles and cousins going back generations. It shows up in family resemblances.

We may get married and practice coitus in which "the two become one flesh." In his theology of the body the late Pope John Paul II spoke of "the spousal meaning of the body."[3] Since Genesis teaches that it is not good for man to be alone, we are rescued from our solitude by a complementary existence as man and woman. Pope John Paul II calls the capacity of the male body and the female body to serve mutual self-giving the spousal or nuptial meaning of the body. The God who, in trinitarian theology, is a community of persons creates human beings for community: the union of man and woman produces an offspring (or several), who then also have a biological relationship as children and siblings.

At a deeper level, of course, we are all biologically related as the human species. But more than that, the deeper we go into our own bodies the more we are able to relate to others in their bodies by way of a somatic empathy. Often when we have a serious illness or physical disability, others with the same illness or disability share their situation and a community develops among those going through similar treatment. I can testify that when I was going through chemotherapy and thereafter I felt a bond with others who were going through cancer treatment. I was eager to find out what treatment was prescribed, how it was going, and to share my own experiences by way of support and encouragement, just as I was happy to receive support and encouragement from other cancer patients when I was going through

---

3. John Paul II, *Man and Woman He Created Them: A Theology of the Body*, trans. Michael Waldstein (Boston: Pauline Books & Media, 2006), 178–91.

treatment. As long as someone's illness is a concept, we have little real feeling for their situation. But if we have experienced their illness in our body, we immediately have an empathetic reaction to their story. It is true, as Reginald Ray writes, that "the more we descend into our body, the more we uncover a very vast and expanding interpersonal world of connections with other people."[4]

What creates the deep sense of identity that Christians feel with fellow believers? I think it has to do with a shared embodiment. When we are just dealing with concepts, with ideology, relationships remain abstract. We have little feeling for the lives of other people. But, as I said about empathy for those who experience the same illness we have experienced, the more we can feel in our own bodies the pain and suffering others are experiencing, the more empathy we have with their situation. If we ourselves have experienced in our own bodies the joys and the sorrows of life, we can identify with others who are experiencing similar joys and sorrows. We can "rejoice with those who rejoice, weep with those who weep" (Rom 12:15). It is possible to feel an empathetic bond with fellow suffering human beings.

This sense of connectedness by interpersonal bodies is not something to be taken for granted. The "original sin" not only broke human communion with God; it also broke relationships between people. Having disobeyed the divine word by eating the forbidden fruit, Adam and Eve hid from God because they were naked. This was not something they had ever noticed before! "Who told you that you are naked?" asked the Lord God. "Have you eaten from the tree of which I commanded you not to eat?" (Gen 3:11). Like children caught in some forbidden activity, they began to blame one another instead of taking responsibility for their own actions. With utter realism, the first chapters of Genesis show humankind going from bad to worse with Cain's murder of Abel out of jealousy. This is the story of humankind taken captive by sin. Making a feeble attempt to band together on a common project, humans build a colossal tower reaching to the heavens but end up being scattered by their different languages.

In God's effort to overcome sin and bring together a people to be his own people, the Lord God liberated Israel from bondage in Egypt so that they might serve him rather than Pharaoh. The Lord gave Israel a sacrificial system by which atonement for sin could be accomplished, and he engraved his laws on stone tablets so that the people would

---

4. Reginald A. Ray, *Touching Enlightenment: Finding Realization in the Body* (Boulder, CO: Sounds True, 2008), 279.

know God's will. A model for forgiveness and reconciliation was established in the sacrificial system of the Old Testament. In the fullness of time, God sent his own Son to atone for the sins of the world, and then sent their Spirit to write God's law on the hearts of his people so that they may be in union with God and with one another. Corporately and individually our bodies are God's temple, and God's Spirit dwells in us (1 Cor 3:16; 6:19). But we share "one and the same Spirit" (1 Cor 12:11).

St. Paul goes on to speak about how "in the one Spirit we were all baptized into one body—Jews or Greeks, slaves or free—and we were all made to drink of one Spirit" (1 Cor 12:13), drinking here undoubtedly referring to the Lord's Supper, which the apostle just discussed in chapter 11. In Holy Baptism people are given God's Spirit to form them into a new humanity. What is initiated in Holy Baptism by water and the Spirit is brought to full expression in Holy Communion. The church is formed into the body of Christ in the world by sharing together (koinonia) the body of Christ in the sacramental meal.

As St. Paul shows in 1 Corinthians 10:16–17, there is a relationship between the sacramental body of Christ and the ecclesial body of Christ. The many become one body in the sharing of the one loaf and in drinking from the one cup. Commenting on this text St. Augustine of Hippo said in *Sermon* 227 to the newly baptized who had been baptized at the Easter Vigil the night before,

> You ought to know what you have received, what you are about to receive, what you ought to receive every day. That bread which you can see on the altar, sanctified by the word of God, is the body of Christ. That cup, or rather what that cup contains, sanctified by the word of God, is the blood of Christ. It was by means of these things that the Lord Jesus wished to present us with his body and blood, which he shed for our sake for the forgiveness of sins. *If you receive them well, you are yourselves what you receive.* You see, the apostle says, "We who are many are one body, for we all partake of the same bread" (1 Cor. 10:17). That's how he explained the sacrament of the Lord's table; one loaf, one body, is what we all are, though many we be.[5]

Not only are all the baptized joined into one body in the Eucharist, but John Chrysostom observed that in this meal "every distinction, every difference in status is here swept away." The rich in their finery and beggars in their rags "are placed on the same footing." Moreover, in

---

5. Augustine, *Sermon* 227 (*Sermons 184–229Z*, ed. John E. Rotelle, OSA, trans. Edmund Hill, OP, Works of St. Augustine III/6 [New York: New City Press, 1993], 254).

Constantinople "the emperor—wearing the diadem and clad in purple garments, in charge of the government of the world—as well as the poor, sitting and begging for alms, partake of one table."[6] The Eucharist is a banquet to which all the baptized are invited, and baptism is a leveling sacrament. There is no difference between Jews and Greeks, slaves and free, men and women, children and adults, rich and poor (see Gal 3:28).

The Role of the Holy Spirit

Such a community formed in Communion doesn't happen without divine synergy. The purpose of the epiclesis in the Eucharist is to invoke the power of God to make communion and community happen. The exercise of that power of God is the work of the Holy Spirit.

The great authority on the relationship of the Holy Spirit to the Eucharist was the late Roman Catholic liturgist John H. McKenna, beginning with his magisterial study of the epiclesis in the eucharistic prayers.[7] In his later work that sums up his life's work, he asserts that "the data of the early liturgical texts form a necessary basis of interpretation for scholars in search of a theology of the epiclesis."[8] McKenna moves from "a brief sketch of possible forerunners of the developed epiclesis" to an examination of the "more developed epiclesis as found in the early anaphoras."[9] Among the "possible forerunners," McKenna includes several New Testament texts—Hebrews 9:14; Jesus's farewell discourse in John 15–17; Luke 1:35; John 6:63; and 1 Corinthians 16:22—along with Jewish *berakhot* formulas.[10] He notes that the some scholars would see in the expression "Maranatha," quoted at the conclusion of 1 Corinthians, "a '*Christus-epiklese*' and an ancestor of the developed epiclesis."[11]

---

6. Cited in J.-M.-R. Tillard, *Flesh of the Church, Flesh of Christ: At the Source of the Ecclesiology of Communion*, trans. Madeleine Beaumont (Collegeville, MN: Liturgical, 2001), 68.
7. John H. McKenna, *Eucharist and Holy Spirit: The Eucharistic Epiclesis in Twentieth Century Theology*, Alcuin Club Collections 57 (Great Wakering, UK: Mayhew-McCrimmon, 1975). Anne McGowan, *Eucharistic Epicleses, Ancient and Modern: Speaking of the Spirit in Eucharistic Prayer* (Collegeville, MN: Liturgical, 2014) extends the survey of epicletic prayers and theology into the twenty-first century.
8. John H. McKenna, *The Eucharistic Epiclesis: A Detailed History from the Patristic to the Modern Era*, 2nd ed. (Chicago: Hillenbrand, 2009), 3.
9. Ibid., 2–3.
10. Ibid., 4.
11. McKenna mentions four such authors—Rudolf Stählin, "Der Herr ist Geist," and Karl Bernhard Ritter, "Bemerkungen zur eucharistischen Epiklese," both of which are in *Kosmos und Ekklesia (Festschrift für W. Stählin)*, ed. Heinz Dietrich Wendland (Kassel: J. Stauda-Verlag, 1953), 40–54, 163–73; Kurt Goldammer, "Die Eucharistische Epiklese in der Mittelalterlichen Abendländischen Frömmigkeit" (Phd diss., Marburg, 1941); and Johannes Betz, *Die Eucharistie in der Zeit der Griechis-*

As for the Jewish *berakhot*, McKenna traces "the broad lines of the *berakah*" and notices "how the *berakah-anamnesis* often unfolds into supplication or prayer."[12] He notes among the meal *berakhot* (*birkat ha-mazon*) the supplication (*berakah rahem*) together with its embolism (the *ya'aleth we-yabho*) that formed the basic model for the Christian eucharistic epiclesis.

> Have mercy, YHWH, our God, on your people Israel, on your city Jerusalem, on Zion, the dwelling place of your glory, on the kingdom of the house of David your servant, and on the great and holy house upon which your name is invoked. Feed us, nourish us, sustain us, provide for us, relieve us speedily from our anxieties, and let us not stand in need of the gifts of mortals, for their gifts are small and their reproach is great, for we have trusted in your holy, great and fearful name. And may Elijah and the Messiah, the son of David, come in our life-time, and restore the kingdom of the house of David to its place, and reign over us, you alone, and save us for your name's sake. And bring us up in it and gladden us in it and comfort us in Zion your city.[13]

On special feast days a "proper" petition is added asking YHWH our God to "visit us on this day for blessing and save us on this day unto life. And by a word of salvation and mercy, spare, favor us and show us mercy, for our eyes look to you, for you are a gracious and merciful God and King."[14] The divine visitation occasions the plea for mercy that will become the Kyrie Eleison response to petitions in the Christian litany prayers.

Likewise, McKenna suggests that another *berakah* text, the *berakah Avodah* from the so-called eighteen blessings (the *Shemoneh Esreh*) plays a role in the formation of epiclesis. One version of this prayer contains a distinctly sacrificial—and therefore, with respect to the early epiclesis, a transformative—element when it asks YHWH our God to "readily accept in love and favor the fiery offerings of Israel and their prayer."[15] Eventually, McKenna explains, "the Christians coupled the contents of this prayer, with its sacrificial theme, to the supplication stemming from the paschal meal *berakoth*." He continues, "With the adoption of

---

chen Väter, vol. 1/1, *Die Aktualpräsenz der Person und des Helswerkes Jesu im Abdenmahl nach der Vorephesinischen Griechischen Patristik* (Freiburg: Herder, 1955).

12. McKenna, *Eucharistic Epiclesis*, 4.
13. Ibid., 5. The English translation is adapted from David Hedegaard, *Seder Rav Aram Gaon* (Lund: Gleerup 1951), 1:151–52.
14. McKenna, *Eucharistic Epiclesis*, 5.
15. Ibid., 6.

this sacrificial element the primitive significance of the epiclesis thus underwent a transformation."[16]

McKenna regarded Louis Ligier[17] "among the particular proponents of this hypothesis," although for Ligier the church never lost sight of the basic signification of the epiclesis as "the restoration and gathering together of the people of God around the *Shekinah*, or the divine presence."[18]

With respect to God's presence with his people, McKenna finds "noteworthy" the effort of W. O. E. Oesterley "to link the Jewish concept of the divine *Shekinah* . . . with the epiclesis." According to Oesterley, McKenna asserts, "The conception of the *Shekinah*, familiar as it was to all Jews, would have been the obvious one to suggest a prayer for the sanctification of the worshippers, gathered together in the name of God, by means of the descent of the Divine Spirit upon them." Thus he concludes, "It may be reasonably maintained that from the beginning what was later known as the *Epiclesis* was in its essence a prayer for the Divine Presence among the worshippers during their most solemn act of worship."[19]

This prayer for the divine presence may be seen in the meal prayers of the *Didache* in which the petition for "your holy Name enshrined in our hearts" functions as a kind of epiclesis. But the East Syrian Anaphora of Addai and Mari invokes the Holy Spirit to rest on the offering, "and bless and sanctify it, that it may be to us, Lord, for the remission of debts, forgiveness of sins, and the great hope of resurrection from the dead, and new life in the kingdom of heaven, with all who have been pleasing in your sight."[20]

The anaphora in the *Apostolic Tradition* also invokes the Holy Spirit "upon the offering of your holy Church; that, gathering her into one, you would grant to all who receive the holy things (to receive) for the fullness of the Holy Spirit for the strengthening of faith in truth."[21] The Spirit works through the oblation (bread and wine) to gather the church and strengthen faith. McKenna advises that "this explicit mention of the Holy Spirit does not, however, entirely exclude the possibility that for Hippolytus [sic] the terms 'Holy Spirit' referred to the

16. Ibid.
17. Louis Ligier, "De la Cène de Jesus l'Anaphore de l'Eglise," *La Maison Dieu* 87 (1966): 7–51.
18. McKenna, *Eucharistic Epiclesis*, 6.
19. Ibid., 6. McKenna is quoting from W. O. E. Oesterley, *The Jewish Background of the Liturgy* (Oxford: Clarendon, 1925).
20. R. C. D. Jasper and G. J. Cuming, *Prayers of the Eucharist: Early and Reformed*, 3rd ed. (Collegeville, MN: Liturgical, 1992), 43.
21. Ibid., 35.

Logos, the Second Person of the Trinity."[22] No effects of the sending of the Spirit on the oblation are specified. The petition only asks that those partaking be gathered together into one and that they be filled with the Holy Spirit for the confirmation of their faith in truth so that they might in turn praise and glorify God.[23]

The Anaphora of Sarapion of Thmuis clearly invokes the Logos or Word instead of the Holy Spirit on the bread and cup, which are the likenesses of Christ's body and blood, that have been offered in thanksgiving, that "the bread may become the body of the Word" and the cup "may become the blood of the Truth; and make all who partake to receive a medicine of life for the healing of every disease, and for the empowerment of all advancement and virtue; not for condemnation, O God of truth, nor for censure or reproach."[24] Between the words over the bread and over the cup Sarapion places a citation of the *Didache* prayer, that "as this bread was scattered over the mountains, and was gathered together and became one, so gather your holy Church out of every nation and every country and every city and village and house, and make one living catholic Church."[25]

The Egyptian Anaphora of St. Basil invokes the Holy Spirit "upon us and upon these gifts that have been set before you, and may sanctify them and make them holy of holies. Make us all worthy to partake of your holy things for sanctification of soul and body, that we may become one body and one spirit, and may have a portion with all the saints who have been pleasing to you from eternity."[26]

The Moment-of-Consecration Debate

The epiclesis in the Egyptian Anaphora of St. Basil serves to consecrate the elements. Indeed, the West Syrian/Byzantine anaphoras acquire a consecratory character. The major focus of McKenna's work is to show how the debate over the "moment of consecration" came to consume discussion of the role of the epiclesis and the Holy Spirit in the eucharistic prayer.[27]

The Anaphora of St. John Chrysostom has: "Make this bread the precious body of your Christ [changing it by your Holy Spirit—added later],

22. McKenna, *Eucharistic Epiclesis*, 7.
23. Ibid.
24. Jasper and Cuming, *Prayers of the Eucharist*, 77–78.
25. Ibid., 77.
26. Ibid., 71.
27. McKenna, *Eucharistic Epiclesis*, 42–94, and much of part 2 of his book.

Amen; and that which is in this cup the precious blood of your Christ, changing it by your Holy Spirit, Amen; so that they may become to those who partake for vigilance of soul, for fellowship with the Holy Spirit, for the fullness of the kingdom of heaven, for boldness toward you, not for judgment or condemnation."[28]

The Roman canon lacked an epiclesis of the Spirit. The Western scholastic theologians regarded the words of institution as consecratory. Then in the growing rift between the Roman and the Byzantine churches the Byzantine theologians pointed to the epiclesis as the moment of consecration. Succumbing to this scholastic concern to pinpoint a "moment of consecration" was a mistake for the Eastern church, in the view of Alexander Schmemann. In the Eastern view, based on that of the church fathers, Schmemann maintained that the entire liturgy from beginning to end is a praise of the Father, a remembrance of the Son, and an epiclesis of the Holy Spirit. The eucharistic prayer focuses this pervading reality in its various sections. Schmemann suggests that "the purpose of the Eucharist lies not in the change of the bread and wine, but in our partaking of Christ, who has become our food, our life, the manifestation of the church as the body of Christ."[29]

This scholastic controversy over the moment of consecration should also not obscure what my teacher Fr. Aidan Kavanagh taught about the purpose of the epiclesis, that it is basically a prayer for unity with God the Father and with one's fellow communicants through the sacrament of the body and blood of Christ: "a prayer for the community's assimilation or integration with God above all things and the members one with another through this action of thanksgiving in Christ. . . . What is ultimately being prayed for is oneness with the Father—that oneness he has made available in Jesus and extends to all men through Jesus' body, the Church."[30]

Commemorations and Intercessions in the Eucharistic Prayer

This unity in the eucharistic fellowship is expressed in the Syro-Byzantine anaphoras by the commemorations of the saints and intercessions for the living that follow the epiclesis. In St. John Chrysostom "this reasonable service" is offered "for those who rest in the faith"

---

28. Jasper and Cuming, *Prayers of the Eucharist*, 133.
29. Alexander Schmemann, *The Eucharist*, trans. Paul Kachur (Crestwood, NY: St. Vladimir's Seminary Press, 1987), 226.
30. Aidan Kavanagh, "Thoughts on the Roman Anaphora," *Worship* 40 (1966): 7–8.

in all their categories from the Old and New Testaments, "especially our all-holy, immaculate, highly glorious, Blessed Lady, Mother of God and ever-virgin Mary" and "all those who have fallen asleep in hope of resurrection to eternal life" (here the diptychs of the faithful departed are read); and the Lord is asked to remember all the Orthodox bishops, presbyters, and deacons, the whole church throughout the world, the rulers, cities, and all who dwell in them (here the diptychs of the living are read), travelers, those who do good works, and the poor.[31] We share this eucharistic meal with the whole church in heaven and on earth.

The Syro-Byzantine anaphoras list general categories of saints, but the Roman canon lists names. "In union with the whole church" the Roman Church honors Mary the ever-virgin mother of Jesus Christ, the apostles and martyrs Peter and Paul, Andrew, James, John, Thomas, James, Philip, Bartholomew, Matthew, Simon and Jude, and the particular martyrs venerated in the Roman Church—Linus, Cletus, Clement, Sixtus, Cornelius, Cyprian, Lawrence, Chrysogonus, John and Paul, Cosmas and Damian, as well as all the saints. It asks a share in the fellowship of the apostles and martyrs, naming John the Baptist, Stephen, Matthias, Barnabas, Ignatius, Alexander, Marcellinus, Peter, Felicity, Perpetua, Agatha, Lucy, Agnes, Cecilia, Anastasia.

In the Syro-Byzantine anaphoras the commemorations and intercessions are linked to the epiclesis of the Holy Spirit. In spite of the interest in the structure of the West Syrian anaphoras in twentieth-century liturgical renewal, Protestants have been reluctant to include intercessions and commemorations within their eucharistic prayers. Perhaps commemorations and intercessions had been so bound up with the cult of the saints and the practice of votive Masses (Masses offered for special intentions for which mass stipends were paid) that the Protestant Reformers rejected commemorations and intercessions in connection with Holy Communion out of hand. There had been a proposal of a common eucharistic prayer based on the Egyptian Anaphora of St. Basil, which was also the basis of Roman Eucharistic Prayer IV, but the Inter-Lutheran Commission on Worship rejected including it in the *Lutheran Book of Worship* (*LBW*)—largely, I suspect, because of its length but also because of the inclusion of the intercessions.[32] The closest

---

31. Ibid., 133–34.
32. This text is Eucharistic Prayer C in Holy Eucharist II in *The Book of Common Prayer . . . according to the Use of The Episcopal Church* (New York: Seabury, 1977), 373–75, and Great Thanksgiving F in the Presbyterian *Book of Common Worship* (Louisville, KY: Westminster John Knox, 1993), 146–49.

the *LBW* came to commemoration and intercession in the eucharistic prayer is this petition:

Join our prayers
with those of your servants
of every time and place,
and unite them
with the ceaseless petitions
of our great high priest
until he comes
as victorious Lord of all.[33]

The Corporate Body

Already in the *Didache* we saw this prayer for the unity of the community here and now in the present celebration of this meal and even more fully in the future kingdom of God. This desire to see the unity of the church in the Eucharist would explain how even the *Supra quae* and *Supplices te* in the Roman canon could be regarded as an "epicletic unit," forming a petition for the divine acceptance of the church's offering to bring about a deeper union between the assembled church and God and among the assembled themselves. This view would explain why it seemed so logical in the new Roman Eucharistic Prayers in the missal of Pope Paul VI to invoke the Holy Spirit as the bond of unity and the source of *koinonia*, first on the bread and cup before the words of institution and then on the faithful after the institution text and anamnesis, and then to follow this invocation with commemorations of the saints and intercessions for the living. The commemorations and intercessions take their place in the eucharistic prayer as an expansion of the epiclesis, with its petition for unity with Christ and with one another, along with the forgiveness of sins that makes such unity possible, as gifts of Communion.[34]

The sharing of the Eucharist manifests the church, and the epiclesis with its commemorations and intercessions calls attention to its concrete reality. As Greek Orthodox theologian John D. Zizioulas writes, "In the Eucharistic assembly . . . the Word of God does not dwell in the human mind as rational knowledge or in the human soul as a mysti-

33. *Lutheran Book of Worship*, pew ed. (Minneapolis: Augsburg Publishing House, 1979), 70–71.
34. See Frank C. Senn, "Intercessions and Commemorations in the Anaphora," in *New Eucharistic Prayers: An Ecumenical Study of Their Development and Structure*, ed. Frank C. Senn (Mahwah, NJ: Paulist, 1987): 195–209.

cal inner experience, but as communion within a community."[35] The Eucharist establishes the embodied connectedness that occurs when the Holy Spirit is invoked in the epiclesis to convey to the communicants the gifts of forgiveness of sins and communion as community and forms them corporately into the body of Christ in the world when they eat the body of Christ and drink his blood.

In 1 Corinthians 12 and Romans 12 St. Paul describes the church as the "body of Christ." He is clearly speaking metaphorically since he discusses various members being parts of the body, like hands or feet, with Christ as the head. Yet if the church is constituted as the body of Christ in the Eucharist, this must be more than a metaphor. We are gathered together in the liturgical assembly as actual bodies actually eating the same bread and drinking the same cup, with these same elements going into our separate bodies and connecting us by what we eat and drink. We enter into union with the crucified and risen Christ by physically eating bread and drinking wine as Christ's body and blood. If we are what we eat, as the materialist philosopher Ludwig Feuerbach said, and as biochemistry proves, then we actually become Christ according to his human nature. As J.-M.-R. Tillard demonstrates from the writings of the church fathers, in Communion the "flesh of the church" becomes the "flesh of Christ" in the world. "To describe 'the flesh of the church' as a network of relationships between brothers and sisters in which the individuals renounce their self-centeredness in the sacrifice of *agape* which makes them, as Christians, inseparable from others, is to refuse to see the church as the sum or the juxtaposition of 'justified' individuals."[36] Certainly within this Communion there is "a wide space" for the personal encounter with Christ. But from the standpoint of the ecclesiology of communion the church becomes actually, and not only figuratively or metaphorically, the physical body of Christ in the world.

The Spirit-Filled Body

The body of Christ in the world is activated by the Holy Spirit. In 1 Corinthians 3:16 and 6:19 Paul speaks of the body as God's temple, the temple of the Holy Spirit. Again, this is a metaphor. Our bodies are not temples made of wood and stone. Yet the Holy Spirit takes up residence

---

35. John D. Zizioulas, *Being as Communion* (Crestwood, NY: St. Vladimir's Seminary Press, 2004), 115.
36. J.-M.-R. Tillard, *Flesh of the Church, Flesh of Christ: At the Source of the Ecclesiology of Communion*, trans. Madeleine Beaumont (Collegeville, MN: Liturgical, 2001), 135.

in our bodies, and this cannot be understood metaphorically. Whatever is the residence of divinity is the temple of that divinity. And Paul is quite clear that the Spirit dwells within us. "Therefore glorify God in your body" (1 Cor 6:20).

This understanding that the Holy Spirit is resident in our bodies is made clearer when we consider that the Spirit is the *rûah*, the *pneuma*, the *spiritus*, the breath or wind or energy of God. We owe our existence to the wind or breath of God, as do all living creatures. A focus on the breath can remind us of being joined together with all who live and move and have their being in God, as St. Paul cited from a pagan poet on the Areopagus in Athens (acts 17:28). We can be conscious of this connection with all living beings on every inhale and exhale.

Yoga philosophy has a sophisticated understanding of the breath (*prana*) and wind (*vayu*) as energy that enters the body in inhalation (*prana vayu*), flows upward (*Udana vayu*), circulates through the body as we breathe (*Vyana vayu*), balances the body (*Samana vayu*), and is expelled from the body in exhalation (*Apana vayu*).

Here is a simple way to experience the movement of breath or wind into, throughout, and out of our bodies. Either standing or sitting press your palms together in prayer position in front of your heart, inhale as you extend your arms outward and continue to inhale as you bring your arms upward over your head, exhale as you bring your hands back to prayer position, and continue to exhale as you fold your torso over your legs. This requires parceling both the intake and outflow of breath so as not to interrupt the flow of vayu in or out.

This subtle flow of energy through the body prompts me to wonder: Can we not also understand the Holy Spirit as the life-giver who enlivens our bodies and makes them fit for the service of God? Could we conceive of a subtle movement of the Holy Spirit in our physical bodies the way yoga thinks of the *nadis* and Chinese medicine thinks of the meridians as subtle bodies within our physical bodies?

In any case, St. Paul brought the incarnational and the spiritual together in his concept of the "spiritual body" (*sōma pneumatikos*). This is the kind of body we expect in the resurrection. Our bodies will be spiritual and glorified, but still be bodies capable of communication with other bodies, like the risen body of Christ.

It is not surprising that St. Paul's great chapter on the resurrection of the body closes out his First Letter to the Corinthians. The problem with the knowledgeable members of the Corinthian congregation is that they were too spiritual, perhaps even gnostic. They did not discern the body, and so they allowed class distinctions to fracture the church in their observance of the Lord's Supper.

The idea that God can be approached through mystical experience or esoteric knowledge does violence to Christ's real presence in the body and in body-to-body relationships within the social order of the church. The work of the Spirit in, with, and through the sacraments is not just spiritual; it is incarnational. The Spirit gives us faith to discern all the bodies—the body of Christ in the sacrament, the body of Christ in the individual bodies that receive the sacramental body, and the social body of the church that is formed by sharing together in the sacramental body.

The Spirit is the energy that causes the social and individual bodies of Christ to go from the eucharistic assembly, fueled by the sacramental body and blood of Christ, to erect signs of the kingdom of God by caring for bodies in need of food, clothing, shelter, healing, and loving care. Quantitatively, ministry to bodies in all their needs has been the primary mission of the church throughout history in terms of social ministries, medical missions, and health and wellness concerns. The Eucharist has been the source of this mission. It is noteworthy that the earliest Lutheran church orders simultaneously reformed the Mass and made provision for the care of the poor and needy through a common chest. Monies once devoted to paying for votive Masses "to help the dead in their movement toward union with God 'in heaven' were now redirected to a common chest 'on earth' where daily bread could be distributed to the hungry poor."[37] In the post-Communion prayer of his *German Mass* Luther's prayer prayed that "this thy salutary gift" may "strengthen us through the same in faith toward thee, and in fervent love among us all."[38]

The Extension of the Sacramental Body and the Social Body

The eucharistic body and blood are also taken to the hospitalized and ill to connect the bodies of some isolated communicants with the social body of Christ in the faith community by administering to them the same sacramental body that was administered in the whole assembly. It is for this reason that the consecrated elements are reserved after the celebration of the Eucharist. This practice goes back at least to the

37. Samuel Torvend, *Luther and the Hungry Poor: Gathered Fragments* (Minneapolis: Fortress, 2008), 108.
38. Martin Luther, "The German Mass and Order of Service," in *Luther's Works*, ed. Ulrich S. Leupold (Philadelphia: Fortress, 1965), 53:84.

report of Justin Martyr in the middle of the second century. After the Great Thanksgiving "the distribution, and reception of the consecrated [elements] by each one, takes place and they are sent to the absent by the deacons."[39]

Space precludes describing orders for the administration of Communion to the sick, for which we have no formularies before the eighth century.[40] The important thing is that the earliest and primary purpose for reserving the consecrated bread and wine after Mass was Communion of the sick and the dying (*viaticum*).[41] The sending of the consecrated elements (*fermentum*) from the pope's Mass to the station churches in Rome in *Ordo Romanus Primus* (ca. 700) also served to extend the eucharistic fellowship, but for a different purpose: the joining of the separate gatherings of the bishop's flock in the bishop's Eucharist.[42]

Places of reservation could include a cupboard in the sacristy, an ambry in the side wall of the apse, a hanging pyx, a sacrament house, or, by the late sixteenth century, a tabernacle on the altar mensa. While these places of public reservation became sites of eucharistic devotion outside of the Mass, their first purpose had been reservation for pastoral care.

At the time of the Reformation the practice of reservation became controverted because of Protestant rejection of the doctrine of transubstantiation. There are three instances where the practice of taking the consecrated elements from the congregation's Mass to the house of the sick was retained: in *The Manual* of Swedish Reformer Olavus Petri (1529); in the Mark Brandenburg Church Order (1540), in a procession that included bell and torches; and in the 1549 Prayer Book of King Edward VI.[43] This practice was abandoned in the 1552 Prayer Book, but provision was made for the celebration of Holy Communion in the house of the sick person with other household and family members present. Lutheran arguments centered on what constituted the "true use" of the sacrament according to the confessional axiom in the Formula of Concord (1577): "Nothing has the character of a sacra-

---

39. Justin Martyr, *First Apology* 67 (*Early Christian Fathers*, trans. and ed. Cyril C. Richardson, Library of Christian Classics 1 [Philadelphia: Westminster, 1953], 287.
40. See Nathan Mitchell, OSB, *Cult and Controversy: The Worship of the Eucharist outside Mass*, Studies in the Reformed Rites of the Catholic Church 4 (New York: Pueblo, 1982), 112.
41. See Archdale King, *Eucharistic Reservation in the Western Church* (New York: Sheed & Ward, 1965), 4–7.
42. See Mitchell, *Cult and Controversy*, 56–59.
43. See Frank C. Senn, "Holy Communion outside the Assembly: Two Models," in *A Stewardship of the Mysteries* (Mahwah, NJ: Paulist, 1999), 194–95.

ment outside of the use instituted by Christ," and the duration of the sacramental union.[44] It was thought that the issue was resolved by having a celebration of the service of Holy Communion (abbreviated according to the circumstances) in the presence of the sick or dying. This remained typical Lutheran and Anglican practice until revisions of worship and prayer books in the 1970s. *The Book of Common Prayer . . . according to the Use of The Episcopal Church* (1977) and *Occasional Services: Lutheran Book of Worship* (1982) provided orders for an extended distribution of Holy Communion from the congregation's Eucharist by the pastor/priest or a deacon/designated lay Communion minister.[45]

These two forms of Communion accomplish different purposes. The celebration of Holy Communion provides for the ministration of the sacrament to the sick or dying communicant and to any who might be attending. The extended distribution of the sacrament also connects the communicant with the social body of Christ, the church, through the reception of the eucharistic elements. I would argue that this is a "true use" of the sacrament in the Lutheran understanding: it is for eating and drinking. The sacramental union endures for the sake of potential uses and therefore does not evaporate when the closing benediction is given. The consecrated elements should be reserved in a suitable place for their availability in pastoral care. Excess bread and wine should consumed by those who have communed or reverently disposed of. Any disposal practices that compromise the doctrine of the real presence would, I assure you, arouse the wrath of Dr. Luther![46]

---

44. Ibid., 193–94. See the doctoral dissertation of Edward F. Peters, "The Origin and Meaning of the Axiom, 'Nothing Has the Character of a Sacrament outside of the Use,' in Sixteenth-Century and Seventeenth-Century Lutheran Theology" (PhD diss., Concordia Seminary, 1968).
45. Senn, "Holy Communion," 198–203.
46. See Edward F. Peters, "Luther and the Principle: Outside of the Use There Is No Sacrament," *Concordia Theological Monthly* 42 (1971): 643–52.

Figure 5. Mid-nineteenth century drawing by the artist Eduard von Steinle, "Priest carries the Holy Sacrament over the mountains," with the face of the pious Bishop Nikolaus von Weis of Speyer. The priest is taking Communion to the sick or Viaticum to the dying. This is an extension of the administration to Holy Communion to those not present in the assembly using the elements from the reserved sacrament.

6

———

Doxology: An Orthodox Worldview

We come to the concluding portion of the anaphora, the Great Thanksgiving, which is the doxology. Jewish prayers typically ended with a blessing or praise of God. It was perhaps this piety that persuaded a Christian scribe to add a concluding doxology to the Lord's Prayer in Matthew 6. One form of doxology is included at the end of the Lord's Prayer in *Didache* 8: "For power and glory are yours."[1] In the style of Jewish table blessings, each prayer in chapters 9 and 10 ends: "To you be glory forever."[2]

The East Syrian Anaphora of Addai and Mari, in its original form, seems to be addressed to God the Father at the outset. It begins, "Worthy of glory from every mouth and thanksgiving from every tongue is the adorable and glorious name." The phrase "of the Father and of the Son and of the Holy Spirit" is probably a later addition. Following the cosmological introduction to the Sanctus the Anaphora goes on to address the "Lord" who "put on our human nature to give us life through your divine nature," who is presumably the Son. But then it addresses the "true God and Father" who "sent our Lord Jesus Christ, your beloved Son." It concludes with an added-on doxology that offers up "praise, honor, thanksgiving and adoration to your living and life-

---

1. Kurt Niederwimmer, *The Didache: A Commentary*, trans. Linda M. Maloney, Hermeneia (Minneapolis: Fortress, 1998), 134.
2. Ibid., 144, 155.

giving name" without specifying that name.[3] A number of scholars have suggested that this prayer probably was originally addressed to Christ without oscillating back and forth with an address to the Father, as we see in the Maronite *Sharar* or Anaphora of St. Peter. It is verbally similar to Addai and Mari, but addresses Christ throughout the entire text from the Sanctus through the concluding doxology.[4] There should be some theological correspondence between the beginning and the ending of a prayer in terms of who is the One addressed, but if a prayer has been subjected to a long and continuous use, emendations take place for various reasons.

The Anaphora in the *Apostolic Tradition* has the advantage of being a model prayer that may not have been actually used in liturgical assemblies before liturgical scholars in the twentieth century became enamored of it. It is addressed to the Father through his Child, "the Word inseparable from you," and concludes: "that we may praise and glorify you through your Child, Jesus Christ, through whom be glory and honor to you, Father and Son with the Holy Spirit, in your holy church, both now and to the ages of ages (Latin text)."[5]

The Roman canon, which begins in its preface with thanksgiving addressed to "Lord, holy Father, almighty eternal God, through Christ our Lord" concludes "through Christ our Lord." "Through him, Lord, you ever create, sanctify, quicken, bless, and bestow all these good things upon us. Through him and with him and in him all honor and glory is yours, O God the Father almighty, in the unity of the Holy Spirit, through all the ages of ages."[6] The Roman prayer retains the ancient Christian emphasis on the mediatorial role of Christ in liturgical prayers even in its expanded Trinitarian form.

The West Syrian Byzantine eucharistic prayers developed in the wake of the Arian controversy on Christology and the doctrine of the Trinity and therefore stated in the response of the people to the invitation to "give thanks to the Lord" that "it is fitting and right (to worship the Father, the Son, and the Holy Spirit, the consubstantial and undivided Trinity)." The Anaphora of St. John Chrysostom concludes, "and grant us with one mouth and one heart to glorify and hymn your

3. R. C. D. Jasper and G. J. Cuming, *Prayers of the Eucharist: Early and Reformed*, 3rd rev. ed. (Collegeville, MN: Liturgical, 1992), 42–44.
4. Maxwell E. Johnson, *Praying and Believing in Early Christianity: The Interplay between Christian Worship and Doctrine* (Collegeville, MN: Liturgical, 2013), 35–37.
5. Paul F. Bradshaw, Maxwell E. Johnson, and L. Edward Phillips, *The Apostolic Tradition: A Commentary*, Hermeneia (Minneapolis: Fortress, 2002), 40.
6. Jasper and Cuming, *Prayers of the Eucharist*, 163, 166.

all-honorable and magnificent name, the Father, the Son, and the Holy Spirit (now and always and to the ages of ages)."[7]

The concluding doxologies, especially after the Councils of Nicaea and Constantinople (326, 381), affirmed Trinitarian orthodoxy. *Orthodoxia* has been defined "right doctrine" (from *orthos*, "correct," and *dokeo*, "teaching"). Maxwell Johnson rather insists on this.[8] But in an understanding that belief and prayer (*lex credendi, lex orandi*) are correlative, orthodoxy (*orthodoxia*) also implies "right praise."[9] The praise is right if it is directed to the right God. The Orthodox East reinforced Nicene-Constantinopolitan orthodoxy by addressing prayers to the Father, Son, and Holy Spirit, mentioning the names of the three persons simultaneously, rather than observing the Roman protocol of addressing prayers *to* the Father, *through* the Son, *in* the Holy Spirit.

The Feminist Critique

The impact of the feminist movement on liturgy in recent years has resulted in revisions of eucharistic prayers and other texts in the liturgy. While admitting that the Trinity is central to Christian faith and worship, feminist theology holds that Trinitarian language should be gender-neutral.[10] Exclusively masculine language for God without corresponding feminine language is perceived as a major problem, a legacy of a patriarchal culture that was proving to be exclusionary to women newly liberated in contemporary Western society. Feminist theology has seen several developments over the last generation, especially toward "emancipatory" God-language,[11] which frees liturgical language to use additional names and images of God that include feminine as well as masculine associations. Gail Ramshaw suggested "Abba, Servant, Paraclete" in place of "Father, Son, and Holy Spirit" as more

---

7. Ibid., 131, 134.
8. Johnson, *Praying and Believing in Early Christianity*, xvi.
9. I learned this from Alexander Schmemann in the course I took at LSTC on Ecumenical Dialogue: East and West, noting that the Russian word for "orthodoxy," *pravoslavie*, means "true glory." Jaroslav Pelikan, *The Melody of Theology: A Philosophical Dictionary* (Cambridge, MA: Harvard University Press, 1988) also says that "The historic meaning of 'orthodoxy' has included both correct doctrine and correct worship; that was the intention behind the formula for the doctrinal authority of worship, *lex orandi lex credendi*" (p. 187).
10. See Ruth C. Duck and Patricia Wilson-Kastner, *Praising God: The Trinity in Christian Worship* (Louisville: Westminster John Knox, 1999), 2.
11. See Marjorie Procter-Smith, *In Her Own Rite: Constructing Feminist Liturgical Tradition* (Nashville: Abingdon, 1990), 85–115.

gender neutral.[12] The names "Father" and "Son," being masculine gender, have been especially problematic for feminist liturgists.

In general, as regards the issue of gender and God, feminist theology rejects the notion of "God" being male gender, and so God is not referred to using male pronouns. So, for example, in place of the Roman "through him, with him, and in him" feminist theology has proposed, and now many prayers end, "through Christ, with Christ, and in Christ." Feminist spirituality also objects to images of God that are perceived as authoritarian, disciplinarian, or warlike and instead emphasizes attributes regarded as "maternal" such as nurturing, accepting, and creative. Monarchical designations of God as "king" and "lord" are also eschewed. This has had consequences for the emendation of many hymn texts[13] and has also influenced eucharistic doxology.

The Trinity in Western Theology

I think we must admit that Western theology was unprepared to respond to the feminist critique, especially its assault on the Trinitarian name. To be sure, we used Trinitarian language in worship and confessions of faith. But a Trinitarian worldview has eluded Western Christianity. This might be attributed to Augustine's influence on Western theology. Robert Jenson has pointed out that Augustine, in his Trinitarian theology, emphasized the oneness of the three persons of the Godhead rather than the threeness of the one, as in the Cappadocian theology, which saw God less as a monarch and more as a community of persons.[14]

We must also recognize that Trinitarian and christological controversies did not rage in the West as they did in the East. Other issues dominated theological controversy in the West, such as sin and grace, understandings of eucharistic presence, and theories of atonement. Yet it can't be said that the Western church experienced no Trinitarian struggles. In the fifth century the Western Roman Empire was overrun by Gothic tribes who had been converted to Christianity by Arian missionaries from Constantinople, who also encouraged them to continue moving west. The Catholic Church in the West struggled for two cen-

---

12. Gail Ramshaw-Schmidt, "Naming the Trinity: Orthodoxy and Inclusivity," *Worship* 60 (1986): 491–98.
13. The hymn based on Francis of Assisi's Canticle of the Sun, "All creatures of our God and King," was rendered "All creatures, worship God most high" in *Evangelical Lutheran Worship* (Minneapolis: Augsburg Fortress, 2006), #835.
14. See Robert W. Jenson, *The Triune Identity* (Philadelphia: Fortress, 1982), 103–59.

turies to convert these new people to the orthodoxy of the Catholic Church. It was as a part of this struggle against Arianism that the canticle Te Deum Laudamus, and the teaching creed that begins *Quicunque vult salus esse* (Whoever wishes to be saved—the so-called Athanasian Creed), emerged in southern Gaul in the fifth century. Terminations of collects, usually addressed to "God" (*Deus*), were also expanded beyond "through Jesus Christ our Lord" with the addition of "who lives and reigns with you and the Holy Spirit, one God, world without end."[15] The conversion of the Visigothic king Richard to Catholicism in 589 CE occasioned the recitation of the Nicene Creed in the Western liturgy. This proved to be a popular addition and was so ordered by Charlemagne for use in the Frankish church. Only in the eleventh century was the Nicene Creed added to the Roman liturgy, at the behest of the German emperor Henry II, but it was only to be recited on Sundays and festivals, not on weekdays and days of devotion.

Reduced Awareness of the Trinity

Another issue is that liturgical changes in the new liturgical books since the 1970s reduced the quantity of references to the Trinity and the Trinitarian name. The Sunday canticle since the fifth century has been the Gloria in Excelsis, a great Trinitarian text. But in the 1978 *Lutheran Book of Worship* a newly written canticle based on texts in the Apocalypse, Worthy is Christ ("This is the feast of victory for our God"), could be sung as an alternative during the Easter season—or any other song of praise could be sung, and none at all during Advent and Lent, since the traditional practice was to suppress the Gloria in Excelsis during these penitential seasons. The Common Service tradition had included the Gloria Patri in the traditional introit of the day, but with the elimination of the historic introits in favor of an entrance hymn the Gloria Patri was lost. For whatever reason, a decision was made not to conclude the psalms with the Gloria Patri, either in the service of Holy Communion or in the prayer offices (for which psalm collects were provided). So the use of this Trinitarian formula is restricted to the end of the New Testament canticles. But *Evangelical Lutheran Worship* (2006) removed the Gloria Patri from all the biblical canticles. Opportunities to sing the Te Deum Laudamus are limited and the *Quicunque Vult* (the

---

15. See Joseph A. Jungmann, *The Place of Christ in Liturgical Prayer*, trans. A. Peeler (1925; repr., Collegeville, MN: Liturgical, 1989), 200–212.

so-called Athanasian Creed) isn't even included in the book, although it was in *Lutheran Book of Worship*.

Reduced opportunities to experience worship as directed to God the Holy Trinity, Father, Son, and Holy Spirit, have undoubtedly contributed to the situation today that most Christians do not consciously relate to God as Trinity. Christian people relate to Jesus because he is like them—human. In countless hymns and songs addressed to or about Jesus, they call him friend, brother, Savior, even the Son of God. They pray to the Father because Jesus prayed to the Father and taught his disciples to do likewise. Western Christians generally don't know quite what to do with the Holy Spirit. They see the Holy Spirit as somehow operating independently of the Father and the Son. They don't understand the Spirit as the bond between the Father and the Son who proceeds from the Father (the Western church added "and the Son") to create a human community that reflects the divine community.

Retrieval of the Trinity in Recent Theology

Given the focus on the Second Person of the Trinity in Western Christianity, even on the human Jesus, some theologians have thought that the only meaningful way to retrieve the doctrine of the Trinity is to get to the Trinity through Jesus. In the late twentieth century Karl Rahner attempted to do it in this way. Theology has historically differentiated between the "economic Trinity"—what God is in relation to Godself—and the "immanent Trinity"—what God is in relation to God's work in creation. Rahner proposed that the economic Trinity *is* the immanent Trinity, and vice versa. That is, who God is as God is in Godself cannot be separated from who God is as God reaches out to God's creation. God has reached out to God's creation through the Logos, through whom the world was created and in whose incarnation the world is redeemed. Rahner explicated this relationship in terms of sacramental reality. Using an ancient understanding of sacraments as "real symbols" (the Platonic notion that symbols participate in the reality to which they point), Rahner proposed that the Trinity is the foundation for all symbolic reality and efficacy.[16] Sacraments bring us together (*symballein*) with God who is Trinity. Jesus, the Logos with us, is the real symbol of the Logos with God. What Jesus does for us and for our salvation reveals the indwelling nature of the Logos as the self-expressing Word of God. As we are connected with Jesus in his human

16. See Karl Rahner, *The Trinity*, trans. J. Donceel (New York: Herder, 1970), 32–33.

nature, so because Jesus is the sacrament or real symbol of the Logos we are connected with the divine Logos in the Trinity.

The late Jesuit theologian Edward J. Kilmartin also begins with a Trinitarian Christology but takes it further. If human beings sanctified in holy baptism share in "the grace of Christ," there must be a grace inherent in Jesus that is communicable, a grace that is not unique to the incarnate Word. This cannot be the grace of the hypostatic union, because that is unique to that union and not shared. Kilmartin concludes that the grace communicated from Christ to those who are being saved is the anointing of the Holy Spirit. The grace of the Holy Spirit, "who sanctifies the humanity of Jesus, created by the Godhead as such, elevating that humanity to union with the Word who assumes it," can be communicated to other human persons, making them "sons and daughters of the Father in the unique Son."[17] In other words, to share in the Spirit-bestowed grace given to Jesus in his baptism is to be drawn into the life of the Holy Trinity.

Catherine LaCugna, late professor of theology at Notre Dame, regarded Rahner's (and perhaps also Kilmartin's) approach as too easily reflecting the modern notion of individualistic personhood, instead of a relational and interdependent model. She favored the doctrine of the Trinity in the Cappadocian fathers because, she said, it "made person rather than substance the primary ontological category."[18] Since to the Greek mind persons "are defined by their 'relation of origin,'" God is confessed to be primarily a relational being. Furthermore, the equally shared monarchy of the Trinitarian persons "contained the seeds of a radical social order."

In contrast, Latin theology placed substance over personhood. "Augustine began with the unity of Father, Son, and Spirit according to the divine substance."[19] Augustine's human analogies of the Trinity (for example, Love, the Beloved, the Lover) "had the effect of locating God's economy not in the history of salvation but within each human person."[20] This kind of abstraction and individualism depicts God as detached and self-sufficient. Latin theology thus projects blatant patriarchal values onto God whereas in Greek theology the coequality of

17. Edward J. Kilmartin, SJ, *Christian Liturgy: Theology and Practice* (Kansas City, MO: Sheed & Ward, 1988), 1:161–62.
18. Catherine Mowry LaCugna, "God in Communion with Us," in *Freeing Theology: The Essentials of Theology in Feminist Perspective*, ed. Catherine Mowry LaCugna (San Francisco: HarperSanFrancisco, 1993), 86.
19. Ibid., 87.
20. Ibid., 88.

the three is reflected in the coequality of the sexes, and indeed the coequality of all human persons in the eyes of God the Creator. Therefore LaCugna turned to the Cappadocian understanding of person as a relationship among equals and showed the significance of the Trinity in the economy of salvation as a model for all personal relationships.

LaCugna tackled head-on the issue of our changed understanding of person as a self-conscious, self-sufficient, self-possessing individual. She observed that, in the economy of salvation, God's whole energy is devoted to the movement of the material to the spiritual. "The law of personhood is that the only way one 'has' oneself at all is by giving oneself away."[21] The essence of life is to love another, to suffer with another, to unite oneself with another as equal peer in the communion of love.

Within this context, LaCugna explored the concept of perichoresis, the reciprocal presence of the three divine persons in one another, as described in the classic doctrine of the Trinity. She applied the rediscovery of this aspect of the immanent Trinity (the love of each person for the other expressed in mutual giving and receiving, without domination or subordination) to the church as the sacrament of the Triune God. Perichoresis has been understood in a literal sense as dancing around. It suggests the intertwining of persons. As God through the Holy Spirit reaches out to create a new redeemed community, it implies an intertwining of persons in their lives and loves. This is the basis of the communitarian worldview projected by the Christian understanding of God as Trinity. It should at least be manifested in the life of the church as the new humanity in Christ.

However, LaCugna does not find the distinction between the "immanent" Trinity and the "economic" Trinity to be helpful. She says that God is known immanently (ontologically) only through God's self-revelation in the economy of salvation, and that "theories about what God is apart from God's self-communication in salvation history remain unverifiable and ultimately untheological."[22]

Within the "economic" Trinity, she holds that each person has a distinct mission. This strikes me as moving toward modalism. Not surprisingly, she suggests that in the descriptions of these distinct missions it is possible to use alternative language that comes out of our own experience of the Trinity to complement the traditional language. As a

---

21. Catherine Mowry LaCugna, *God for Us: The Trinity and Christian Life* (New York: HarperCollins, 1991), 398.
22. Ibid., 231.

faithful Christian feminist, she proposed that the "insights of Trinitarian theology should free our imaginations without forcing us to abandon our tradition."[23]

However, she saw problems in the tradition. The doctrine of the Trinity has been abused to legitimize and perpetuate the subordination of women. This problem is especially vexing in Latin theology. She claimed that Greek theology, on the other hand, aids the feminist cause because it distinguishes hypostasis and ousia, fatherhood and Godhood. LaCugna critiques the appeal to "Father, Son, and Holy Spirit" as the unalterable revealed name of God. To make such an appeal, she wrote, is to ignore the "conditioned character of biblical testimony and the patriarchal context of biblical writings."[24] She typically recommended the addition of other images to counter exclusively male names. But she regarded "Creator, Redeemer, Sustainer" as far too abstract and functional to express the personhood of God.

God Has a Name

I have rehearsed here the Trinitarian theology of Catherine LaCugna, who died at the untimely age of forty-four from cancer, because I think we can appreciate her recovery of the personal in "the Triune identity" and the implications of perichoresis for a Trinitarian worldview. But, just so, if the relationships within the Trinity are person-to-person and if our human relationship to God is personal in that sense, we need to be able to communicate person-to-person. For starters, we need to be able to speak to one another, to address one another. And to do that we need something more specific than "O God" (which god?) or "hey you" (which "you"? Adam, Catherine, Frank?).

At the point in salvation history when the God who identifies himself in the biblical narrative as the God of Abraham, the God of Isaac, the God of Jacob is about to redeem his people Israel from slavery in Egypt and form them into his own people free to worship him, he calls Moses through the burning bush and commissions him to go back into Egypt and lead the people out of Egypt. Moses is to bring the people to this holy mountain (Sinai) where they can worship him. The command is specific: "You shall worship God on this mountain" (Exod 3:12). Gods need worshipers if they are to be real to the world. Many ancient gods are no longer real because they no longer have worshipers. Who wor-

---

23. Ibid., 106.
24. *Freeing Theology*, 102.

ships Zeus today? Zeus lacks worshipers, so Zeus isn't real. Perhaps the God of Abraham, Isaac, and Jacob was acting at this point in time because he was losing worshipers and therefore also his reality in the world. But Moses asks the logical question: "If I come to the Israelites and say to them, 'The God of your ancestors has sent me to you,' and they ask me, 'What is his name?' what shall I say to them?" (Exod 3:13). The God of the ancestors plays a bit with Moses, saying "I am who I am." "Say to the Israelites, 'I am has sent me to you'" (Exod 3:14). This is not a name as much as a warning that this God is not to be trifled with. The mystery of God cannot be penetrated. But in the very next verse Moses is told, "Thus you shall say to the Israelites, 'the Lord [YHWH], the God of your ancestors, the God of Abraham, the God of Isaac, the God of Jacob, has sent me to you'" (Exod 3:15).

Here is the revelation of this God's name. As Jenson says, "What the word 'Yahweh' may once have meant we do not know. Since historical Israel did not know either, the loss is not theologically great."[25] Jenson is not being flippant. While it is true that many names in the Bible are given because they have great significance (and sometimes names are changed to reflect new situations), the important thing about names is that they are handles by which we can identify the person with whom we are trying to communicate. I think I know why my parents named me Frank (although several variant reasons exist), but if I fail to pass on that knowledge to my wife or children they will not cease to call me by my proper name.

The name of God in the Bible is not "God" (ʾəlōhîm). Although that term is used, especially in the so-called Priestly document in the Pentateuch, it is not used in the context of the covenant. When Moses descended from Sinai and presented the commandments to the people, the Lord accompanied him and proclaimed his own name to the people.

> The Lord, the Lord,
> a God merciful and gracious,
> slow to anger,
> and abounding in steadfast love and faithfulness. (Exod 34:6)

When the covenant needed to be renewed, this God again said through his prophet Ezekiel, "I will establish my covenant with you, and you shall know that I am the Lord" (Ezek 16:62); also through the Isaiah of the exile,

25. Jenson, *The Triune Identity*, 5.

I am the Lord, your Holy One,
the Creator of Israel, your King. (Isa 43:15)

YHWH, usually translated in English as "Lord," is the covenant name of God. Googling indicates that it occurs 6,823 times in the Old Testament and is by far the most frequent usage of any name for God.

When we come to the New Testament, Jesus explicitly taught his disciples to call God Abba when they asked him how to pray (Matt 6:9; Luke 11:2), which is a familiar form of "father" or "daddy." This is the One who called Jesus "Son" at his baptism (Matt 3:17; Mark 1:11; Luke 3:22). Paul already refers to Christians praying "Abba! Father!" as prompted by the Holy Spirit, before any of the gospels were written (Rom 8:15).

Let us note that Jesus specifically did not teach his disciples to call God YHWH. There's a reason for this. The name of God is holy, so it is to be protected from profanation, as we see in the Ten Commandments (Exod 20:7; Deut 5:11), and it is to be sanctified by proper use, as Jesus taught in the Lord's Prayer (Matt 6:9; Luke 11:2). In the Jewish tradition the concern to protect God's name from profanation was so great that it was not even spoken. "Adonai" became a substitution for speaking the name "YHWH." Even if we could be sure that "Yahweh" was the original pronunciation of YHWH, we need to recognize not only that this name is never pronounced but also that this silence is part of the actual tradition of the Scriptures. This is why the ancient translations generally did not transliterate it, but provided instead a translation of the substitute word 'ădōnāy—kyrios—in the Septuagint.

People don't seem to get that. But it really goes to the actual revelation of God himself. This name is the verbal or linguistic equivalent of the holy of holies. You just don't go there whenever you feel like it. In fact, it could be pronounced only once, on only one day of the year, in only one place (the holy of holies), and only by the holiest man (the high priest). There is but one God, and we believe that YHWH and Abba are the same God. But Jesus, as a pious Jew, would never have used YHWH out loud, and he did not teach us to do so.

It is when we take seriously this chaste approach to the speaking of God's name that the teaching of Jesus to call God "Father" stands out as utterly remarkable. Not only is Abba an intimate form of address, but we are to *say* the name. In this sense, Abba (Father) is not exactly the Christian equivalent and stand-in for YHWH (Lord), even though ontologically Abba is the same God as YHWH. It is a new revelation made known in the fullness of time in Christ Jesus, a change of names to reflect the new situation of the new covenant.

It is true, however, that "Lord," the translation of ʾădōnāy, is used of all three persons of the Trinity. St. Paul generally uses "Lord" to indicate the Father and "our Lord" to indicate the Son. He references the early Christian creed that affirms, "Jesus is Lord [kyrios]." The Nicene Creed says, "one Lord, Jesus Christ," and "the Holy Spirit, the Lord and giver of life." The so-called Athanasian Creed, Quicunque Vult, teaches that "the Father is Lord; the Son is Lord; the Holy Spirit is Lord: And yet there are not three Lords but one Lord."[26] Whatever it means to be God, the Father, Son, and Holy Spirit are equally that. And within the Trinity the Second Person is true man as well as true God.

This creed, which is most helpful in sorting out the relations within the Trinity, begins with the statement, "We worship one God in three persons and three persons in one God." We don't worship the Trinity as a theological concept, but the three persons who are one God. These persons have names, and those names are the handles—the identity of God—given to us so that we can call on God in prayer, praise, and thanksgiving. One cannot have a personal relationship with someone without a way to address that person by name. We do not have a personal relationship with the Godhead. We have personal relationships with the Father to whom we pray as Jesus taught us, with the Son who is our mediator and advocate, and with the Holy Spirit who empowers our prayer. In other words, we have a personal relationship with each person of the Trinity.

The names all come together in only a few places in the New Testament. Paul often begins his letters with greetings in the Name of "God the Father" and "our Lord Jesus Christ." The closing benedictions mention no name or only the name of Jesus, except in 2 Corinthians 13:13, where for some reason (not readily apparent) Paul concludes with "The grace of the Lord Jesus Christ, the love of God, and the communion of the Holy Spirit be with all of you." The most explicit Trinitarian naming of God is in the baptismal formula in Matthew 28, where the disciples are commissioned to "make disciples of all nations, baptizing them in the name of the Father and of the Son and of the Holy Spirit."

It has been proposed that this full Trinitarian formula developed from earlier unitary or binary formulas such as "in Jesus's name" or "in the name of God and the Lord Jesus." I don't see much evidence

26. Lutheran Book of Worship (Minneapolis: Augsburg, 1978), 54.

of that in the extant early literature. Acts 8:14–16 indicates that baptism "in the name of the Lord Jesus only" was inadequate. The *Didache*, reflecting usage at the end of the first century, probably in Antioch, says: "baptize in the name of the Father and of the Son and of the Holy Spirit, in running water" (7.1). Justin Martyr reports to the Roman Senate in his *Apology* around 150 CE that the candidates for baptism are "washed in the water in the name of God the Father and Master of all, and of our Savior Jesus Christ, and of the Holy Spirit." The *Apostolic Tradition*, reflecting a practice that may be as early as the beginning of the third century but which was also a living liturgical document as reflected in various later church orders, uses as the baptismal formula an embryonic form of what later developed into the Apostles' Creed, with the candidate saying "I believe" to each article and being immersed after each profession of belief in God the Father, Christ Jesus the Son of God, and the Holy Spirit and the holy church. It is especially in liturgy, when we do not just talk about God but also speak to God in prayer or proclaim God's word, that we need to have access to God's name. It is especially in connection with the sacraments of Holy Baptism and Holy Communion that the Trinitarian name of God has been important.

Our problems with the Trinitarian name arise because we don't really "get" the Trinity in the first place. For some it's just an arbitrary abstraction, and they find it easy to replace it with other arbitrary abstractions. However, for the New Testament and the early church, the reality that came to be named Trinity is not an abstraction. It's the essence of our life in Christ. In baptism we become "sons and daughters in the Son," as some of the church fathers expressed it. We say "Abba," "Father," because we are taught by Christ to do so, as some liturgies of the church instruct us, right before the Lord's Prayer. But this "teaching" that Christ gives us is not some kind of external knowledge; it is an unfolding within us of Christ's own Spirit, relating us to the One he called "Abba, Father" by introducing us into *his* actual relationship with the Father. The Spirit of God bears "witness with our spirit that we are children of God" (Rom 8:16). We call God "Father" not only *because* of Christ, but *in* Christ and *with* Christ and *through* Christ.

Jesus and Abba

Jesus did not address his Father as "Creator" or even as "Lord" or by any of the other titles that have been proposed in recent years to avoid using the name "Father." These titles all fall short of indicating that profound relation of origination and generation that *only* a familial term conveys, as when humans speak of their identities in human language, using such terms as father/mother, daughter/son.

The names "Father" and "Son" were not embraced in Christian prayer and worship because of some penchant for patriarchalism in the early church. We use these given names because the relations of the Trinity *must* be expressed in the familial terms used by Christ and by the tradition that is rooted in him. The Council of Ephesus (431) affirmed that Mary is Theotokos, God-bearer. Jesus did not call God "Mother" because his mother is Mary; and he is not God's "Daughter" because he's not a "daughter" in any sense of the word. The scandal of particularity is that the divine Word was enfleshed in a Jewish male. So we are left with his usage—Abba, Father—and the Father's designation of Jesus as "Son" as the indelible imprint of the incarnation on human speech. We have to take the incarnation seriously. It is revelation. That means we must accept the "father-son" relationship, as it was appropriated first of all in Christ's own being and then as it was given expression in his self-reflection and on his tongue. The theological task is to explore the meaning of Christ's incarnation as a male Jew, not to suggest alternative ways of conceiving him because we don't like patriarchalism.

But patriarchalism is indeed an issue. It was a concept that emerged in seventeenth century England in defense of the absolutist claims of the Stuart monarchy.[27] Patriarchalism was thus related to monarchy and triumphalism, three interrelated concepts that feminist theology rightly eschews. This theological model held a certain liturgical attraction in the age of political absolutism (especially in France during the reign of the "sun king" Louis XIV) because it evokes a feeling of awe and reverence.[28] One thinks of the Baroque altars in Catholic churches with their tabernacles resembling thrones of Christ the King. Some Protestant pulpits in the Baroque era were also pretty impressive. This reminds us that liturgy is more than words. It is also sacred space and sacred music and roles of the assembly. The model of liturgical renewal, reflecting modern sensibilities, has been communitarian rather than hierarchical, and God language has been more relational

---

27. Gordon J. Schochet, *Patriarchalism in Political Though: The authoritarian family and political speculation and attitudes especially in seventeenth-century England* (New York: Basic, 1975).

28. See the Baroque concept of liturgy described by Louis Bouyer, *Liturgical Piety* (Notre Dame: University of Notre Dame Press, 1954), 1–9.

than abstract. This may be part of what got us into this situation in the first place. A review of the prayer texts for the Roman Rite prepared by the International Commission on English in the Liturgy (ICEL) in 1973 shows a greater use of the term "Father" in addressing God than was warranted by the more prevalent Latin "Deus" in the Roman liturgical books. But this reflected the concern at that time to be more concrete in our prayers and less theologically abstract.

It has been asked: What is important to maintain about the Father-Son relationship that cannot be expressed, for example, by "Parent-Child"? Apart from the fact that "Parent" sounds awfully bureaucratic, I reiterate: we are not talking about images or metaphors, which might well be employed in prayers and in hymns, but about the divine name. We have been given the divine name, as Martin Luther teaches in his catechism, so that we can call on God in prayer, praise, and thanksgiving (*Small Catechism*, part 1, Second Commandment). This is *orthodoxia*. It is identifying and calling on the right God. Calling on the right God is aided by having the right name of God to use in prayer and proclamation.

Orthodoxy and Doxology

The classical Latin collects are generally not directed to the Father but simply to "God" (*Deus*), "through Jesus Christ our Lord." As I said, the Trinitarian expansion of the termination of the collects was added in response to Arianism (in Gaul, not in Rome) since the Arians could appeal to prayer to God through Christ to prove that the Son is subordinate to the Father. Yes, that is true as regards his humanity, said the *Quicunque Vult*, but not as regards his divinity. In the face of theological confusions, which seem to be replicated today, the collects were expanded with full Trinitarian terminations. Thus Roman protocol dictated that prayers would be addressed *to* the Father, *through* the Son, *in* the unity of the Holy Spirit, ever *one* God, world without end, thus preserving both the immanent and the economic Trinity. This care has not been demonstrated in prayers in current use. I take the eucharistic prayers in *Evangelical Lutheran Worship* (*ELW*) as a case in point.[29]

Many Lutheran Mass orders retained that part of the Roman Anaphora known as the preface. In the English-language version of the

---

29. The ten eucharistic prayers are in every setting of the Holy Communion liturgy in *Evangelical Lutheran Worship*, leader's desk ed. and altar book (Minneapolis: Augsburg Fortress, 2006), see 194–205. II is the text of the Words of Institution.

Common Service, after the opening dialogue the prayer begins, "It is meet, right, and salutary, that we should at all times, and in all places, give thanks unto thee, O Lord, Holy Father, Almighty, Everlasting God." Some of the proper prefaces include the clause "through Jesus Christ our Lord, who ..." if the proper concerns the work of Christ rather than the work of the Father in promising, sending, giving, or raising the Son. So it continued in contemporary English speech in the *Lutheran Book of Worship* (*LBW*). In *ELW* the preface begins, "It is indeed right, our duty and our joy, that we should at all times and in all places give thanks and praise to you, almighty and merciful God." The Father is not named. Some of the propers continue "through our *Savior* Jesus Christ," thus avoiding also "Lord" and also "your Son." Among all the proper prefaces, only the one for the Epiphany and the Baptism of our Lord makes reference to the Son—it was unavoidable there in an allusion to the biblical text.

In terms of the doxological conclusions, Eucharistic Prayer I, based on the text drafted by Luther Reed for the *Service Book and Hymnal* (1958), and inspired by Eastern as well as Western sources, has an Eastern-type termination: "To you, O God, Father, Son, and Holy Spirit, be all honor and glory in your holy church, now and forever." But Prayer III, for Advent through the Epiphany of our Lord, has: "All praise and glory are yours, Holy One of Israel, Word of God incarnate, Power of the Most High." Those biblical images might be added to "Father, Son, and Holy Spirit," but should not replace the divine name. Prayer IV, for Lent through the Day of Pentecost, has: "With [names and] your holy ones of all times and places, with the earth and all its creatures, with sun and moon and stars, we praise you, O God, blessed and holy Trinity, now and forever." Since the eucharistic prayer includes everything from the preface through the doxology, no specific God is named in Prayers III and IV. Of the remaining eucharistic prayers in the *ELW* leader's edition, Prayer V came from the *LBW Occasional Services* and is okay; Prayer VI is the "rose canon" (the rose-shaded column) in the *LBW* pew edition and is okay. Prayer VII concludes: "we feast forever in the triumph of the Lamb: through whom all glory and honor is yours, O God, O Living God, with the Holy Spirit." The Father and the Son are not named at all in this prayer. Prayer VIII is from *This Far by Faith* and is okay. Prayer IX does not name the Father at all. Prayer X is effulgent with images of God that seem to be drawn from Gail Ramshaw's writings,[30] and ends: "O God most majestic, O God most motherly, O God our strength and our song, you show us a vision of the tree of life with fruits for all and leaves that heal the nations. Grant us such life, the life of the Father to the Son, and the life of the Spirit of our risen Savior, life in you, now and forever." I think this is acceptable. Prayer XI is the so-called Anaphora of Hippolytus from the *Apostolic Tradition*, which is a model of orthodox eucharistic praying (as it was originally intended to be) since it is addressed to the Father, through the Son (actually "Child" in the Latin text), in the Holy Spirit.

I could go through the eucharistic prayers in other recent worship books in some other denominations and find similar confusions. Many contemporary eucharistic prayers are addressed to "God" through "Christ." No "Son" to imply a "Father." What is at stake here? Nothing less than an orthodox worldview—the right worship of the right God.

Many people turn to religion to make sense out of life, and there's a lot in the Trinitarian understanding of God and the Trinity's relationship to the world that makes sense. Many people today live fragmented and sometimes isolated lives. They long for a sense of connection and integration that comes through a true sense of community. The dogma of the Trinity is all about a communitarian view of reality.

John of Damascus, who grew up under Muslims in Damascus and spoke Arabic, said that "the Muslims call [us Christians] associators because, they say, we introduce beside God an associate to Him by saying that Christ is the Son of God and God."[31] The Christian Triune God is not a solitary God but an associating God. God the Father, Son, and Holy Spirit associates with Godself as three persons within the one Godhead and with us in the incarnation of the Word and through the Spirit of the Father and the Son, who brings the church into an association with God by means of the sacraments. It has been said that the doctrine of the Trinity embraces both transcendence and immanence. I think it is more apropos of our own age to say that Trinity creates community. Faith in our Trinitarian God requires us to be in relationships with God, with others, and with the world created by the word of the Lord through the Word (Logos) by the Spirit.

This is a communitarian view of reality. It is a worldview that comes to focus in the eucharistic prayer over the bread and wine that we will receive as the means of union with Christ in our own bodies. We lift up our hearts in thanksgiving to the Father, join with all creation in praise, in remembrance of the Son who gives us his body and blood,

---

30. See Gail Ramshaw, *Treasures Old and New: Images in the Lectionary* (Minneapolis: Augsburg, 2002).
31. In *The Fount of Wisdom; Patrologiae Graecia* 94:768. Cited in Robert Louis Wilken, *Remembering the Christian Past* (Grand Rapids: Eerdmans, 1995), 63.

by invoking the Spirit, who joins us bodily into the body of Christ, as we commemorate all the saints who have gone before us, pray for the world, and praise God the eternal three-in-one, Father, Son, and Holy Spirit, now and through all the ages of ages. In the sweep of the Great Thanksgiving we evoke a cosmology, take into account a sinful world and human suffering, and express the dimensions of community, all within the embrace of God the Holy Trinity.

A Doxological Body

We have emphasized in this book worship that is more than words. Worship of the Holy Trinity is also expressed by the body. We have mentioned bodily and physical gestures within the Anaphora: gestures in the preface dialogue, bowing during the Sanctus and Hosanna, and the use of the orans position during the praying of the Anaphora, in which the presiding minister might be joined by others in the assembly. The presider takes hold of the bread and the cup during the words of Christ over each. The faithful have sometimes knelt or genuflected during these words. The presider extends her or his hands over the bread and cup during the invocation of the Holy Spirit. And the bread and cup are elevated during the final doxology to proclaim the presence of the body and blood of Christ.

But the body of the worshiper responds to the Trinitarian name in doxologies by bowing. This is not a nod of the head, as is done at the mention of the name of Jesus, but a deep bow from the waist, to which is added by the Orthodox worshiper the sign of the cross over one's whole body with fingers touching the floor. The sign of the cross is made at invocations of the Trinitarian name because that is the name placed on the Christian in Holy Baptism. One must be standing to perform this posture and gesture. Many Christian hymns conclude with a Trinitarian doxology as the final stanza. If the congregation is seated they stand for the doxological stanza so that they may bow at the name of the Father, Son, and Holy Spirit. One bows in reverence and makes the sign of the cross only for the divine name, not for a theological concept such as "holy and blessed Trinity."

I have engaged in an act of body worship of the Trinity using the yoga half sun salutation in this way.

Figure 6. Fifteenth-century icon of the Holy Trinity by the Russian iconographer Andrei Rublev. God cannot be pictorially portrayed in Orthodoxy. These are the three strangers or angels who visited Abraham and Sarah by the Oaks of Mamre. Like the Trinity, the three angels appear in harmony, yet each is unique. They are offered the hospitality of food and drink by Abraham. In the center of the icon is a chalice with a calf or lamb resting in it, symbolizing Christ who is a sacrificial lamb whose body and blood we receive in Holy Communion.

Begin in standing or mountain pose. Extend arms overhead and think or say "Glory." Do a backward bend "to the Father." Do a forward fold to the floor "to the Son." Do monkey pose "to the Holy Spirit." Conclude with standing pose and hands in prayer over the heart center with "Amen."[32] *Do this three times.*

In doing this vinyasa I build into my body's memory my devotion (*bhakti*) to the Holy Trinity. As we do this doxological yoga sequence daily, and connect it with the profound liturgical bow at every Trinitarian doxology, we are reminded that God is available to us through God's own sacramental embodiment in Christ, and through the sacraments of Christ God is embodied in us. The Holy Spirit dwells in our bodies as a temple and we are glorifying God in our bodies (1 Cor 6:19) by our profound bow at the mention of the holy name as well as by our arms raised in praise.

---

32. In *Embodied Liturgy* I provide a complete sun salutation (*Surya namaskara*) on pp. 106-8.

7

Communion: Presence and Embodiment

In the months following my first Communion on Easter Sunday 1957, my life in my body took a positive turn. I was in the boys gymnastic show at school. My soprano voice held out long enough to sing in the spring concert of the Singing Boys of Buffalo at Kleinhans Music Hall and to perform in the children's operetta at the Buffalo Science Museum. I played a piano solo at my eighth grade graduation—a piece by Tchaikovsky. The boys who had bullied me on the way home from school went to a different high school and I didn't have to deal with them any longer. My parents' tenant who felt he could come into my bedroom unannounced moved out. These things would have happened without my first Communion. But I do not doubt that I was also spiritually uplifted by the event.

In describing my first experience of receiving Holy Communion I mentioned the early adolescent body issues that were fresh on my mind during that Lent and Holy Week and on that Easter morning. I believed that the sacrament conveyed the gifts of forgiveness of sins, life, and salvation, as taught in my recently memorized catechism, and that my sins were forgiven by virtue of receiving Holy Communion in faith. But in the following months I came to think that there is more.

Yes, the sacrament is a means of grace; its benefits include the forgiveness of sins. But this could be accomplished just by meditating on the atoning sacrifice of the cross as we receive the sacramental signs. Eating and drinking the sacramental signs assert to us bodily that the body of Christ was given for us and the blood of Christ was shed for us (words that are used in the administration of the sacrament in Lutheran practice) and we are put in mind of his atoning sacrifice. We have learned from cognitive mind theory that the mind is part of the body, not separate from it, and that what the body experiences affects the mind.[1] If we eat the bread and drink from the cup, hearing the words "the body of Christ, given for you. The blood of Christ shed for you" (note that several senses plus the motor actions of eating and drinking are involved here), we will be put in mind of what is proclaimed concerning Christ's offering of himself—body given and blood shed for you for the forgiveness of sins. I think this body-mind connection squares with the Reformed (high Calvinist) view of the Eucharist; it is an understanding also shared by Lutherans and Roman Catholics. Yet I came to believe that more is involved in that we actually consume in our bodies the body and blood of Christ. We receive Christ bodily as bread and wine.

Consuming the Body of Christ

As I continued to receive Holy Communion in the months to come (albeit only once a month when it was offered in my home church), the realization came to me that the body of the Lamb of God who takes away the sins of the world *comes into my body*, and that my humble little adolescent body had been honored by the body of Christ entering into it. If my body had been defiled, it was now cleansed; if it had been rendered impure, it was now sanctified—not because of anything I have done on my part, but because my body absorbs the body of Christ.

I believed the Lutheran teaching I learned in confirmation class that Christ's body and blood is present in the sacrament in, with, and under the bread and wine. I later pondered the question: Why does Christ come to us in bread and wine? I concluded: apart from the historical "accidents" of bread and wine being food stuff used at the Passover Seder at which Jesus instituted the Lord's Supper, these are "substances" that can be assimilated by the body. I came to believe that Christ comes bodily into our bodies to make them holy and to connect our bodies as well as our minds with his. This is what it means to speak about being "in union with Christ."

---

1. See George Lakoff and Mark Johnson, *Philosophy in the Flesh: The Embodied Mind and Its Challenge to Western Thought* (New York: Basic, 1999), 16–44, 97.

This view was reinforced when I read Alexander Schmemann's *For the Life of the World* as a college student. He begins with a statement by the German materialist philosopher Friedrich Feuerbach that "man is what he eats."[2] Schmemann agreed with Feuerbach, noting that the Bible begins with humankind as hungry beings and the whole world given to them as food. He saw the need to eat and drink as central to our religious identity as creatures of God who nevertheless have the means of being in communion with God. By that time I knew a little about bio-chemistry and I thought: yes, we are what we eat, and if we eat bread and drink wine that are received as the body and blood of Christ, does that not make us, in a kind of spiritual biology, a part of Christ? And does that not have moral consequences?

In the early 1960s the social dimension of the Eucharist was being emphasized. The Eucharist was called "social dynamite" that broke racial barriers. I was caught up in the excitement of the civil rights movement. Some pastors asked: How could those who ate and drank together at the Lord's Table eat and drink separately in the cafeteria? I thought: by receiving the body and blood of Christ into our bodies we actually became one with Christ. We become, as Luther said, "little Christs to our neighbors." We are the hands of Christ for reaching out to others, the legs of Christ for getting up and marching in the civil rights demonstrations, the heart of Christ for beating compassion for the oppressed, the mind of Christ for working out justice for all people, the body of Christ manning the barricades, or at least integrating white suburban swimming pools in New Jersey with black kids from Camden in the summer of 1963.

This incarnational spirituality and its liturgical embodiment began with a sense that dignity was given to my body by receiving the body and blood of Christ into it. Into the 1970s I was very focused on the importance of the body in worship. Liturgical renewal for me had to do with recovering a positive view of ritual, which is outward bodily behavior, and the sensory aspects of worship, and the use of physical postures to put one in mind of the presence of God. When my teacher Aidan Kavanagh introduced his liturgy students to the role of ritual in human life, I was very much attuned to this.[3] And when I published my

---

2. Alexander Schmemann, *For the Life of the World: Sacraments and Orthodoxy* (Crestwood, NY: St. Vladimir's Seminary Press, 1973), 11.
3. See James D. Shaughnessy, ed., *The Roots of Ritual* (Grand Rapids: Eerdmans, 1973).

first book, a liturgical manual, this is what it emphasized.[4] I believed that the actions of worship were as important as the words.

As I think about my own emerging awareness as a youth of the honor given to our bodies by receiving sacramentally the body of Christ, I wonder about those Catholic children and youth who were sexually abused by Catholic priests—or, for that matter, the Catholics whose bodies were tortured by fellow Catholics during the dictatorship of General Augusto Pinochet in Chile, as reported by William Cavanaugh.[5] Robert Orsi reports that many of the victims of clergy abuse continued to attend Mass and receive Communion. Orsi demonstrates in his book, *History and Presence,* how deep-seated is the Catholic belief in the real presence of Christ in the Eucharist.[6] He wrote his book to do history from the standpoint of the experience of divine presence rather than the secular (largely Protestant-engendered) assumption of the absence of the "gods" (as he called the divine). He believes that this is the only way to write a social history of Catholicism because a sense of real presence is the defining characteristic of Catholic faith and piety. Just so, I wonder: Did those victims of sexual abuse feel that their abused bodies were sanctified by receiving the body of Christ into their abused bodies?

Following Lee Palmer Wandel's study *The Eucharist in the Reformation,*[7] Orsi contrasts the Catholic experience of bodily presence with the Protestant experience of bodily absence, making allowance for the Lutheran position of the real presence of Christ's body and blood "in, with, and under" bread and wine. (Orsi is married to Christine Helmer, a recognized Luther scholar, so he is aware that the Lutheran idea of the real presence is quite different from the Reformed idea.) He admits that the simple equation—Catholicism = presence, Protestantism = absence—is a caricature and an oversimplification, but it is the way many Catholics have seen Protestantism and many Protestants have seen Catholicism.[8]

Orsi presents the case for how Catholics feel connected with Christ in the Eucharist. I wonder how a Protestant feels connected to Christ

4. Frank C. Senn, *The Pastor as Worship Leader: A Manual for Corporate Worship* (Minneapolis: Augsburg, 1977).
5. William T. Cavanaugh, *Torture and Eucharist: Theology, Politics, and the Body of Christ* (Malden, MA: Blackwell, 2000).
6. Robert A. Orsi, *History and Presence* (Cambridge, MA: The Belknap Press of Harvard University Press, 2016), 1–11.
7. Lee Palmer Wandel, *The Eucharist in the Reformation: Incarnation and Liturgy* (Cambridge: Cambridge University Press, 2006).
8. Orsi, *History and Presence,* 25.

when he or she receives Communion. Is he or she connected with Christ through the mind or through the body? Would a Protestant experience the sanctification of the body as well as the transformation of the mind by receiving Holy Communion?

Views of the Real Presence

Wandel says that the Roman Catholic, Lutheran, and Reformed traditions "all held that Christ was 'really' present, though each defined 'real presence' differently."[9] For the Catholic Church the presence of Christ came by way of the Host—the little round wafer. For the Reformed, the unleavened flour-and-water wafer had no scriptural basis; so in their Communions they used real loaves of leavened bread as the earthly signs leading them to Christ's body in heaven. For the Lutherans the ingredients in the earthly signs were not important, although most Lutherans continued to use wafers. But Lutherans believed that they received Christ's body corporeally according to his word. All the churches used wine, although in the Roman Catholic Church the cup was withheld from lay communicants under normal circumstances. Lutherans and Anglicans continued to use metal patens and chalices; the Reformed and later Puritans used wooden platters and pewter cups. Silver flagons became required vessels in Lutheran and Reformed Communions as the number of communicants increased in Lutheran congregations and the whole congregation communed in the quarterly or monthly Reformed Communions. None dispensed with the earthly signs of bread and wine that were required to have a sacrament, and all traditions strove to connect the presence of Christ with the earthly elements, although in different ways.

The Roman Catholic Church affirmed at the Council of Trent the doctrine of transubstantiation promulgated at the Fourth Lateran Council (1215), which taught that the bread and wine change into body and blood. The Protestants rejected transubstantiation. But Lutherans held that the body and blood of Christ are received and consumed "in, with, and under" the bread and wine (the sacramental union). The Reformed, following Calvin, believe that the eating and drinking of the bread and wine lead one to a "real, spiritual" communion in Christ's body and blood in heaven.

The promulgation of the dogma of transubstantiation in 1215 was a response to controversies over the eucharistic presence in the West-

---

9. Wandel, *The Eucharist in the Reformation*, 258.

ern church that went back to debates between two monks of Cor-
bie—Ratramnus and Paschasius Radbertus—in Carolingian times (ninth
century). In a sense it was a conflict between an older Platonic worldview espoused by Augustine of Hippo, that the symbol participates in
the reality to which it points—the "symbols" or "figures" of bread and
wine sharing in the "reality" of body and blood—and the empirical
worldview of the emerging Western culture—what you see is what
you get.[10] A "symbolic" interpretation of the Eucharist was no longer
tenable in the "realistic" West, and various formulas were
devised—inflicted on the hapless Berengar of Tours in the eleventh
century—to affirm that we eat the true body of Christ and drink his
blood. Eucharistic miracles stories of Hosts turning into flesh or drops
of blood appearing on corporals helped to nail the view that at the
words of Christ—"this is my body," "this is my blood"—the bread and
wine change into body and blood. Lateran IV promulgated as dogma
what was generally believed by that time. It was left to Thomas Aquinas
and the scholastic theologians to invoke the newly discovered Aristo-
tle's categories of substance and accidents and propose that the substance or essence of bread and wine change into the substance or
essence of body and blood while the accidents or outward appearances
of bread and wine remain unchanged. In the wake of Protestant challenges to this dogma, the Council of Trent affirmed Lateran IV's affirmation of transubstantiation or "change of substance."

An interesting aspect of Trent's deliberations, as Wandel notes, is
the disproportionate concern with Zwingli out of all the Reformers.
When the council deliberated on the "articles of the heretics" concerning the Eucharist in 1547, Zwingli's influence had waned. There
was no church or theological movement named after him. His place
in the Reformed tradition had been superseded by Bucer and Oecolampadius and Calvin and Bullinger. But the council fathers recognized
that Zwingli had opened a path that, if not contested by doctrine and
church discipline, would lead to God's real absence from the world.
Therefore the first heretical article was Zwingli's, Oecolampadius's,
and the sacramentarians' teaching that "in the Eucharist is present not
the body and blood of Jesus Christ but a sign only." Second, these same
heretics erroneously held that "in the Eucharist Christ is exhibited, but
eaten solely spiritually through faith." The third article recognizes that
Luther held to the presence of the body and blood of our Lord Jesus

---

10. See Frank C. Senn, *Christian Liturgy—Catholic and Evangelical* (Minneapolis: Fortress, 1997), 241–53.

Christ, "but at the same time as the substance of the bread and wine, that is, not through transubstantiation, but in a hypostatic union of Christ's humanity and the substance of the bread and wine" (citing Luther's *Confession Concerning the Lord's Supper*, 1528).[11]

Wandel gets Luther and the Lutheran church wrong when she writes that they taught a doctrine of consubstantiation.[12] The Lutheran confessions nowhere espouse the term "consubstantiation," nor does the Council of Trent use that term. The only place Luther mentioned what could be construed as an alternative philosophical understanding to transubstantiation that could be termed "consubstantiation" was in *The Babylonian Captivity of the Church.* In this 1520 treatise he knocked down the three walls the Romanist had erected around the Eucharist: the withholding of the cup from lay communicants, the doctrine of transubstantiation, and the use of the Mass as a good work and sacrifice. In debunking the doctrine of transubstantiation he mentioned having read the opinions of "the learned Cardinal of Cambrai" (Peter d'Ailly, a student of Ockham), who "argues with great acumen that to hold that real bread and real wine, and not merely their accidents, are present on the altar, would be much more probable and require fewer superfluous miracles—if only the church had not decreed otherwise." After "floating in a sea of doubt" Luther "found rest for my conscience" in this view, "namely, that it is real bread and real wine, in which Christ's real flesh and real blood are present in no other way and to no less a degree than the others assert them to be under their accidents."[13]

This is where Luther settled in his understanding of the eucharistic presence of Christ until he was drawn into debate with the Swiss Reformer Ulrich Zwingli, because "sacramentarian" ideas were unsettling South German churches. Luther's controversy with Zwingli over the real presence of Christ in the Eucharist split the Protestant movement. Their differences came to focus in the Marburg Colloquy in 1529, convened by Landgrave Philip of Hesse to resolve disputes between the Reformers and create a united Protestant front. Zwingli focused on John 6:63: "It is the spirit that gives life, the flesh is of no avail"; that is, "sacramental eating is by faith not by mouth." Martha Moore-Keish holds that for Zwingli the benefits of receiving the sacrament

---

11. Wandel, *The Eucharist in the Reformation*, 217.
12. Ibid., 258.
13. Martin Luther, *The Babylonian Captivity of the Church* (1520), in *Luther's Works*, trans. A. T. W. Steinhaeuser, rev. Fredrick C. Ahrens and Abdel Ross Wentz, ed. Abdel Ross Wentz (Philadelphia: Fortress, 1959), 36:28–29.

do not come from consuming the elements but as a direct gift of the Holy Spirit.[14] Luther, on the other hand, argued that we cannot overlook the material elements because God has willed that "forgiveness of sins, eternal life, and the kingdom of heaven are, by the Word of God, attached to these low and, as it would seem, carnal things."[15]

Zwingli emphasized the ascension of Christ, which is based on interpretation of John 6:62–63 ("Then what if you were to see the Son of Man ascending to where he was before? It is the spirit that gives life; the flesh is useless."). Since the body of Christ is in heaven at the right hand of God it "is not eaten essentially, really, and in a carnal way" in the Lord's Supper.[16] Rather, he insists on a spiritual eating in the Lord's Supper.

Luther agreed with Zwingli's spiritual eating. Pressing this, Oecolampadius asked: "As we have the spiritual eating, why should there be any need for a bodily eating?" Luther answered:

> We do not deny the spiritual eating; on the contrary we teach and believe it to be necessary. But from this it does not follow that the bodily eating is either useless or unnecessary. It is not our business to judge whether it is useful or not. We have the command "Take, eat; this is my body." Christ gives Himself to us in many ways; first, in the preaching of the word; secondly, in baptism; thirdly, in brotherly consolation; fourthly, in the sacrament as often as the body of Christ is eaten, because He Himself commands us to do so. If He ordered me to eat dung, I would do it.[17]

Although Zwingli has some sympathy with Luther's thought, which is based on Scripture as the Word of God, he suggests some of Luther's words seemed "pretty childish, as e.g.: 'If God ordered me to eat dung.'"[18] Luther responds that "wherever the Word of God is, there is spiritual eating. . . . If, however, He [God] adds bodily eating to that, we are bound to obey. . . . While the mouth receives the body of Christ, the soul believes the words when eating the body."[19] Zwingli does not entirely deny Christ's presence in the Lord's Supper. He states: "We, too, speak of a sacramental presence of the body of Christ, which means that the body of Christ is in the Supper representatively."[20]

14. Martha L. Moore-Keish, *Do This in Remembrance of Me: A Ritual Approach to Reformed Eucharistic Theology* (Grand Rapids: Eerdmans, 2008), 17–18.
15. Ibid., 18. See also the record of the Marburg Colloquy in Hermann Sasse, *This Is My Body: Luther's Contention for the Real Presence in the Sacrament of the Altar* (Minneapolis: Augsburg, 1959), 234.
16. Sasse, *This Is My Body*, 238.
17. Ibid., 236–37.
18. Ibid., 238–39.
19. Ibid., 239.

Luther will not have just a representative or figurative presence of the body of Christ in the sacrament (the earthly signs). He appealed to the "communication of attributes" (*communicatio idiomata*) and held that since the human body of Jesus shares in the attributes of the divine Christ, including omnipresence, Christ's body and blood can be present in the bread and wine according to his word. According to Zwingli and Oecolampadius, God is indeed omnipresent, but they argued that the Scripture reveals that "Christ is always in a particular place, as in the manger, in the temple . . . at the right hand of the Father."[21]

A telling exchange occurred between Oecolampadius and Luther.

Oecolampadius: You should not cling to the humanity and the flesh of Christ. But rather lift up your mind to his divinity.

Luther: I do not know of any God except Him who was made flesh, nor do I want to have another.[22]

Both Luther and Zwingli based their arguments on interpretations of Scripture. While they agreed on much (fifteen articles), they could not agree on the real presence. Hermann Sasse suggested that Zwingli's rationalism as a humanist scholar made it difficult for him to transcend what was empirically evident, namely, that a body cannot be present in two places at the same time, much less simultaneously present on thousands of earthly altars. This became a major impasse.

With the untimely death of Zwingli in battle in 1531, Martin Bucer, the Reformer of Strassburg,[23] saw an opportunity to mediate between the German and Swiss Reformations in the interest of a united Protestant front. Sasse contends that at first Bucer's perspective on Christ's presence was closer to Zwingli's than to Luther's because he believed that "nothing material can help the soul." But since Bucer understood eating (*edere*) the body of Christ as believing (*credere*), Sasse argues that Bucer did not entirely agree with Zwingli's perspective of spiritual participation in the Lord's Supper.[24] The reason is that Bucer still retained Erasmus of Rotterdam's idea that the spiritual eating and drinking does not simply depend on the communicant's belief but also implies the

---

20. Ibid., 256.
21. Ibid.
22. Ibid., 252.
23. Strassburg in the sixteenth century was a German city with a large French minority. When I write of Bucer's work with the German congregations I use the German name "Strassburg;" when I write of Calvin's work with the French-speaking congregation I use the French name "Strasbourg."
24. Ibid., 303–4.

incomprehensible "mysterious presence."[25] Moreover, the religious and political agreement of South German cities with the Lutheran territories of Germany in presenting and subscribing to the Augsburg Confession helped to push Bucer's thought of Christ's presence closer to Luther's position of the "sacramental union" of the bread and wine with Christ's body and blood.[26]

Nevertheless, Gordon Jensen argues that Bucer's conception of the presence of Christ does not entirely embrace the Lutheran concept of "sacramental union," even though Bucer supports Luther's thought on Christ's presence in the bread and wine. Specifically, Bucer has a different understanding from Luther in terms of "who eats" the bread and wine. While Bucer and Luther generally agree with "what is eaten"—Christ's body and blood when the participants eat and drink the bread and wine—Luther held for the communion of the ungodly (*communicatio impiorum*) whereas Bucer was only willing to accept the communion of the unworthy (*communicatio indignorum*).[27] The difference is that for Luther one receives the true body and blood of Christ whether one believes it or not, because the real presence depends on the word of Christ, not on the faith of the communicant. This is a more "objective" approach to the sacrament compared with Bucer's more "subjective approach" of eucharistic reception.[28] He was concerned that Luther's perspective on the Eucharist was too close to the Roman. Bucer argued that receiving Christ's presence depends on the situation of the participant's faith when he or she partakes of the bread and wine.[29] That is, for Bucer the recipients' receiving with faith was a more important issue than for Luther. Furthermore, Bucer does not want to use the German text of the Augsburg Confession but rather the Latin text. This is because he translated the Latin word *exhibere* as "shown," while Luther interpreted it as saying that Christ's body and blood are simply "offered" or "distributed" to the participants.[30] Bucer believes Christ's body and blood are shown in the bread and wine in terms of a "mystical presence"; but he never gives up the importance of the participants' faith in terms of receiving the body and blood of Christ.

Bucer became a mentor to Calvin when the latter came to Strasbourg

25. Ibid., 308.
26. Ibid., 306–7.
27. Gordon A. Jensen, "Luther and Bucer on the Lord's Supper," *Lutheran Quarterly* 27, no. 2 (2013): 167–87, here 175.
28. Ibid., 176.
29. Ibid.
30. Ibid.

to serve as minister to the French Reformed congregation (1539–1541). But Calvin had already been working on his *Institutes of the Christian Religion* (the first edition was published in 1536), and he had given thought to his understanding of the Lord's Supper and the presence of Christ before coming to Strasbourg. Sasse contends that Calvin, like Bucer, does not want to minimize "the efficacy of this sacred mystery . . . it is accomplished by the secret and miraculous virtue of God" during the partaking of the bread and wine.[31] Sasse notes Calvin's use of the terms "really," "truly," "essentially," "substantially" in regard to receiving the body of Christ from his 1536 edition of the *Institutes*.[32] Further, Calvin emphasizes the role of the Holy Spirit and the Sursum Corda ("Therefore lift up your hearts on high, seeking the heavenly things in heaven . . .)" in participating in the body and blood of Christ at the Lord's Supper. This is because Calvin, like Zwingli, believes the physical body of Christ to be in heaven.[33] But unlike Zwingli, Calvin does not consider the bread and wine as mere signs. Owing to human frailty they are necessary. God works through earthly means that affect the body and therefore the mind. Specifically, the Holy Spirit works through these means to draw our hearts and minds to Christ, who is at the right hand of God.

Bard Thompson argues that we cannot ignore the importance of the Communion exhortation in Calvin's liturgy. It can be compared with the exhortations in Bucer's liturgy. Bucer has influenced Calvin's liturgical ideas on the Lord's Supper, but Calvin has his own theological understandings.[34] The exhortation in the Communion service in Calvin's Geneva shows Calvin's understanding of faith. We hear

> His [Christ's] word to us, to invite us to His table . . . we do not have perfect faith . . . nevertheless, since our Lord has granted us the grace of having His gospel graven on our hearts . . . that we may follow His righteousness and His Holy commandments, let us be assured that the sins and imperfections that remain in us will not prevent Him from receiving us and making us worthy partakers of his spiritual table.[35]

Calvin reveals here a different perspective from Bucer on the role of "faith" in receiving Communion. Bucer's receptionism makes the real

---

31. Sasse, 324.
32. Ibid., 325.
33. Ibid. Bard Thompson, *Liturgies of the Western Church* (1961; repr., Philadelphia: Fortress, 1989), 187.
34. Thompson, *Liturgies of the Western Church*, 189.
35. *John Calvin: Writings on Pastoral Piety*, ed. and trans. Elsie Anne McKey, Classics of Western Spirituality (Mahwah, NJ: Paulist, 2002), 132.

presence of Christ dependent on the faith of the communicant. For Calvin, the body of Christ is not received *because* of the faith of the participants, because Calvin perceives the weakness of faith in human beings. Nevertheless, our "sins and imperfections" will not prevent Christ from receiving us at his spiritual table.

Moreover, for Calvin "faith" is not the primary requirement to receive the bread and wine. Calvin contends that all participants in Holy Communion are sinful and imperfect. He is more concerned with those who receive the bread and wine "without discerning the body [of Christ]," following the Pauline admonishment (1 Cor 11:29). "Discernment"—knowledge, understanding—is more important to Calvin than faith. Wandel notes that in philosophic terms epistemology—how we know—is important in Calvin's *Institutes*. Furthermore, she notes, for Calvin the Lord's Supper is not "a single act" but a repeated action intended to deepen and develop "a process" of faith development in discerning the body of Christ.[36] Calvin's main focus is to avoid "wrong understanding" by the communicants in partaking and experiencing the body and blood of Christ in the Lord's Supper.[37] Calvin's fencing of the table serves the purpose of excluding ungodly and immoral persons and helping participants examine themselves before they partake the body and blood of Christ.

Calvin taught that the earthly signs are received by the body to focus the mind on Christ, who is in heaven, and that the Holy Spirit lifts up our minds to where Christ is. Hence he taught a "real spiritual presence" because the Holy Spirit is at work to join us in union with Christ through the sacrament. In that sense Calvin could agree with Lutherans that we receive the body and blood of Christ *with* the bread and wine (the preposition in the *variata* edition of the Augsburg Confession prepared by Melanchthon in 1540), but not *in* the bread and wine (the *invariata* edition in 1530).

John Knox, the assumed author of the "Black Rubric" in the 1552 Prayer Book of King Edward VI of England (about which more later), profited from Calvin's tutelage when he was a refugee in Geneva during the reign of the Catholic Mary Tudor. He prepared for the worship of the English exiles in Geneva *The Forme of Prayers* (1556), which was "approved by the famous and godly learned man, John Calvin."[38] At the death of Queen Mary and the accession of the Protestant Elizabeth,

---

36. Wandel, *The Eucharist in the Reformation*, 140.
37. Ibid.
38. Thompson, *Liturgies of the Western Church*, 295.

Knox was not welcome back in England because he had written a tract against "the monsterous reign of women." So he returned to Scotland. There he influenced the first Scots Confession, which "utterly damn[s] the vanity of those who affirm sacraments to be nothing else but naked and bare signs." The approved doctrine as set forth in that confession is fully seen in the Communion exhortation in *The Forme of Prayers*: "We spiritually eate the flesh of Christ, and drink his bloude; then we dwell in Christ, and Christ in us; we be one with Christ, and Christ with us."[39]

The English situation and the Anglican Reformation is more complicated. The leading English Reformer was Thomas Cranmer, archbishop of Canterbury. He was also the principal author and editor of the Book of Common Prayer in its 1549 and 1552 versions. But all of the Protestant views on the Eucharist on the Continent made their way to England. Cranmer himself was at various times in personal contact with the leading Continental Reformers, including Lutheran pastor Andreas Osiander in Nuremberg, Martin Bucer (who was offered and accepted a professorship at Oxford at the end of his life), and other Swiss Reformers. But other leading churchmen in England had their own views, some more traditional and others more radical than Cranmer's. While Cranmer rejected transubstantiation, he did hold with Cyprian "that we be partakers of the Spirit of God, and most purely joined unto Christ, and spiritually fed with his flesh and blood; so that now the said mystical bread is both a corporal food for the body, and a spiritual food for the soul."[40] This strikes me as close to a Calvinist view of the sacrament. The same concept is found in the exhortation to the communicants to repent of one's sins before eating and drinking since "the benefit is great, if with a truly penitent heart and liuely faith, we receiue that holy Sacrament (for then we spirituallye eate the fleshe of Christ, and drynke hys bloud, then we dwel in Christ and Christ in us, we be one with Christ and Christ with us)."[41]

The Book of Common Prayer was not solely authored by Cranmer; there was a committee, even though Cranmer exerted considerable leadership by reason of his library, knowledge, and international contacts. The finished product had to be steered through the convocation of the church and finally required acts of uniformity passed by Parliament and the approval of the king. Cranmer's personal views were a

39. Ibid., 292.
40. Thomas Cranmer, *A Defense of the True and Catholic Doctrine of the Sacrament of the Body and Blood of Our Savior Christ* (1550), ed. Charles H. H. Wright (London: Charles J. Thynne, 1908; reprint Eugene, OR: Wipf & Stock, 2004), 75.
41. *The First and Second Prayer Books of Edward VI*, Everyman's Library 448 (London: Dent, 1910), 385.

work in progress, and when he changed his mind and in what theological direction has been much debated. Comparing the textual, structural, and rubrical changes between the 1549 Prayer Book and the 1552 Prayer Book makes an interesting exercise in liturgical theology.[42] But whatever Cranmer's personal views, he must be viewed as a political as well as a theological figure, with a high sense of responsibility for the well-being of the realm. The Reformation in England went as far as circumstances would allow at any given time, and sometimes farther than some pockets of the population would tolerate, as witness the rebellions in the north country during Henry VIII's reign and in Cornwall and Devonshire during the reign of Edward VI.

Since I am concerned here with the understanding of eucharistic presence in the various traditions, I will simply note the changes in the words of administration of the sacrament in the successive editions of the Prayer Book.

> 1549: The body of our Lorde Jesus Christs whiche was geuen for thee, preserue thy bodye and soule unto euerlasting lyfe.

> The bloude of our Lorde Jesus Christe which was shed for thee, preserue thy bodye and soule unto euerlastyng lyfe.[43]

> 1552: Take and eate this, in remembraunce that Christ dyed for thee, and feede on him in thy hearte by faythe, with thanksgeuing.

> Drinke this in remembraunce that Christ's bloude was shed for thee, and be thankfull.[44]

The 1549 formula allows for a belief in the real presence. The 1552 formula seems Zwinglian, in that the signs are not even named beyond "this" and eating and drinking are reminding us of Christ's death but not connecting us now with Christ in his body and blood. The 1559 Prayer Book was the 1552 Prayer Book restored at the beginning of the reign of Elizabeth I by a third Act of Uniformity passed by Parliament. However, the two previous formulas of administration were joined together, allowing for a belief in the real presence. This com-

---

42. Here I note only two important studies: Aidan Kavanagh, *The Concept of Eucharistic Memorial in the Canon Revisions of Thomas Cranmer, Archbishop of Canterbury 1533-1556* (St. Meinrad, IN: Abbey Press, 1964); Colin Buchanan, *What Did Cranmer Think He Was Doing?* (Bramcote, UK: Grove, 1976).

43. *First and Second Prayer Books*, 225.

44. Ibid., 389.

bined formula continued in subsequent editions of the Book of Common Prayer (1604, 1662).

We should note that in 1784 John Wesley prepared a Communion service for the American Methodists that was based on the 1662 Book of Common Prayer that used the same words of administration.[45] John Wesley's understanding of the eucharistic presence was typically Anglican, and Charles Wesley's eucharistic hymns reference Christ's real presence, including the presence of Christ's sacrifice, as in the hymn "Victim Divine, your grace we claim," which ends with the line "and show your very presence here."

The extent to which the teachings of the Reformers are held today by their spiritual descendants, five centuries removed, would be a worthy study. I note as an example that in the nineteenth century when John Williamson Nevin of the German Reformed Seminary in Mercersburg, Pennsylvania, published his book on *The Mystical Presence* (1846)[46] to teach Calvin's eucharistic theology, the Presbyterian Charles Hodge at Princeton Theological Seminary thought it was heresy within the Reformed tradition. The debate between them centered on the interpretation of the various orthodox Reformed confessions promulgated between 1559 and 1563.[47] Hodge viewed these confessions as a compromise between Zwingli's memorialist views and Calvin's emphasis on sacramental signs. Nevin held that these confessions are pure Calvinist and that for Calvin terms such as "sign" and "signify" always include the conviction in Calvin's mind of the actual presence of the thing signified. To Hodge, this was moving toward the Catholic view of presence.

From my informal survey of students in courses I have taught (both in North America and in Asia) as to what their congregants think about the Lord's Supper, it would seem that many Protestants around the world are Zwinglian in their understanding and regard the Lord's Supper simply as a memorial reenactment of Jesus's last supper with his disciples to put the communicants in mind of Jesus's passion. However, James White pointed out that when we label current beliefs "Zwinglian" we have to factor in the change of worldviews between

---

45. Thompson, *Liturgies of the Western Church*, 432.
46. John Williamson Nevin, *The Mystical Presence: A Vindication of the Reformed or Calvinistic Doctrine of the Holy Eucharist* (1846; repr, Hamden, CT: Archon, 1963).
47. See Jonathan G. Boromo, *Incarnation and Sacrament: The Eucharistic Controversy between Charles Hodge and John Williamson Nevin* (Eugene, OR: Wipf & Stock, 2010). Nevin found support for his views in the Confession of Basel, art. 6; First Helvetic Confession, art. 20 and 23; Gallican Confession, art. 36, 37; Second Helvetic Confession, art. 21; Heidelberg Catechism, q. 75, 76; Westminster Confession 29.7; Westminster Larger Catechism, q. 168, 170.

the early sixteenth century and the post-eighteenth-century Enlightenment era. Zwingli lived and worked within a sacralized universe; Western people today no longer do. "The world of Zwingli saw God, far from being absent, as *intervening* in the midst of the worshiping congregation."[48] For Zwingli, God was present and active in the preaching of the Word and the administration of the sacraments. He also believed that Christ was present in the congregation. The church was the body transformed by the celebration of the Lord's Supper, not the elements.

In this regard, Jeffrey Truscott points out that some Baptists believe that the memorial of Christ's death in the Lord's Supper has the effect of spiritually nourishing believing participants, but "this presence is not different from the Lord's presence in any other act of worship or devotion."[49] The same may be said of Pentecostals, who see the Holy Spirit at work in many concrete ways. Most Baptists and Pentecostals refer to the Lord's Supper as an "ordinance" rather than as a sacrament. In many Protestant congregations, especially among the evangelicals, the Lord's Supper does not receive primary place in their worship. It may be celebrated monthly. Even many Lutheran congregations in North America do not offer Holy Communion every Sunday. But I would like to believe that Lutherans still cling to Luther's dogged defense of the real presence of the body and blood of Christ received in the bread and wine.

In that regard the *way* in which the sacrament is received becomes very important, since, as I have emphasized, what we do with our bodies affects our minds. As Calvin so clearly understood, bodily actions and repeated behavior form theological belief.[50]

Administration of the Sacrament

How we receive the sacrament bodily is determined by how it is administered. In the Eastern churches communicants receive the consecrated sacramental bread broken into a large chalice of consecrated wine. The communicants form a line and approach the priest or bishop and receive the body and blood of Christ from a common spoon. They

---

48. James F. White, *Protestant Worship: Traditions in Transition* (Louisville: Westminster John Knox, 1989), 60.
49. Jeffrey A. Truscott, *The Sacraments: A Practical Guide*, Christian Heritage Rediscovered 22 (New Delhi, India: Christian World Imprints, 2016), 309.
50. This is demonstrated in a practical way, and with reference to Calvin's understanding, in Hwarang Moon, *Engraved upon the Heart: Children, the Cognitively Challenged, and Liturgy's Influence on Faith Formation* (Eugene, OR: Wipf & Stock, 2015).

receive the elements standing in honor of the risen Christ. This is still the common practice.

In the Catholic Church of the West, according to *Ordo Romanus Primus* (ca. 700), communicants at a pontifical Mass went to a Communion station, received a piece of consecrated bread, and drank the consecrated wine from a vat using a straw (*syphus*). By the late Middle Ages communicants came forward to the altar steps and knelt (a posture that variously displayed humility or penitence) to receive only the body of Christ. The chalice was not usually administered to lay communicants. All Christians received Communion on Easter Sunday. But most received Communion only a few times a year. This was the situation the Reformers encountered.

All the Protestant Reformers restored the cup to lay communicants. Zwingli gave attention to further changes when he implemented liturgical changes in Zurich in 1525. Thompson describes Zwingli's emphasis on the participation of the congregation in his ordering of the Lord's Supper. Zwingli states specifically that the Communion Table be placed "at the front of the nave, in the midst of the people who were seated round about."[51] Further, he notes that the place of the Table does not mean the offering place of the priest alone to God but "a congregational table for the new family of God." After the narrative institution, the delivering of the bread and wine is clearly seen by the congregation since the plates and cups are passed through the congregation and the administration is accompanied by no music and no more speaking. Zwingli wanted to help the congregation to deeply experience "itself as the Body of Christ" without any distractions.[52]

A year later, in his treatise *The German Mass and Order of Service*, Luther suggested that "In the true mass . . . the altar should not remain where it is, and the priest should face the people as Christ doubtlessly did in the Last Supper. But let that await its own time."[53] Its own time was long in coming in Lutheran practice. No matter where the altar was placed, Lutheran ministers continued to face the altar for the consecration, and the communicants continued to come forward and kneel to receive the bread and cup.

Martin Bucer brokered a typical compromise between Zwingli and the Lutherans in Strassburg. A Communion Table was set up at the

---

51. Thompson, *Liturgies of the Western Church*, 145.
52. Ibid.
53. Martin Luther, *Liturgy and Hymns*, in *Luther's Works*, ed. Ulrich S. Leupold (Philadelphia: Fortress, 1965), 53:69.

front of the nave, the ministers stood behind it for the consecration, and the people came forward and received the bread and cup standing.

In England, in 1550, an ordinance required the removal of all stone altars and ordered a plain wooden table to be set up "lengthwise" in the choir. In the divided choirs of English churches communicants would assemble in the south choir stalls and the priest would stand on the north side of the table facing them for the consecration. The rubric to kneel at the table was left in the 1552 Prayer Book at Cranmer's insistence, although over Knox's vehement opposition.[54] A Declaration concerning Kneeling, printed in black instead of the usual red for rubrics, was inserted as the Prayer Book was going to print. It was an attempt, without the authority of Parliament, to deny any connection between kneeling and the corporal presence of Christ in the sacramental elements of bread and wine. The 1552 declaration read, in part, in relation to kneeling at the time of receiving the bread and wine:

> Leste yet the same kneelyng myght be thought or taken otherwyse, we dooe declare that it is not ment thereby, that any adoracion is doone, or oughte to bee doone, eyther unto the Sacramentall bread and wyne there bodily receyued, or unto anye reall and essencial presence, there beeyng of Christ's naturall fleshe and bloude. For as concernynge the Sacramentall bread and wynee, they remayne still in theyr verye natural substaunces, and therefore may not be adored, for that were Idolatrye to be abhorred of all faythfyll Christians. And as concernynge the natural body and blood of our savior Christ, they are in heauen and not here. For it is against the trueth of Christes true natural bodye, to be in more places then in one, at one tyme.[55]

This "Black Rubric" was removed in the Elizabethan Prayer Book of 1559, and Anglicans continued to kneel for reception of Holy Communion.

The Reformed were more consistent in forbidding kneeling to receive Communion. Although Calvin was ever mindful of what liturgical practice could do to form faith, and recognized that kneeling stimulated prayer and was pleasing to God, he knew that kneeling for Communion was associated with eucharistic adoration and discouraged it.[56] The practice was vehemently condemned in the 1563 Heidelberg Catechism (expanded version).

54. Diarmaid MacCulloch, *Thomas Cranmer: A Life* (New Haven: Yale University Press, 1996), 525–30.
55. *First and Second Prayer Books*, 393.
56. Benjamin Charles Milner, *Calvin's Doctrine of the Church*, Studies in the History of Christian Thought 5 (Leiden: Brill, 1970), 159–61.

Figure 7. Lithograph of "The Lord's Supper in a Scanian Church" (southern Sweden) by Bengt Nordenberg, 1860s. Holding a paten with hosts the priest invites the communicants to draw near to receive Holy Communion. They kneel in adoration of the presence of Christ in the sacrament at the communion rail covered with a houseling cloth. Notice the life size crucifix above the altar with Mary of Mother of our Lord next to the cross. Reprinted from *The Church of Sweden: Past and Present* (Allhem: Malmö, 1960).

Kneeling before the altar remained the posture for receiving Communion in the Catholic, Lutheran, Anglican, and Methodist Churches until the liturgical renewal after the Second Vatican Council. Low Communion railings were installed that enabled people to kneel with greater ease. Both Catholics and Lutherans laid cloths over these rails as they would over a table. These houseling cloths provided a semblance of eating and drinking at a table, albeit on one's knees. By the late twentieth century it became more common for communicants to process to Communion stations, usually at the head of the center aisle but sometimes also off to the side, and receive the elements standing. However, in all of these traditions kneeling to receive the sacrament remains the custom. In my congregation in Evanston, Illinois, kneeling was customary, but during the fifty days of Easter (with a nod to canon 20 of the Council of Nicaea, which forbade Christians from kneeling on Sundays and during the Paschal season[57]) we administered the sacrament to communicants who stood at the chancel step. Standing to receive Communion was encouraged by removing the chancel railings and the kneeling cushions. But one elderly woman continued to kneel anyway without the railing or a cushion. In following years, out of concern for the elderly who would try to kneel even without the aid of the rails to steady themselves, we left the rails in even during Eastertide. Piety and habit can trump both tradition and innovation.

---

57. See Gabriel Radle, "Embodied Eschatology: The Council of Nicaea's Regulation of Kneeling and Its Reception across Liturgical Traditions (Part 1)," *Worship* 90 (2016): 345–69.

8

Fencing the Table: Eucharistic Initiation, Fellowship, Reconciliation

Christianity entered the world as a meal fellowship.[1] There has never been a time when the Eucharist, the Mass, the Lord's Supper (as it is variously named) has not been at the center of the church's life, even if it has not been celebrated on every Lord's Day in some Christian traditions. When John Calvin, for example, settled on the Antecommunion as the main Sunday service in Geneva because he could not get the city council to approve celebrating the Lord's Supper every Lord's Day, it was with the idea that this liturgy of the Word pointed toward completion in the full Communion service, even if that completion occurred only four times a year. This liturgical decision was also embraced by Lutherans and Anglicans in the Reformation era. In Lutheran practice, if there were no communicants the service of the Word ended after the sermon with the litany or a general prayer, the Lord's Prayer, and a benediction. But Luther and his colleagues preached to encourage the faithful to receive Communion more frequently. As long as there were

---

1. Gordon Lathrop, *The Four Gospels on Sunday: The New Testament and the Reform of Christian Worship* (Minneapolis: Fortress, 2012), 39–59. See also Frank C. Senn, *The People's Work: A Social History of the Liturgy* (Minneapolis: Fortress, 2006), 34–42, and Paul F. Bradshaw and Maxwell E. Johnson, *The Eucharistic Liturgies: Their Evolution and Interpretation* (Collegeville, MN: Liturgical, 2012), 1–24.

communicants registered, after being examined and absolved, the full Mass was celebrated on Sundays and festivals (Apology of the Augsburg Confession, article 24).

Just because the Lord's Supper, the Mass, the Eucharist has been at the center of the church's life, there has been a concern throughout the history of the church to guard its special character, its holiness, its integrity. This has involved "fencing the table." Who is invited to the meal? Who is excluded? We will see in the ancient church that the unbaptized were excluded from participating in the Eucharist. Heretics and penitents were also barred from the Table. Never in the history of the church has the invitation to receive Communion been extended to everyone until recent times when some pastors and congregations have practiced an "open table" in the name of "radical hospitality."

Radical Hospitality

What has led to this new open access to the table? No church body made this radical form of "open Communion" an official policy before pastors begin practicing it. They reason: we invite people to come to church. The church sign says, "All Are Welcome." But as the frequency of celebration of Holy Communion increases in Protestant churches, we have a situation in which people who respond to our open invitation to attend worship have to wonder whether they are also welcome to partake of the eucharistic meal. There has been a feeling that guests should not feel excluded. It goes against the grain of our culture to invite people to an event at which there is food and drink and then tell them that it is not for them. Some have thought that Holy Communion can even be a gateway leading to fuller participation in the life of the church and perhaps to baptism. This, of course, would be a reversal of the traditional journey from font to table.

Methodists in particular have argued that John Wesley regarded the Eucharist as a "converting sacrament." But this did not imply that he was using it for evangelism purposes. The people to whom Wesley was preaching and who were drawn into the Methodist societies were already baptized. Rather, the sacrament was for the strengthening of the faith and the continuing transformation of the baptized. Yet Methodists, along with some Anglicans, ELCA Lutherans, Presbyterians, and the United Church of Christ have been at the forefront of the "open table."

A theological rationale has been developed that points to the inclusiveness of Jesus's meals in the gospels with tax collectors and sinners as well as scribes and Pharisees and his feeding of multitudes on the hillsides of the Sea of Galilee. (Given the two feedings of multitudes of five thousand and four thousand in Matthew and Mark, this was undoubtedly done more than once.)

In this regard, a book that has been persuasive to many advocates of the "open table" is Richard Beck's *Unclean*. He is an experimental psychologist who admits that he is not an exegete or a theologian, although he says he tried to do his homework in writing a book on a psychological theme for church people. Beck begins with Jesus's words to the Pharisees in Matthew 9:13, "Go and learn what this means, 'I desire mercy, not sacrifice.'" Jesus assumed that those who were scandalized by his presence at the table with "many tax collectors and sinners" had not learned the lesson of Hosea, "I desire mercy, not sacrifice" (Hos 6:6). Beck aims to follow Jesus's direction and unravel this puzzle using both contemporary psychological research and theological reasoning. He sees mercy and sacrifice as "two impulses pulling in opposite directions" and as "intrinsically incompatible." Mercy reaches outside the boundaries of human societies to be inclusive and welcoming and is inherently hospitable. Sacrifice withdraws for the sake of maintaining its boundaries of purity. Beck proposes that the psychological issue involved here is disgust or revulsion at what is unclean. "The central argument of this book," he writes, "is that the psychology of disgust and contamination regulate how many Christians reason with and experience notions of holiness, atonement, and sin. In a related way, the psychology of disgust and contamination also regulate societal boundaries and notions of hospitality within the church."[2]

There is a lot of value in Beck's "meditations" for a fresh consideration of the church's approach to hospitality and inclusion. He sees implications of this divide between mercy and sacrifice in all areas of the church's life, but especially at every eucharistic table. Who is included? Who is excluded? What are the limits of mercy? What are the failings of sacrifice? He understands the purpose of sacrifices, in the ancient sense, to purify the individual or the community making them, and therefore they should be protected from contamination by a zone of holiness.

What Beck does not bring out so clearly is that God instituted the

---

2. Richard Beck, *Unclean: Meditations on Purity, Hospitality, and Mortality* (Eugene, OR: Wipf & Stock, 2011), 4.

sacrificial cult in the Old Testament precisely as a merciful act. The sacrifices were means of grace by which God's people could draw near to God to receive a blessing since sinful human beings could not directly approach a holy God. But one had to be in a state of ritual purity to offer the sacrifices (which, let's face it, were disgusting spectacles from our cultural perspective who seldom see how animals are slaughtered for our meat). The Lord's Supper too, Beck rightfully notes, has a disgusting motif at its center: eating Jesus's body and drinking his blood. No matter how much we sanitize our ritual practices, for example, by using individual wafers and glasses of wine to keep from being contaminated by someone else's germs in sharing a common meal, the sacrament is still about body and blood.

Radical Intimacy

A ritual issue we need to consider is that not all meals are the same in terms of hospitality. There is no question that the evangelists, writing decades after the time of Jesus's ministry, wove eucharistic overtones into their narratives of the mass feedings (especially in John 6). But on the literal level Jesus was tending to the needs of those who had followed him out to these deserted areas to hear his teaching; he would not send them home empty. By this gesture he showed himself as the messianic king who took care of the needs of the people. In fact, in John 6:15 Jesus has to escape the crowd because they wanted to make him king.

But the "Last Supper" was different. This was an intimate gathering of Jesus and his disciples in an upper room to observe the Passover Seder (according to the Synoptic Gospels) or a meal before the Passover (as the Fourth Gospel states). Jesus knew that his betrayal, arrest, trial, and execution were imminent. The Gospel of John, which does not describe the meal itself, provides Jesus's "Farewell Discourse" to the disciples in chapters 14–17, concluding with his "high priestly prayer" in chapter 17 "that they may be one" as he and the Father are one.

The gospels also report other meals between Jesus and his disciples after his resurrection. These include the supper at Emmaus in Luke 24 with two disciples whose hearts were warmed as he opened to them the Scriptures as they walked along the road. But they didn't recognize him as their Master until he "broke bread," undoubtedly saying the blessing (berakah) over the bread that was typical of Jewish custom, but which perhaps Jesus had made his own. The exact prayer formularies for the meals that we have in the Mishnah (ca. 200 CE) were not fixed at the time of Jesus. Jesus also served breakfast on the beach in John 21 to the fishermen disciples who had followed his instruction to return to Galilee after his resurrection, where they would see him. The purpose of this meal was reconciliation with the disciples, who had abandoned him at the time of his arrest, trial, and crucifixion. The very act of providing meal hospitality demonstrated his gesture of reconciliation. There was also the matter of the rehabilitation of Simon Peter, who had denied him three times. Three times, therefore, Jesus asked Simon Peter, "Do you love me?" After each affirmation of Peter, "Yes, Lord, you know that I love you," Jesus told him, with increasing intensity, to "feed my sheep," "tend my lambs."

The implications of Jesus's institution of this special meal ("Do this for the remembrance of me") is that it is a way for Jesus to remain connected with his disciples between the time of his ascension and his return in glory. The earliest iteration of Jesus's instituting command is in 1 Corinthians 11:23–25. The apostle Paul comments on the Lord's Supper tradition (*paradosis*), which he received and passed on to the Corinthians, "For as often as you eat this bread and drink the cup, you proclaim the Lord's death until he comes" (1 Cor 11:26).

Of course, St. Paul recites this tradition of the Lord's Supper in the context of addressing problems with the practice of the Lord's Supper in the Corinthian congregation. It was a meal laden with difficulties as the early church tried to figure out how to order its socially inclusive life and observe a common meal for all its members.

We have seen that the social-cultural context of the Lord's Supper in the early church was a meal (*deipnon*) with a symposium, a drinking party with discussion. This cultural backdrop undoubtedly also influenced the development of the Jewish Passover Seder in the diaspora.[3] The canonical gospels present a symposium on the night Jesus was betrayed that left the disciples drowsy and not able to watch with Jesus in the Garden of Gethsemane while he prayed to the Father that the next cup would pass from him. The symposium structure can best be seen in John 13–17. In the context of a meal, which is mentioned but not described, Jesus performs the dramatic action of washing his disciples' feet. This serves as the basis for discussion of the new commandment Jesus lays on his disciples (now called "friends"), that they love

---

3. Blake Leyerle, "Meal Customs in the Greco-Roman World," in *Passover and Easter: Origin and History to Modern Times. Two Liturgical Traditions*, vol. 5, ed. Paul F. Bradshaw and Lawrence A. Hoffman (Notre Dame: University of Notre Dame Press, 1999), 29–61.

one another as he has loved them. Because this is a "last supper," there is also much discussion about Jesus's impending departure from his disciples, concluding with Jesus's high priestly prayer to his Father.

There is no reason not to think that the Lord's Supper in the Corinthian church also followed the format of a meal (*deipnon*) with a symposium (*symposion*). The cup with its thanksgiving in Paul's text is "after supper." Is it possible that the words of Jesus over the cup cited by Paul—"Do this, as often as you drink it, in remembrance of me"—refer to the multiple cups of the symposium, and not to the frequency of the gatherings to share the meal, since a comparable specification "as often as you *eat* this" does not accompany the command "do this" in connection with the bread? In other words, this banquet as a whole is the Lord's Supper, and the Lord himself is received—in his body and blood—throughout the meal in the bread that is broken and the multiple cups that are shared. References in 1 Corinthians 11:21 to some becoming drunk (as did the guests in Plato's *Symposion*) suggest that this was a real possibility. Hence, restraint is called for, not only in waiting for the slaves to arrive before the patrons and clients begin to eat, but also in the amount of wine consumed. There were obviously a lot of problems with the celebration of the Lord's Supper at Corinth. This advises us against taking the early church as a model for our liturgical practices today. It took the church a while to get the meal right, and the church has had a tendency to go off track all through its history. But who were the participants included in this Lord's Supper in the context of a *deipnon* with a symposium?

Eucharist as Initiation

St. Paul mentions the sharing of the various gifts of the members at this assembly of the church, including speaking in tongues. His concern in 1 Corinthians 14:23 that the tongue-speakers might baffle outsiders who might enter the gathering unless their utterances were interpreted raises the question of who attended this supper-symposium. Might the host have invited guests who were not in the congregation? It is unlikely that people would have walked into a private dinner party from off the street. Did the meal guests include some who were unbaptized? Or did nonmembers of the church come only for the symposium? Was the wine imbibing that might have occurred all during the symposium considered a part of the Lord's Supper, or was it unrelated to the sacramental meal, which ended with a thanksgiving over the final cup of the supper?

We don't know the answers to these questions, and we can't argue from silence one way or the other. But it is interesting that the issue of the unbaptized attending the Lord's Supper was raised in the *Didache* at the end of the first century/beginning of the second. The eucharistic prayers in chapters 9 and 10 of the *Didache* indicate that the Lord's Supper was still being eaten in the context of an actual community meal, because the heading above chapter 9 says "Concerning the Eucharist." The compiler of this oldest church manual says, "You must not let anyone eat or drink of your Eucharist except those who are baptized in the Lord's Name" (*Didache* 9.5).[4]

Half a century later Justin Martyr reports to the Roman Senate (ca. 150 CE) that no one is allowed to partake of "the food we call Eucharist" except one who "believes that the things we teach are true, and has been washed with the washing that is for the forgiveness of sins and rebirth, and is living as Christ enjoined" (*First Apology* 66).[5]

The *Apostolic Tradition*, which earlier scholars dated in the early third century but more likely was compiled in the early fourth century, although some material may be as old as the second,[6] not only excludes the unbaptized (catechumens) from the Eucharist but also excludes them from the offering and the kiss of peace ("their kiss is not yet pure"). But after their water bath they will be received by the bishop in the banquet hall with the laying on of hands and chrismation and will then receive their first Communion with the faithful. They will receive cups of water and milk and honey as well as the cup of wine, signifying that the Eucharist is an internal cleansing corresponding to the outward cleansing of baptism and that they have arrived in the promised land.[7]

What we see emerging in ancient Christianity is a process of initiation in which those who came into the orbit of the church's life were led by stages from their old life as pagans to their new life in Christ.

4. Kurt Niederwimmer, *The Didache: A Commentary*, trans. Linda M. Maloney, Hermeneia (Minneapolis: Fortress, 1998), 144. Niederwimmer is not able to see the eucharistic meal described in chapters 9 and 10 as a sacramental meal; that meal follows in chapter 14. I do not see any distinction between a community meal and the Lord's Supper. Chapter 14 in my view refers to the discipline of fencing the table, not to a sacramental meal that is not otherwise discussed in this manual that discusses all the ordinances of the church.

5. Cyril C. Richardson, ed. and trans., *Early Christian Fathers*, Library of Christian Classics 1 (Philadelphia: Westminster, 1953), 286.

6. Paul F. Bradshaw and Maxwell E. Johnson, *The Eucharistic Liturgies*, 40.

7. Paul F. Bradshaw, Maxwell E. Johnson, and L. Edward Phillips, eds., *The Apostolic Tradition: A Commentary*, Hermeneia (Minneapolis: Fortress, 2002), 120.

There was a clear sense of a boundary between "this world" and the life of the world to come that had to be crossed in the process of Christian initiation.

In the process of initiation in any society the initiates come to the realization that the conventional view of reality that they had taken for granted is not the real view. The purpose of rites of initiation is to bring initiates, especially young people, into living contact with this ultimate reality. To accomplish this, the initiates are removed from society and are sequestered with a group of initiates under the supervision of the elders of the tribe. They go through learning and ordeals and are eventually incorporated into their new status in the social group.[8]

Arnold van Gennep compared all rites of passage to the process of taking a journey.[9] The ritual structure includes leave-taking (preliminal rites), passage or transition (liminal rites), and arrival (rites of incorporation). Victor Turner focused on the value of the betwixt-and-between liminal rites.[10] The initiates who go through the ordeal form a common bond that Turner called "communitas." Those who experience communitas in the liminal experience become a source of renewal for the whole social group. The catechumenate in the ancient church, and potentially as revived in the current rites of Christian initiation of adults (RCIA), provides a liminal experience that not only serves the needs of formation of new Christians but also the renewal of the Christian community with an influx of well-formed new members.

In the liturgies that developed after the fourth century the catechumens were dismissed from the assembly after the liturgy of the Word (which came to be called "the liturgy of the catechumens") with a blessing and exorcism. They were remanded to the supervision of the catechists. They could not participate in the kiss of peace, the offering, or receive Communion. The kiss of peace and offertory marked the transition to "the liturgy of the faithful." Holy Communion was the meal of the baptized.

The Communion Table continued to be fenced off, especially in the Eastern liturgies, with the dismissal of the catechumens with a blessing before the offertory and the deacon's announcement, "Let all catechumens depart." Then: "the doors, the doors"—close the doors. The

---

8. See Mircea Eliade, *Rites and Symbols of Initiation: The Mysteries of Birth and Rebirth*, trans. Willard R. Trask (New York: Harper & Row, 1958).

9. Arnold van Gennep, *The Rites of Passage*, trans. Monika B. Vizedom and Gabrielle L. Caffee (Chicago: University of Chicago Press, 1960).

10. Victor Turner, *The Ritual Process: Structure and Anti-structure* (Chicago: Aldine, 1969), 94–130.

invitation/admonition "Holy things for the holy people" before the administration of the sacrament indicates that only the initiated may partake. One becomes holy—a person dedicated to God—in Holy Baptism. In this sacrament one is reborn by water and the Holy Spirit (John 3:5). The distinctive thing about Christian baptism is not so much the bath; other religions also have water purification rites. The distinctive thing about Christian baptism is that one receives the gift of the Spirit to be able to discern "the things that are above" (Col 3:1).

In the ritual process of Christian initiation, baptism leads to the eucharistic meal. Holy Communion is actually the goal of Christian initiation. One is not fully a member of the church until one receives first Communion. The ancient church orders indicate how much time and attention was given to preparing seekers for church membership through the processes of the catechumenate, which might last several years, or, in the case of some public officials, a lifetime. The emperor Constantine, for example, was baptized (and therefore communed) on his deathbed. Ambrose was elected bishop of Milan while he was still a catechumen, and had to be baptized before he was ordained a bishop. His famous baptismal candidate Augustine of Hippo was made a catechumen when he was an infant, beginning his journey toward new life by receiving the sign of the cross; but he was not baptized until he was thirty years old.[11] The forty-day season of Lent (Quadragesima) developed as the time in which the catechumens became the elect (candidates chosen for Holy Baptism) and received their final preparation for Holy Baptism and first Holy Communion at the Easter Vigil. Other times for solemn public baptism were Pentecost and Epiphany (especially in the Eastern churches). These days remained occasions for solemn public baptism even as the practice of infant Communion became more normative in the Middle Ages.

In the Western church the bishop retained his prerogative of placing the seal of the Holy Spirit on all the baptized. But the bishop could not be present at every baptism. For the postbaptismal rite that came to be called the sacrament of confirmation the child had to be taken to the bishop or the bishop had to confirm baptized children when he visited the parishes. Over the course of the centuries the interval between the water baptism and confirmation by the bishop generally lengthened.[12] The idea was gradually accepted that infants were not appro-

---

11. See Garry Wills, *Font of Life: Ambrose, Augustine, and the Mystery of Baptism* (New York: Oxford University Press, 2012).

12. J. D. C. Fisher, *Christian Initiation: Baptism in the Medieval West* (London: SPCK, 1965), 120–40.

priate candidates for confirmation. The theological rationale was that the additional gift of the Holy Spirit given in confirmation provided the strengthening one needed to live a mature life of faith. This led to a problem with first Communion. Could a child receive first Communion at baptism, or would first Communion be delayed until after confirmation?

So integral a part was first Communion in the ritual process of Christian initiation—indeed, as I said, it was the goal of Christian initiation—that infants were communed at their baptism. This has remained the practice of the Eastern churches. In the medieval West, however, infant Communion ceased through no fault of the infants. Infants and young children could be communed from the cup, either by sucking the wine off the priest's finger or by intincting the bread in the cup for older children who could swallow the bread. If infants received the wine alone, medieval theology appealed to the doctrine of concomitance, which taught that one received the whole Christ under either element. But growing scrupulosity over spilling the blood of Christ in the transmission of the cup led to the removal of the cup from lay communicants. To this was added the growing practice of individual confession. At the Fourth Lateran Council (1215) auricular confession to a priest before receiving Communion became a requirement for all communicants who had reached an age of discretion (around age seven).[13] In a sense, then, first confession became a part of the process of Christian initiation leading to first Communion. But these developments eliminated the practice of infant Communion in the West.

As initiatory discipline was tightened, especially after the Council of Trent, no child in the Catholic Church would receive first Communion until he or she had been confirmed and had made a confession. The age of first Communion would be minimally age seven. This remains normative Roman Catholic practice. An argument can be made, in terms of Catholic understanding, that confirmation is a completion of baptism, and therefore reserving first Communion until after confirmation makes sense in this sacramental economy.

In the Protestant churches of the Reformation the age of first Communion was even increased because of the emphasis placed on catechesis. In the Reformed churches first Communion followed the confirmation of young adolescents who were between the ages of twelve and fifteen. At first Lutherans abolished a rite of confirmation but insti-

13. Ibid., 101–8.

tuted catechesis of all the youth. First Communion was administered when it seemed right in terms of preparation. When Lutherans instituted a rite of confirmation during the eighteenth century, first Communion followed confirmation.[14]

In these Protestant traditions in the late twentieth century first Communion was removed from the rite of confirmation, which has been construed as an affirmation of baptism,[15] and has been steadily lowered, first to age ten and then downward to very young children. While there are those who have argued for the Communion of all the baptized (including me[16]), there are not many Protestant congregations that practice the Communion of infants at their baptism.[17] In those congregations that practice the open table but do not commune baptized infants it is possible that non-Christians are invited to a Eucharist that does not include all the baptized.

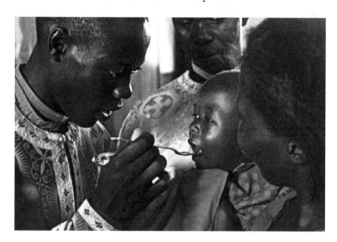

Figure 8a. Communion of an infant in an Orthodox Church.

The Eucharist as a Sign of Church Membership and Fellowship

Since Holy Communion is a sacrament of initiation, what is the status of the unbaptized who partake of the sacramental elements? By receiv-

---

14. See Arthur C. Repp, *Confirmation in the Lutheran Church* (St. Louis: Concordia, 1964).
15. See Jeffrey A. Truscott, *The Reform of Baptism and Confirmation in American Lutheranism* (Lanham, MD and Oxford: Scarecrow Press, 2003), 147–71.
16. Frank C. Senn, "Infant Communion and Church Statements," *Dialog* 18 (1979): 86–87.
17. Jeffrey A. Truscott, *The Sacraments: A Practical Guide* (New Delhi, India: Christian World Imprints, 2016), 362–68. See also Eric W. Gritsch, *Who Gets to Eat? Issues of Admission to the Lord's Table*, ed. Lawrence A. Recla (Delhi, NY: ALPB Books, 2015).

ing the body of Christ into their own bodies, they are united to Jesus Christ. Whether that is for their benefit or detriment must be discerned, as it must be for any communicant. The church has taken seriously the admonition of St. Paul in 1 Cor 11:29, "For all who eat and drink without discerning the body [other ancient authorities read *the Lord's body*], eat and drink judgment against themselves." Interpretations have differed as to whether this means discerning the sacramental body, the ecclesial body, or both, depending on how one understands "the body" (τό σῶμα). Eric Gritsch, in writing about "Issues of Admission to the Lord's Supper: A Lutheran View," cites Günther Bornkamm in support of his view that "Paul related church and sacrament closely." "The body of Christ, which we receive in the bread, implies for Paul directly 'the body of Christ' in which we are bound together in the sacrament. In it we receive the body of Christ and, by receiving it, are and show ourselves to be the body of Christ."[18]

Since those who eat and drink are being joined to the body of Christ, they must be considered to be members of the church. Participation in the Eucharist determines membership in the church as the body of Christ. This is clearly stated in a post-Communion prayer in the 1979 Book of Common Prayer, Holy Eucharist II:

> Almighty and everliving God,
> We thank you for feeding us with the spiritual food
> of the most precious Body and Blood
> of your Son our Savior Jesus Christ;
> and for assuring us in these holy mysteries
> that we are living members of the Body of your Son,
> and heirs of your eternal kingdom.
> And now, Father, send us out
> To do the work you have given us to do,
> To love and serve you
> As faithful witnesses of Christ our Lord.
> To him, to you, and to the Holy Spirit,
> Be honor and glory, now and for ever. Amen.[19]

The practice of communing the unbaptized seemingly makes baptism unnecessary since those who participate in the Lord's Supper are de facto members of the body of Christ. From a theological perspective,

---

18. Eric W. Gritsch, *Who Gets to Eat? Issues of Admission to the Lord's Supper: A Lutheran View*, ed. Lawrence R. Recla, STS (Delhi, NY: ALPB Books, 2015), 31–32. The source of the Bornkamm quote is not given.
19. *The Book of Common Prayer . . . according to the Use of The Episcopal Church* (New York: The Church Hymnal Corporation and Seabury, 1977), 366.

of course, Christian baptism cannot be unnecessary because it conveys the Holy Spirit, who gives the gift of faith needed to discern the body of Christ, both the sacramental and the ecclesiastical bodies of Christ. That the Holy Spirit might work apart from particular means of grace is always possible; the Spirit works faith where and when the Spirit chooses. But we don't know about that. We only know that one must be born again by water and the Holy Spirit (John 3:5). This regeneration has been celebrated in rites of Christian initiation. If the church surrenders an initiatory process for its members, it deprives them of what religions and traditional societies have all provided: access to the spiritual reality that lies behind the cultural facade of the social institution. Only through the process of initiation can Christians come into contact with the purpose of their spiritual traditions and the truth these traditions encode. It serves no good purpose for the church to be composed of uninitiated members. But that is what unbaptized communicants are.

Some advocates of radical hospitality argue that the experience of Communion can lead one to request baptism. This would reverse the direction of initiation from font to table to one of table to font. But if our churches embrace the rites of Christian initiation of adults (RCIA) as a model for making Christians (Tertullian famously said that "Christians are made, not born," and this has been a slogan of the catechumenal process[20]), what do we do with those who have already been communing? Ask them to absent themselves from the table for a season while they go through the catechumenate? Those communicants who become catechumens will, in any event, be dismissed before the liturgy of the faithful with a blessing as the deacon says, "Let all catechumens depart." They will depart to their catechumenal sessions.

Today the concern for extending eucharistic hospitality takes place in religiously pluralistic societies in which people marry those from other Christian denominations or of other faiths. This is not a new concern. From early times local Christian communities had to decide how they would welcome into their eucharistic fellowship at least baptized Christians visiting from other localities.

Werner Elert shows how the Eucharist came to define church fellowship.[21] The idea that the unity of the local church is expressed in the bishop's Eucharist is as old as Ignatius of Antioch (110–115 CE). In his

---

20. See Murphy Center for Liturgical Research, *Made, Not Born: New Perspectives on Christian Initiation and the Catechumenate* (Notre Dame: University of Notre Dame Press, 1976).
21. Werner Elert, *Eucharist and Church Fellowship in the First Four Centuries* (St. Louis: Concordia, 1966).

Letter to the Philadelphians Ignatius warns the congregation, "Be careful . . . to observe a single Eucharist. For there is one flesh of our Lord Jesus Christ, and one cup of his blood that makes us one, and one altar, just as there is one bishop along with the presbytery and the deacons, my fellow slaves. In that way whatever you do is in line with God's will."[22]

Local churches were in fellowship with other local churches if their bishops were in fellowship. If the bishops excommunicated each other (for example, as the bishops of Rome and Asia Minor did during the second century because of disagreement over the dating of Easter—a schism later resolved by Irenaeus of Lyons), their churches were out of fellowship. Individual Christians traveling throughout the Roman world brought letters from their bishop requesting admission to the Eucharist in the churches they visited on their travels. Receiving Communion in the Catholic Church even today means that the communicant is in communion with a local bishop who is in communion with the bishop of Rome. The same eucharistic ecclesiology is practiced in the Eastern Orthodox churches. In this practice you receive Communion only in churches whose bishops are in communion.

We are joined into the fellowship of the church by sharing the sacrament of the body and blood of Christ. But there also emerged the issue in the early church of whether one shares Holy Communion with heretics. Baptism was a fundamental fencing of the table, but another concerned being in one faith at the table. This is reflected in the insertion of the Nicene-Constantinopolitan Creed into the eucharistic liturgy. This was first done in the Byzantine liturgy by Patriarch Timothy of Constantinople (511–518), and it spread to all the Eastern liturgies. It was located after the dismissal of the catechumens, the prayers of the faithful, the kiss of peace, and the entrance with the gifts, so it was clearly intended as the gate to the eucharistic sacrifice. The creed was inserted into the Visigothic liturgy by King Reccared in 589 when he renounced Arianism. It was located right after the Our Father and before Communion. The custom was spread in the Frankish lands under Charlemagne. But the creed was not inserted into the Roman Mass until 1014 under Pope Benedict VIII, who gave into the request of the German emperor Henry II that it be included. Since its place in the Roman Mass was after the Gospel, and it was recited only on Sundays and feast days, the creed was probably serving a more catechetical purpose than a disciplinary one.[23]

---

22. Ignatius of Antioch, *To the Philadelphians* 4 (Richardson, *Early Christian Fathers*, 108–9).

Churches still express fellowship with one another on the basis of whether they can share Holy Communion together. An extension of the fact that one does not eat the Lord's Supper with heretics led to the idea that one does not share Holy Communion with Christians of other denominations. This has been the case among Protestants themselves as well as between Catholics and Protestants. The Orthodox do not share Communion with any Christians who are not within an Orthodox jurisdiction. To receive Communion in the Catholic Church one must be, as I stated above, in communion with a bishop who is in communion with the bishop of Rome. The Catholic Church is actually a communion of twenty-two different rites, only one of which is the Latin or Roman rite. World communions of Anglican, Lutheran, and Reformed churches also emerged in the twentieth century. Only as a result of the ecumenical movement of the twentieth century has this barrier gradually broken down between denominations through a series of agreements enacting eucharistic hospitality (welcoming other Christians to the table) and altar and pulpit fellowship or full communion (sharing ordained ministers at the table).

I was a member of the Lutheran-Episcopal Dialogue in the USA that led to interim Eucharistic hospitality between the LCA and ALC and The Episcopal Church in 1981 and, as ecumenical officer of my ELCA synod, I promoted the "Concordat of Agreement" that was rejected by the ELCA in 1997 and "Called to Common Mission" that was adopted by the ELCA and The Episcopal Church in 2000. These and other ecumenical agreements in doctrine and procedure have been painstakingly worked out. They take seriously agreement in eucharistic faith and practice.

Eucharist and Reconciliation

There can be disagreements within the family that cause separation at the table. The angry family member gets up and leaves or, in the case of a naughty child, is told to leave. So schism happens not only between Christian communities but also within them for reasons of scandal and sin. When this happens reconciliation must occur. This is undoubtedly what is intended by the instruction in chapter 14 of the *Didache*: "Assembling on every Sunday of the Lord's Day, break bread and give thanks, confessing your faults beforehand, so that your sacrifice may be pure. Let no one engaged in a dispute with his comrade

23. See Joseph A. Jungmann, SJ, *The Mass of the Roman Rite: Its Origins and Development*, trans. Francis A. Brunner, CSSR (Westminster, MD: Christian Classics, 1986), 1:467–70.

join you until they have been reconciled, lest your sacrifice be pro-faned."[24] "Confessing your faults" does not here refer to something like a Brief Order for Confession and Forgiveness or even to private confession, which are medieval developments, but to an act of reconciliation. Later church orders like the *Apostolic Constitutions* specified that bishops should hold court and hear cases on Mondays. This would allow the greatest possible time for disputes to be resolved and for reconciliation to be effected before the Sunday Eucharist. Those who remained unreconciled or unrepentant were not admitted to the Eucharist on Sunday until reconciliation and forgiveness had been achieved.

Reconciliation is what "the peace of the Lord" is all about, which in the Roman rite occurs just before Communion but in other rites occurs before the offering of gifts. In the ancient church the greeting of peace was actually the kiss of peace, as Paul says in 1 Cor 16:20, "Greet one another with a holy kiss." Since this letter was read in the assembly, the kiss was to be enacted right there and then in that eucharistic assembly. It was an act of reconciliation among the faithful in this divided community of faith. *The Apostolic Tradition* held that catechumens could not participate in it until they were baptized, because "their kiss is not yet pure." This kiss was a real kiss enacted by all in the eucharistic assembly.[25]

Not surprisingly the kiss moved from being an action to a procla-mation—although in Solemn High Masses in the Roman rite the clergy kissed the clergy in descending hierarchical order. In the late Middle Ages, especially in France and England, a pax board, which was usually a wooden cross with the image of Christ painted on it, was passed through the congregation and kissed by the worshipers at the *Pax Domine sit semper vobiscum* just before the Communion.[26] The purpose of kissing the pax board was the same as the ancient kiss of peace: those present had to be at peace with one another before receiving the sacrament at Mass. Being in a state of reconciled fellowship remained an important consideration for receiving one's Easter Communion.

Martin Luther regarded "the peace of the Lord" as "a public absolution of the sins of the communicants, the true voice of the gospel announcing remission of sin, and therefore the one and most worthy preparation for the Lord's Table, if faith holds to these words as coming

---

24. Niederwimmer, *The Didache*, 194.
25. Michael Philip Penn, *Kissing Christians: Ritual and Community in the Late Ancient Church* (Philadelphia: University of Pennsylvania Press, 2005).
26. John Bossy, *Christianity in the West 1400–1700* (Oxford: Oxford University Press, 1988), 70.

from the mouth of Christ himself."[27] The purpose of the sacrament, as Luther expressed it in the post-Communion prayer in his German Mass, is "to strengthen us . . . in faith toward thee, and in fervent love among us all."[28] Luther had a social, and not just an individualist, view of the Eucharist, especially in his early writings. In his 1519 Treatise *On the Blessed Sacrament of the Holy and True Body of Christ, and the Brotherhoods*, he makes clear how receiving Communion is always a communal matter, gathering us together into God's ongoing care for the life of the world, inserting each of us into a fellowship of beggars who need mercy from God and must show mercy to others.

> When you have partaken of this sacrament, therefore, or desire to partake of it, you must in turn share the misfortunes of the fellowship. . . . Here your heart must go out in love and learn that this is a sacrament of love. As love and support are given to you, you in turn must render love and support to Christ in his needy ones. You must feel with sorrow all the dishonor done to Christ in his holy Word, all the misery of Christendom, all the unjust suffering of the innocent, with which the world is everywhere filled to overflowing. You must fight, work, pray, and—if you cannot do more—have heartfelt sympathy. . . . It is Christ's will, then, that we partake [of the sacrament] frequently, in order that we may remember him and exercise ourselves in this fellowship according to his example.[29]

As Luther encouraged Christians to receive the sacrament of the body and blood of Christ more frequently, he recognized that forms of personal preparation for receiving Communion such as fasting and private confession had been encouraged and even required since the early centuries and have sometimes been a barrier to reception of the sacrament. In his *Small Catechism* Luther admitted that these were commendable practices, "but he is truly worthy and well prepared who believes these words: 'for you' and 'for the forgiveness of sins.'"[30]

Receiving the sacrament in faith is the most important preparation. He also emphasized the forgiveness of sins as the primary gift of Communion. But it's not just personal sins that are forgiven in the sacrament. There are ruptures in relationships. Families and neighbors were always getting into discord. In Luther's time these were one's fellow

---

27. Martin Luther, "An Order of Mass and Communion for the Church at Wittenberg" (1523), in *Luther's Works*, ed. Ulrich S. Leupold (Philadelphia: Fortress, 1965), 53:28–29.
28. Martin Luther, "The German Mass and Order of Service" (1526), in Leupold, *Luther's Works*, 53:84.
29. Martin Luther, *On the Blessed Sacrament of the Holy and True Body of Christ, and the Brotherhoods*, in *Luther's Works*, ed. E. Theodore Bachman (Philadelphia: Fortress, 1960), 35:54–56.
30. Martin Luther, *The Small Catechism* 6 (*The Book of Concord*, ed. Theodore G. Tappert [Philadelphia: Fortress, 1959], 352).

Christians. So the assembly as a whole has to be prepared to worthily celebrate the Lord's Supper. Practices to facilitate this preparation must be put in place. Article 24 of the Apology to the Augsburg Confession testifies that "among us the Mass is celebrated every Lord's Day and on other festivals, when the sacrament is made available to those who wish to partake of it, after they have been examined and absolved."[31] It was expected that communicants would know the basics of the catechism and would have availed themselves of individual confession and absolution. In historic Lutheran practice Saturday afternoon Vespers became a penitential service attended by those who intended to receive Holy Communion on Sunday. After opportunity for individual confession, absolution was pronounced to all with the laying on of hands in bestowal of the blessing of forgiveness to those who had confessed particular sins that disturbed their consciences.

In the ancient church a practice of public penance developed that involved excommunication during the term of penitence and reconciliation when the time of penitence was over. An order of penitents (*ordo paenitentium*) developed that paralleled the order of catechumens (*ordo catechumenorum*). Not surprisingly, the preparation of the penitents for reconciliation occurred simultaneously with the preparation of catechumens for baptism, and the time of preparation of both orders was during Lent (Quadragesima—the forty days). Baptism of the catechumens occurred at the Easter Vigil and reconciliation of the penitents took place on Maundy Thursday. Those enrolled as public penitents included those guilty of grave sins—apostasy, murder, adultery. Some Christians entered the order of penitents voluntarily as a spiritual discipline.[32] Canonical public penance waned as a pastoral practice in the church, although the liturgical rites of excommunication and reconciliation remained in the books.

Excommunication of public sinners received a new emphasis in the Reformed churches of the sixteenth century as a form of church discipline. This emphasis on the fencing of the table in Reformed practice is seen in the list of those who qualified for excommunication in the Exhortation to Communicants in Calvin's "Manner of Celebrating the Supper" in his *Form of Church Prayers* (1542). After the words of institution the minister says,

---

31. *The Book of Concord*, ed. Robert Kolb and Timothy J. Wengert (Minneapolis: Fortress, 2000), 258.
32. Bernhard Poschmann, *Penance and the Anointing of the Sick*, trans. Francis Courtney, SJ (New York: Herder & Herder, 1964), 38–52, 81–99.

We have heard, brethren, how our Lord celebrated his Supper with his disciples, thereby indicating that strangers, and those who are not of the company of the faithful, ought not to be admitted. Therefore, in accordance with this rule, in the name and by the authority of our Lord Jesus Christ, I excommunicate all idolaters, blasphemers, despisers of God, heretics, and all who form private sects to break the unity of the Church, all perjurers, all who rebel against parents or their superiors, all who are seditious, mutinous, quarrelsome or brutal, fornicators, thieves, ravishers, misers, drunkards, gluttons, and all who lead a scandalous and dissolute life. I declare that they must abstain from this holy table, for fear of defiling and contaminating the holy food which our Lord Jesus Christ gives only to his household and believers.[33]

In Geneva those charged with particular infractions that merited excommunication, or those who had previously been excommunicated, were brought before the consistory and examined to see if they were qualified to receive the sacrament or ready to be readmitted to the supper. In most cases they were, upon expression of contrition and evidence of repentance.[34]

We may be put off by these words from Calvin's liturgy today. Postmodern sensibilities are nonjudgmental. Who are we to guard access to the presence of Christ in the Eucharist? Aren't sinners the ones who are especially in need of the grace the sacrament conveys? But in St. Paul's First Letter to the Corinthians the apostle addresses the case of a man who was sleeping with his father's wife. Paul seems almost less scandalized by this than by the fact that the man has not been removed from the congregation's meal fellowship. "Do not even eat with such a one" (1 Cor 5:11). Though absent in body from the congregation, Paul is present in spirit and pronounces excommunication. "When you are assembled, and my spirit is present with the power of our Lord Jesus, you are to hand this man over to Satan for the destruction of the flesh, so that his spirit may be saved in the day of the Lord" (1 Cor 5:4–5). Paul had apparently written earlier to the congregation "not to associate with sexually immoral persons"—not meaning the immoral persons in the world but immoral persons in the church. Citing Deuteronomy 17:7 he commands the congregation: "Drive out the wicked person from among you" (5:13).

33. R. C. D. Jasper and G. J. Cuming, *Prayers of the Eucharist: Early and Reformed*, 3rd ed. (Collegeville, MN: Liturgical, 1992), 216.
34. See Robert Kingdon, "Worship in Geneva before and after the Reformation," in *Worship in Medieval and Early Modern Europe: Change and Continuity in Religious Practice*, ed. Karin Maag and John D. Witvliet (Notre Dame: University of Notre Dame Press, 2004), 41–61.

Holy Communion is at the center of the church's life because it is needed by the church. It is needed because disciples fail and fall into sin. Sins must be confessed and reconciliation achieved so that communicants participate in the sacrament in a state of peace and unity. Full forgiveness of sins is given in baptism, but we must live out our baptismal covenant in a world in which we are beset by sin, seduced by the world, and accosted by the evil one. Luther said that the Christian life is a daily living out of baptism and so we must return to our baptism daily. There are many ways to return to our baptism, but the primary way is by receiving Holy Communion. So we come to the table in repentance and faith ready to be reconciled with our Lord and with one another.

Presence, Grace, and Judgment

When the apostle Paul discusses the Lord's Supper in 1 Corinthians 11, he says that we must eat the bread and drink from the cup in such a way that we "discern the body" (1 Cor 11:28–29). Discerning the body is not a doctrinal test. It is recognizing the unity of the church that eats and drinks at the Lord's Table. "All who eat and drink without discerning the body, eat and drink judgment against themselves. For this reason many of you are weak and ill, and some have died" (11:29–30). There is a zone of holiness surrounding the Lord's Supper because of the presence of the holy one, just like the zone of holiness surrounding Mt. Sinai when God was present.

Do we believe that Christ himself is present in this meal? However the relationship between the bread and wine and the body and blood of Christ is understood, does eating and drinking the sacramental signs not put us into the presence of the Christ? Do we not believe that the Christ who comes to us in this holy sacrament is the crucified, risen, and ascended Lord who comes again as our judge? We desire the grace this sacrament confers, but we eat in awareness of judgment. The Anaphora of St. John Chrysostom includes the petition in its epiclesis that communion in the body and blood of Christ "may become to those who partake for vigilance of soul, for fellowship with the Holy Spirit, for the fullness of the kingdom (of heaven), for boldness toward you, not for judgment or condemnation."[35] Over and above any considerations of the ritual process of Christian initiation or the polities of church fellowship or acts of reconciliation, this is why it is not a good

---

35. Jasper and Cuming, *Prayers of the Eucharist*, 133.

idea for the uninitiated to participate in the Lord's Supper. In this meal we are in the real presence of Christ, whose coming brings the judgment of condemnation as well as the grace of forgiveness.

People come to Holy Communion with their needs and expectations. How well prepared are they for what they might experience in the intensity of the moment? Robert Orsi has investigated people's actual experiences of divine presence, especially Catholics who receive the Host at Mass. For some, especially victims of clergy sexual abuse, receiving Communion is a painful experience, but they still come, drawn to the divine presence that is both gracious and terrifying. What Orsi writes about these communicants can be applied to any who approach the Table. "Presence is real, but not necessarily good, not necessarily bad, as these words are understood in ordinary social discourse. It is a dreadful thing to be in relationship with the gods really present. Painful and unexpected consequences may ensue. It is not safe to be so raw and vulnerable to real presences, to make desire and need so transparent."[36]

Pastors ought to know this as they exercise their stewardship of the mysteries of Christ and the cure of souls. Perhaps, as in earlier times, people need to be better prepared to receive the sacramental body and blood of Christ in repentance and faith through the disciplines of bodily fasting, self-examination, and confession and absolution when appropriate.

Preparation for Holy Communion

In Luther's *Small Catechism* I learned that "fasting and bodily preparation are in fact a fine discipline, but a person who has faith in these words, 'given for you' and 'shed for you for the forgiveness of sins,' is really worthy and well prepared. However, a person who does not believe these words or doubts them is unworthy and unprepared, because the words 'for you' require truly believing hearts."[37]

Lutheran pastors did a lot in former times to prepare "truly believing hearts." I mentioned the special confessional services on Saturday afternoons as a part of Vespers. There was preaching on the sacrament on Communion Sundays. The hymns sung during the distribution of Holy Communion inculcated a warm piety of devotion to Jesus, who is

---

36. Robert A. Orsi, *History and Presence* (Cambridge, MA: Belknap Press of Harvard University Press, 2016), 5.
37. Martin Luther, *Small Catechism*, "The Sacrament of the Altar," 9–10 (Kolb and Wengert, *Book of Concord*, 363).

really present in the sacrament. But in a supposed evangelical freedom the traditional "bodily preparations" that Luther said were a "fine discipline" were abandoned.

Perhaps in reaction to the Catholic requirement of fasting before receiving Communion, Lutherans and other Protestants did not fast—at least not in relationship to Holy Communion. (Lutherans have sometimes fasted on fast days like Ash Wednesday and Good Friday. Holy Communion might have been celebrated on those days, but the fasting was for the day, not for the sacrament.) Abstinence from marital relations before Communion was not even a consideration. But lost in the abandonment of "bodily preparations" is the idea of preparing one's body to receive into it the body and blood of Christ.

It has been assumed by liturgical scholars that the rigorous practices of fasting and abstinence discouraged frequent Communion on the part of the laity. While the Orthodox pre-Communion ascetic practices remain mostly intact, in the Roman Catholic Church there has been a progressive relaxation of strict fasting rules since Vatican II. But not much thought has been given to why these rules were in place.

I believe that pre-Communion fasting and abstinence point to the initiatory character of Holy Communion. Fasting by the baptismal candidate and those accompanying the candidate was practiced in the ancient church already by the time of the *Didache*. "Before the baptism, let the person baptizing and the person being baptized—and others who are able—fast; tell the one being baptized to fast one or two [days] before" (7.4).[38] It is clear in the later church orders that there was fasting before baptism, that the whole congregation was drawn into this, and that such a practice contributed to the origins of the fasting season of Lent when Easter baptisms became a norm.[39] It is also clear in the church orders that baptism, with its attendant ceremonies, led directly to the celebration of the Eucharist at which the newly baptized received their first Communion. It is possible that the fasting that later became a requirement before all Communions had its origin in the ritual complex of Christian initiation. Every Communion is a renewal of baptism.

In contemporary celebrations of the Eucharist we gather around the baptismal font for a brief penitential office or remembrance of baptism before continuing the pilgrimage "journey into the dimension of the

---

38. Niederwimmer, *The Didache*, 125.
39. See Maxwell E. Johnson, *The Rites of Christian Initiation: Their Evolution and Interpretation* (Collegeville, MN: Liturgical, 1999), 159–76.

kingdom" (Schmemann). We need to be prepared for what our body and mind will receive when we come to the moment of communion with Christ. The church tradition offers historical practices for preparing the body through fasting and abstinence and preparing the mind through confession and absolution that are worth considering. Martin Luther taught in his *Large Catechism* that "fasting, prayer, and the like may have their place as external preparation and children's exercise so that one's body may behave properly and reverently toward the body and blood of Christ. But the body cannot grasp and appropriate what is given in and with the sacrament. This is done by the faith of the heart that discerns and desires such a treasure."[40]

But what will help to open the heart to desire this gift of Communion? Confession and absolution. Luther provided an order for individual confession in his *Small Catechism*, and in some editions of his *Large Catechism* he provided a brief exhortation to confession. He granted that there are various forms of confession: public and corporate, private and individual. But at the end of his exhortation he said, "Therefore, when I exhort you to go to confession, I am doing nothing but exhorting you to be a Christian. If I bring you to this point, I have also brought you to confession. For those who really want to be upright Christians and free from their sins, and who want to have a joyful conscience, truly hunger and thirst already."[41] This is a hunger and thirst that can only finally be satisfied by receiving Christ's body and blood as the gift of Communion.

We need a preparation for Holy Communion that whets the appetite for this meal and engenders a desire to share it with others who have been drawn into the community of the baptized. Holy Communion nourishes us in the baptismal life, and for that reason it is appropriate for all the baptized to receive Holy Communion. At the same time, all communicants need to return again and again to the catechumenate to be reformed in the faith of the church. This is accomplished especially in the liturgy of the catechumens that precedes the liturgy of the faithful. All the elements of the Antecommunion—hymnody, readings, preaching, confession of faith, intercessions, and confession of sins—serve the purpose of preparation for Holy Communion if we keep in mind the destination of the journey: coming into the presence of the Lord in his supper. This is a presence conveyed in earthly elements that we receive into our bodies, joining us in union with Christ and

40. Kolb and Wengert, *Book of Concord*, 470.
41. Ibid., 479.

in union with others who also share the body and blood of Christ, so that together we become what we all receive—the body of Christ in the world.

Figure 8b. Icelandic Communion. Pastor Sigurður Árni Þórðarson of the Church of Iceland invites the congregation to receive Communion. The picture is from a confirmation service in Flatey in western Iceland on June 19, 2016. The young woman serving as a Communion minister is Filippía Jónsdóttir from Reykavík, a member of the congregation of Hallgrimskirkja, where Sigurður serves as a pastor. She wanted to have the confirmation ceremony on the island where her family stays in the summertime. I also had the practice of inviting confirmands to have a liturgical role in the service on their confirmation day.

Bibliography

Athanasius. *On the Incarnation*. Introduction by C. S. Lewis. Crestwood, NY: St. Vladimir's Seminary Press, 1953.

Audet, J.-P. *La Didachè: Instructions des Apôtres*. Paris: Cerf, 1958.

Aulén, Gustaf. *Eucharist and Sacrifice*. Translated by Eric H. Wahlstrom. Philadelphia: Muhlenberg, 1958.

Baldovin, John F., SJ. *Worship: City, Church and Renewal*. Washington, DC: Pastoral Press, 1991.

Beck, Richard. *Unclean: Meditations on Purity, Hospitality, and Mortality*. Eugene, OR: Wipf & Stock, 2011.

Bellah, Robert N. *Religion in Human Evolution: From the Paleolithic to the Axial Age*. Cambridge, MA: Belknap Press of Harvard University Press, 2011.

Bieler, Andrea, and Luise Schottroff. *The Eucharist: Bodies, Bread and Resurrection*. Minneapolis: Fortress, 2007.

Book of Common Prayer . . . according to the Use of The Episcopal Church, The. New York: The Church Hymnal Corporation and Seabury, 1977.

Book of Common Worship. Louisville: Westminster John Knox, 1993.

Boromo, Jonathan G. *Incarnation and Sacrament: The Eucharistic Controversy between Charles Hodge and John Williamson Nevin*. Eugene, OR: Wipf & Stock, 2010.

Bossy, John. *Christianity in the West 1400–1700*. Oxford: Oxford University Press, 1988.

Bouyer, Louis. *Eucharist: Theology and Spirituality of the Eucharistic Prayer*. Translated by Charles Underhill Quinn. Notre Dame: University of Notre Dame Press, 1968.

——. *Liturgical Piety*. Notre Dame: University of Notre Dame, 1954.

Bradshaw, Paul F., and Maxwell E. Johnson. *The Eucharistic Liturgies: Their Evolution and Interpretation*. Collegeville, MN; Liturgical, 2012.

Bradshaw, Paul F., Maxwell E. Johnson, and L. Edward Phillips. *The Apostolic Tradition: A Commentary*. Hermeneia. Minneapolis: Fortress, 2002.

Buchanan, Colin. *What Did Cranmer Think He Was Doing?* Grove Liturgical Study 7. Bramcote, UK: Grove, 1976.

Cavanaugh, William T. *Torture and Eucharist: Theology, Politics, and the Body of Christ*. Malden, MA: Blackwell, 2000.

Chan, Simon. *Liturgical Theology: The Church as Worshiping Community*. Downers Grove, IL: IVP Academic, 2006.

Chesterton, G. K. *The Autobiography of G. K. Chesterton*. San Francisco: Ignatius, 2006.

Common Service Book of the Lutheran Church. Philadelphia: The Board of Publications of the United Lutheran Church in America, 1917.

Cutrone, E. J. "The Anaphora of the Apostles: Implications of the Mar Esa'ya Text." *Theological Studies* 34 (1973), 624–42.

Dix, Gregory. "Primitive Consecration Prayers." *Theology* 37 (1938): 261–83.

_____. *The Shape of the Liturgy. With Additional Notes by Paul V. Marshal*. New York: Seabury, 1983.

Duck, Ruth C., and Patricia Wilson-Kastner. *Praising God: The Trinity in Christian Worship*. Louisville: Westminster John Knox, 1999.

Egeria's Travels. Edited and translated by John Wilkerson. 3rd ed. Warminster, UK: Aris & Phillips, 1999.

Eiseley, Loren. *The Firmament of Time*. New York: Atheneum, 1960.

Elert, Werner. *Eucharist and Church Fellowship in the First Four Centuries*. Translated by N. E. Nagel. St. Louis: Concordia, 1966.

Eliade, Mircea. *Rites and Symbols of Initiation: The Mysteries of Birth and Rebirth*. Translated by Willard R. Trask. New York: Harper & Row, 1958.

_____. *The Sacred and the Profane: The Nature of Religion*. Translated by Willard R. Trask. New York: Harper & Row, 1959.

Evangelical Lutheran Worship. Pew Edition and Leaders Edition. Minneapolis: Augsburg Fortress, 2006.

Feuerstein, Georg. *Tantra: The Path of Ecstasy*. Boston: Shambhala, 1998.

Fink, Peter E., SJ, ed. *The New Dictionary of Sacramental Worship*. Collegeville, MN: Liturgical, 1990.

The First and Second Prayer Books of King Edward VI. Everyman's Library 448. Introduction by Douglas Harrison. 1910. Reprint, New York: Dutton, 1968.

Fisher, J. D. C. *Christian Initiation: Baptism in the Medieval West*. London: SPCK, 1965.

Frere, Walter Howard. *The Anaphora or Great Eucharistic Prayer*. London: SPCK; New York: Macmillan, 1938.

Girard, René. *The Girard Reader.* Edited by James G. Williams. New York: Cross-road, 1996.

Gritsch, Eric W. *Who Gets to Eat? Issues of Admission to the Lord's Table.* Edited by Lawrence A. Recla. Delhi, NY: ALPB Books, 2015.

Hänggi, Anton, and Irmgard Pahl, eds. *Prex Eucharistica: Textus e Variis Liturgiis Antiquioribus Selecti.* Fribourg: Èditions Universitaires Fribourg Suisse, 1968.

Haverkamp, Heidi. "Take and Eat? When Church Members Prefer Just a Blessing." *The Christian Century* 133, no. 16 (2016): 20–22.

Hoffman, Lawrence A. *Beyond the Text: A Holistic Approach to Liturgy.* Bloomington and Indianapolis: Indiana University Press, 1987.

Hogue, David A. *Remembering the Future, Imagining the Past: Story, Ritual and the Human Brain.* Cleveland: Pilgrim, 2003.

Hopkins, Gerard Manley. *A Selection of His Poems and Prose.* Edited by W. H. Gardner. Baltimore: Penguin, 1953.

Jacobi, Jolande. *The Psychology of C. G. Jung.* New Haven: Yale University Press, 1973.

Jammo, Sarhad. "The Anaphora of the Apostles Addai and Mari: A Study of Structure and Background," *Orientalia Christiana Periodica* 68 (2002): 5–35.

Jasper, R. C. D., and G. J. Cuming, eds. *Prayers of the Eucharist: Early and Reformed.* 3rd ed. Collegeville, MN: Liturgical, 1992.

Jenson, Robert W. *The Triune Identity.* Philadelphia: Fortress, 1982.

Jeremias, Joachim. *The Eucharistic Words of Jesus.* Rev. ed. Translated by Norman Perrin. New York: Charles Scribner's Sons, 1966.

John Paul II, Pope. *Man and Woman He Created Them: A Theology of the Body.* Translated by Michael Waldstein. Boston: Pauline Books & Media, 2006.

Johnson, Maxwell E. *Praying and Believing in Early Christianity: The Interplay between Christian Worship and Doctrine.* Collegeville, MN: Liturgical, 2013.

_____. *Rites of Christian Initiation: Their Evolution and Interpretation.* Collegeville, MN: Liturgical, 1999.

Juhan, Deane. "Reaching the Mind with Touch." *Job's Body.* October 12, 2010. http://tinyurl.com/kga3fye.

Jungmann, Joseph A., SJ. *The Mass of the Roman Rite: Its Origins and Development.* 2 vols. Translated by Francis A. Brunner, CSSR. 1951–1955. Reprint, Westminster, MD: Christian Classics, 1986.

_____. *The Place of Christ in Liturgical Prayer.* Translated by A. Peeler. 1925. Reprint, Collegeville, MN: Liturgical, 1989.

Justin Martyr, *First Apology.* In *Early Christian Fathers*, edited by Cyril C. Richardson, 242–89. Translated by Edward Rochie Hardy. Library of Christian Classics 1. Philadelphia: Westminster, 1953.

Kavanagh, Aidan, OSB. *On Liturgical Theology.* New York: Pueblo, 1984.

_____. "Thoughts on the Roman Anaphora." *Worship* 39 (1965): 515–29; 40 (1966): 2–15.

Keightley, Georgia Masters. "The Church's Laity: Called to Be Creation's Priests." *Worship* 84 (July 2010): 309–27.

Kilmartin, Edward J., SJ. *Christian Liturgy: Theology and Practice.* Vol. 1. Kansas City, MO: Sheed and Ward, 1988.

_____. *The Eucharist in the West.* Edited by Robert J. Daly, SJ. Collegeville, MN: Liturgical, 1998.

King, Archdale. *Eucharistic Reservation in the Western Church.* New York: Sheed and Ward, 1965.

Kingdon, Robert. "Worship in Geneva before and after the Reformation." In *Worship in Medieval and Early Modern Europe: Change and Continuity in Religious Practice,* edited by Karin Maag and John D. Witvliet, 41–61. Notre Dame: University of Notre Dame Press, 2004.

Kolb, Robert, and Timothy J. Wengert, eds. *The Book of Concord.* Minneapolis: Fortress, 2000.

Kolk, Bessel van der. *The Body Keeps the Score: Brain, Mind, and Body in the Healing of Trauma.* New York: Viking, 2014.

LaCugna, Catherine Mowry, ed. *Freeing Theology: The Essentials of Theology in Feminist Perspective.* San Francisco: HarperSanFrancisco, 1993.

_____. *God for Us: The Trinity and Christian Life.* New York: HarperCollins, 1991.

Lakoff, George and Mark Johnson. *Philosophy in the Flesh: The Embodied Mind and Its Challenges to Western Thought.* New York: Basic Books, 1999.

Lathrop, Gordon W. *The Four Gospels on Sunday: The New Testament and the Reform of Christian Worship.* Minneapolis: Fortress, 2012.

Leyerle, Blake. "Meal Customs in the Greco-Roman World." In *Passover and Easter: Origin and History to Modern Times,* edited by Paul F. Bradshaw and Lawrence A. Hoffman, 29–61. *Two Liturgical Traditions,* vol. 5. Notre Dame: University of Notre Dame Press, 1999.

Ligier, Louis. "De la Cène de Jesus l'Anaphore de l'Eglise." *La Maison Dieu* 87 (1966): 7–51.

Lubac, Henri de. *Corpus Mysticum: The Church and the Eucharist in the Middle Ages.* Translated by Gemma Simmonds, CJ, with Richard Price and Christopher Stephens. Notre Dame: University of Notre Dame Press, 2006.

Luther, Martin. *The Babylonian Captivity of the Church* (1520). In *Luther's Works,* edited by Abdel Ross Wentz, 36:3–126. Translated by A. T. W. Steinhäuser and revised Frederick C. Ahrens and Abdel Ross Wentz. Philadelphia: Muhlenberg Press, 1959.

_____. *Liturgy and Hymns.* Vol. 53 of *Luther's Works.* Edited and translated by Ulrich S. Leupold. Philadelphia: Fortress, 1965.

_____. "The Marburg Colloquy and The Marburg Articles" (1529) and *Admonition concerning the Sacrament* (1530). In *Luther's Works*, edited and translated by Martin H. Lehmann, 38:3–137. Philadelphia: Fortress, 1971.

_____. *That These Words of Christ, "This Is My Body," etc., Still Stand Firm against the Fanatics* (1527). In *Luther's Works*, edited and translated by Robert H. Fischer, 37:3–150. Philadelphia: Muhlenberg Press, 1961.

Lutheran Book of Worship. Ministers Edition. Minneapolis: Augsburg, 1978.

Lutheran Service Book. St. Louis: Concordia, 2006.

Maag, Karin. *Lifting Hearts to the Lord: Worship with John Calvin in Sixteenth-Century Geneva.* Grand Rapids: Eerdmans, 2016.

McFague, Sallie. *The Body of God: An Ecological Theology.* Minneapolis: Fortress, 1993.

McGowan, Andrew B. *Ancient Christian Worship: Early Church Practices in Social, Historical, and Theological Perspective.* Grand Rapids: Baker Academic, 2014.

McKenna, John H. *Become What You Receive: A Systematic Study of the Eucharist.* Chicago: Hillenbrand, 2012.

_____. *Eucharist and Holy Spirit: The Eucharistic Epiclesis in Twentieth Century Theology.* Alcuin Club Collections 57. Great Wakering, UK: Mayhew-McCrimmon, 1975.

Merleau-Ponty, Maurice. *Phenomenology of Perception.* Translated by Donald A. Landes. London and New York: Routledge, 2012.

Milner, Benjamin Charles. *Calvin's Doctrine of the Church.* Studies in the History of Christian Thought 5. Leiden: Brill, 1970.

Mitchell, Nathan, OSB. *Cult and Controversy: The Worship of the Eucharist outside Mass.* Studies in the Reformed Rites of the Catholic Church 4. New York: Pueblo, 1982.

Moore-Keish, Martha L. *Do This in Remembrance of Me: A Ritual Approach to Reformed Eucharistic Theology.* Grand Rapids: Eerdmans, 2008.

Murphy Center for Liturgical Research. *Made, Not Born: New Perspectives on Christian Initiation and the Catechumenate.* Notre Dame: University of Notre Dame Press, 1976.

Niederwimmer, Kurt. *The Didache: A Commentary.* Translated by Linda M. Maloney. Hermeneia. Minneapolis: Fortress, 1998.

Nischan, Bodo. "Becoming Protestants: Lutheran Altars or Reformed Communion Tables." In *Worship in Medieval and Early Modern Europe: Change and Continuity in Religious Practice*, edited by by Karin Maag and John Witvliet, 84–111. Notre Dame: University of Notre Dame Press, 2004.

Orsi, Robert A. *History and Presence.* Cambridge, MA: Belknap Press of Harvard University Press, 2016.

Pelikan, Jaroslav. *Obedient Rebel: Catholic Substance and Protestant Principle in Luther's Reformation.* New York: Harper & Row, 1964.

Penn, Michael Philip. *Kissing Christians: Ritual and Community in the Late Ancient Church.* Philadelphia: University of Pennsylvania Press, 2005.

Persson, Roland. *Johan III och Nova Ordinantia.* Lund: CWK Gleerup, 1973.

Peters, Edward F. "Luther and the Principle: Outside of the Use There Is No Sacrament." *Concordia Theological Monthly* 42 (1971): 643–52.

_____. *The Origin and Meaning of the Axiom, "Nothing Has the Character of a Sacrament outside of the Use," in Sixteenth-Century and Seventeenth-Century Lutheran Theology.* Phd diss., St. Louis: Concordia Seminary, 1968.

Pfatteicher, Philip H. *Commentary on the Lutheran Book of Worship.* Minneapolis: Augsburg Fortress, 1990.

Plato. *The Portable Plato.* Edited by Scott Buchanan. New York: Viking, 1948.

Pliny. "Letter X (*ad Traj.*)." In *Documents of the Christian Church*, ed. Henry Bettenson, 3–4. 2nd ed. Oxford: Oxford University Press, 1967.

Poschmann, Bernhard. *Penance and the Anointing of the Sick.* Translated by Francis Courtney, SJ. New York: Herder & Herder, 1964.

Power, David N. *The Eucharistic Mystery: Revitalizing the Tradition.* New York: Crossroad, 1992.

_____. "The Eucharistic Prayer: Another Look." In *New Eucharistic Prayers: An Ecumenical Study of Their Development and Structure*, edited by Frank C. Senn, 239–57. Mahwah, NJ: Paulist, 1987.

_____. *Irenaeus of Lyons on Baptism and Eucharist.* Alcuin/GROW Joint Liturgical Study 18. Nottingham, UK: Grove, 1991.

Pratzner, Ferdinand. *Messe und Kreuzopfer. Die Krise der Sakramentalen Idee bei Luther und in der Mittelalterlichen Scholastik.* Wien: Herder, 1970.

Procter-Smith, Marjorie. *In Her Own Rite: Constructing Feminist Liturgical Tradition.* Nashville: Abingdon, 1990.

Radle, Gabriel. "Embodied Eschatology: The Council of Nicaea's Regulation of Kneeling and Its Reception across Liturgical Traditions." *Worship* 90 (2016): 345–71 (Part 1: West), 433–61 (Part 2: East).

Rahner, Karl. *The Trinity.* Translated by J. Donceel. New York: Herder, 1970.

Ramshaw, Gail. *Treasures Old and New: Images in the Lectionary.* Minneapolis: Augsburg Fortress, 2002.

Ramshaw-Schmidt, Gail. "Toward Lutheran Eucharistic Prayer." In *New Eucharistic Prayers: An Ecumenical Study of Their Development and Structure*, edited by Frank C. Senn, 74–79. Mahwah, NJ: Paulist, 1987.

Ratcliff, E. C. "The Sanctus and the Pattern of the Early Anaphora," *Journal of Ecclesiastical History* 1 (1950): 29–36, 125–34.

Ratzinger, Joseph Cardinal (Pope Benedict XVI). *Feast of Faith: Approaches to a Theology of the Liturgy.* San Francisco: Ignatius, 1986.

Ray, Reginald A. *Touching Enlightenment: Finding Realization in the Body.* Boulder, CO: Sounds True, 2008.

Reed, Luther D. *The Lutheran Liturgy.* 2nd ed. Philadelphia: Muhlenberg, 1959.

Repp, Arthur C. *Confirmation in the Lutheran Church.* St. Louis: Concordia, 1964.

Rowley, H. H. *Worship in Ancient Israel: Its Forms and Meaning.* Philadelphia: Fortress, 1967.

Schmemann, Alexander. *The Eucharist: Sacrament of the Kingdom.* Translated by Paul Kachur. Crestwood, NY: St. Vladimir's Seminary Press, 1987.

———. *For the Life of the World. Sacraments and Orthodoxy.* Crestwood, NY: St. Vladimir's Seminary Press, 1973.

Senn, Frank C. *Christian Liturgy—Catholic and Evangelical.* Minneapolis: Fortress, 1997.

———. *Embodied Liturgy: Lessons in Christian Ritual.* Minneapolis: Fortress, 2016.

———. "Infant Communion and Church Statements." *Dialog* 18 (1979): 86–87.

———. "*Liturgia Svecanae Ecclesiae*: An Attempt at Eucharistic Restoration during the Swedish Reformation." *Studia Liturgica* 14 (1980–1981): 20–36.

———, ed. *New Eucharistic Prayers: An Ecumenical Study of Their Development and Structure.* Mahwah, NJ: Paulist, 1987.

———. *The People's Work: A Social History of the Liturgy.* Minneapolis: Fortress, 2006.

———. *A Stewardship of the Mysteries.* Mahwah, NJ: Paulist, 1999.

Serenius, Sigtrygg. *Liturgia svecanae ecclesiae catholicae et orthodoxae conformis: En liturgihistorisk undersökning med särskild hänsyn till struktur och förloagor.* Turku, Finland: Åbo Akademi, 1966.

Service Book and Hymnal of the Lutheran Church in America. Minneapolis: Augsburg, 1958.

Sittler, Joseph. "Called to Unity." *Ecumenical Review* 14 (1962): 175–87.

———. *The Care of the Earth and Other University Sermons.* Philadelphia: Fortress, 1964.

———. *Essays on Nature and Grace.* Philadelphia: Fortress, 1972.

Smith, Dennis E. *From Symposium to Eucharist: The Banquet in the Early Christian World.* Minneapolis: Fortress, 2003.

Smith, John Arthur. *Music in Ancient Judaism and Early Christianity.* Farnham, UK: Ashgate, 2011.

Spinks, Bryan D. *Addai and Mari—The Anaphora of the Apostles, a Text for Students.* Bramcote, UK: Grove, 1980.

_____. *Do This in Remembrance of Me: The Eucharist from the Early Church to the Present Day*. London: SCM, 2013.

_____. "The Integrity of the Anaphora of Sarapion of Thmuis and Liturgical Methodology." *Journal of Theological Studies* 49 (1998): 136–45.

_____. *The Sanctus in the Eucharistic Prayer*. Cambridge: Cambridge University Press, 1991.

Spretnak, Charlene. *The Resurgence of the Real: Body, Nature, and Place in a Hypermodern World*. Reading, MA: Addison-Wesley, 1997.

Swimme, Brian Thomas and Mary Evelyn Tucker. *Journey of the Universe*. New Haven and London: Yale University Press, 2011.

Taft, Robert F., SJ. *The Great Entrance*. Vol. 2 of *A History of the Transfer of the Gifts and Other Preanaphoral Rites of the Liturgy of St. John Chrysostom*. Orientalia Christiana Analecta 200. 2nd ed. Rome: Pontificium institutum studiorum orientalium, 1978.

_____. "The Interpolation of the Sanctus into the Anaphora: When and Where; An Interpretation of the Dossier." *Orientalia Christiana Periodica*, part 1: 57 (1991): 281–308; part 2: 58 (1992): 531–52.

Theissen, Gerd. *The Social Setting of Pauline Christianity: Essays on Corinth*. Edited and translated by John H. Schütz. Philadelphia: Fortress, 1982.

Thompson, Bard. *Liturgies of the Western Church*. 1961. Reprint, Philadelphia: Fortress, 1989.

Tillard, J.-M.-R. *Flesh of the Church, Flesh of Christ: At the Source of the Ecclesiology of Communion*. Translated by Madeleine Beaumont. Collegeville, MN: Liturgical, 2001.

Truscott, Jeffrey A. *The Reform of Baptism and Confirmation in American Lutheranism*. Lanham, MD and Oxford: Scarecrow Press, 2003.

_____. *The Sacraments: A Practical Guide*. New Delhi, India: Christian World Imprints, 2016.

Turner, Victor. *The Ritual Process: Structure and Anti-structure*. Chicago: Aldine, 1969.

Turner, Victor, and Edith Turner. *Image and Pilgrimage in Christian Culture: Anthropological Perspectives*. New York: Columbia University Press, 1978.

Van der Meer, Frederic. *Augustine the Bishop*. Translated by B. Battershaw and G. R. Lamb. London: Sheed & Ward, 1961.

Van Gennep, Arnold. *The Rites of Passage*. Translated by Monika B. Vizedom and Gabrielle L. Caffee. Chicago: University of Chicago Press, 1960.

Vööbus, Arthur. *Liturgical Traditions in the Didache*. Stockholm: Estonian Theological Society in Exile, 1968.

Wandel, Lee Palmer. *The Eucharist in the Reformation: Incarnation and Liturgy*. New York: Cambridge University Press, 2006.

West, Fritz. *Scripture and Memory: The Ecumenical Hermeneutic of the Three-Year Lectionaries.* Collegeville, MN: Liturgical, 1997.

Wilken, Robert L. *Remembering the Christian Past.* Grand Rapids: Eerdmans, 1995.

Willis, G. G. *Further Essays in Early Roman Liturgy.* Alcuin Club Collections 50. London: SPCK, 1968.

Wills, Garry. *Font of Life: Ambrose, Augustine, and the Mystery of Baptism.* New York: Oxford University Press, 2012.

Wisløff, Carl F. *The Gift of Communion: Luther's Controversy with Rome on the Eucharistic Sacrifice.* Translated by Joseph M. Shaw. Minneapolis: Augsburg, 1958.

Worship Supplement. St. Louis: Concordia, 1969.

Wright, N. T. *Surprised by Hope: Rethinking Heaven, the Resurrection, and the Mission of the Church.* San Francisco: HarperOne, 2008.

Yelverton, Eric E. *The Mass in Sweden: Its Development from the Latin Rite from 1531 to 1917.* Henry Bradshaw Society 57. London: Harrison & Sons, 1920.

Zizioulas, John D. *Being as Communion.* Crestwood, NY: St. Vladimir's Seminary Press, 2004.

Index